T0305357

The Life Cycle of New Ventures

We thank CEO Finn Haugan and the Sparebank 1 SMN for
generously supporting this research.

The Life Cycle of New Ventures

Emergence, Newness and Growth

Edited by

Candida G. Brush

Babson College, USA

Lars Kolvereid

Bodø Graduate School of Business, Norway

L. Øystein Widding

Norwegian University of Science and Technology, Norway

and

Roger Sørheim

Norwegian University of Science and Technology, Norway

Edward Elgar
Cheltenham, UK • Northampton, MA, USA

Published by
Edward Elgar Publishing Limited
The Lypiatts
15 Lansdown Road
Cheltenham
Glos GL50 2JA
UK

Edward Elgar Publishing, Inc.
William Pratt House
9 Dewey Court
Northampton
Massachusetts 01060
USA

The information and views set out in this book are those of the authors and do not necessarily reflect those of the Commission of the European Communities.

A catalogue record for this book is available from the British Library

Library of Congress Control Number: 2010922140

ISBN 978 1 84844 697 7

Typeset by Cambrian Typesetters, Camberley, Surrey
Printed and bound by MPG Books Group, UK

Contents

Contributors

I. Elaine Allen is the Research Director of the Arthur M. Blank Center for Entrepreneurship and an Associate Professor of Statistics and Entrepreneurship where she teaches advanced statistics and analytics courses. She is the statistician on several large survey projects including the Global Entrepreneurship Monitor and the Sloan Survey on online education. She is also Director of the Babson Survey Research Group (BSRG), USA. Prior to joining Babson she founded and held executive positions in the healthcare and biotechnology industry, including at Centocor, ARIAD and MetaWorks, Inc. She serves on several National Institutes of Health (NIH) research panels on best practices in statistics and on evidence- and effectiveness-based research. She is a Fellow of the American Statistical Association.

Bjørn Willy Åmo holds a Post Doctor position at Bodø Graduate School of Business, Norway. His research is oriented towards understanding the role of corporate entrepreneurship and intrapreneurship in the development of the organization. He focuses on the innovation behavior of the employee. He is also a member of the Norwegian Global Entrepreneurship Monitor research team working on regional differences regarding entrepreneurship. Some of his publications also relate to entrepreneurship education.

Ekaterina S. Bjørnåli is a senior researcher at NIFU STEP Norwegian Institute for Studies in Innovation, Research and Education in the area of Innovation Studies. Ekaterina has recently completed her PhD studies at the Norwegian University of Science and Technology (NTNU), Department of Industrial Economics and Technology Management, and submitted her dissertation 'Board of directors, top management team and the development of academic spin-off companies'. During the PhD studies Ekaterina was a visiting researcher at Stanford University, USA, and published her first peer-reviewed article in the *Journal of Technology Transfer*. Ekaterina completed an MSc in Business and Administration at Bodø Graduate School of Business, Norway, and obtained a BSc in the field of international industrial management at the Baltic State Technical University, St Petersburg, Russia, where she conducted research in the fields of marketing, internationalization, and competence and learning in knowledge organizations.

Candida G. Brush is a Professor of Entrepreneurship and holder of the Paul T. Babson Chair in Entrepreneurship at Babson College, USA. She is also Chair of the Entrepreneurship Division and a visiting adjunct Professor to the Norwegian School of Engineering and Technology, Norwegian University of Science and Technology (NTNU) in Trondheim, Norway. She is a founding member of the Diana Project International and she was named the 2007 recipient of the FSF–Swedish Research Foundation International Award for Outstanding Research Contributions in the Field of Entrepreneurship. Her research investigates emerging organizations, women entrepreneurship and angel financing.

Tommy Høyvarde Clausen is a senior researcher at the Nordland Research Institute and the University of Oslo, Norway. He earned his PhD in Innovation Studies from the University of Oslo in 2007. His research interests include innovation strategy and firm performance, entrepreneurship (start-ups and spin-offs) and evaluation of technology policies.

Linda F. Edelman is an Associate Professor of Strategic Management at Bentley University, USA. Before coming to Bentley she was a research fellow at the Warwick Business School, UK. She received her MBA and DBA from Boston University, USA. Dr Edelman is the author of 14 book chapters and over 30 peer-reviewed articles. In addition, she has made over 50 scholarly and professional presentations. Her work has appeared in top entrepreneurship journals. She is on the editorial review board of three peer-reviewed journals and her current research examines nascent entrepreneurs and entrepreneurial finance.

Amanda Elam is an entrepreneur and scholar with research interests in patterns of business start-up activity across social groups, entrepreneurial networks, and markets and economies. She holds a PhD in Sociology from the University of North Carolina at Chapel Hill, USA. Her dissertation involved a cross-national, multilevel analysis of gender and entrepreneurship. Recent projects have focused on the application of sociological theory to the study of entrepreneurship and studies of immigrant entrepreneurship. After two years of post-doctoral study at the Queensland University of Technology, Australia, and then Babson College, USA, Dr Elam returned to the trenches for inspiration and a fresh perspective on the entrepreneurship process. She currently leads a clinical testing start-up in Durham, North Carolina, USA.

Truls Erikson received his Doctorate from the University of Manchester, UK, and is presently a professor at the University of Oslo, Norway, where he serves as the Director of the Center for Entrepreneurship – a center which offers both

PhD and Master programs – and is hosting a renowned global entrepreneurship training program. Erikson is also adjunct Professor at both the Norwegian University of Science and Technology (NTNU) and Bergen University College, and has published in international research outlets such as the *Journal of Business Venturing, Negotiation Journal, Venture Capital* – an international journal of entrepreneurial finance, *Technovation, Journal of Small Business Management, International Journal of Entrepreneurship, Journal of Family Business* and *Frontiers of Entrepreneurship Research*, among others.

Bradley A. George is an Assistant Professor of Entrepreneurship at Babson College, USA, and holds the John A. Hornaday P'76 Term Chair in Entrepreneurship. His research focuses on strategic decision making in new ventures, governance impacts on corporate innovation activity, entrepreneurial orientation and research methodology. His research can be found in upcoming issues of the *Journal of Management Studies and Frontiers of Entrepreneurship Research*. Brad received his PhD from Indiana University and holds an MBA from the University of Northern Iowa as well as a BS and MEng from the University of Louisville. Prior to joining academia, Brad spent 15 years in the diesel engine industry working in a variety of roles in engineering and marketing around the world.

Timothy Habbershon is a managing director at Fidelity Investments. Dr Habbershon reports to the Chairman's Office and is involved in matters of organizational design and development for the company. Prior to joining Fidelity in 2006 Dr Habbershon was the founding director of the Institute for Family Enterprising at Babson College in Wellesley, Massachusetts, USA, and an adjunct Professor. Additionally, Dr Habbershon was a founding partner in The TELOS Group, a consulting firm that specializes in transition and strategy consultations to large family firms worldwide. Dr Habbershon received a BA in Psychology from Grove City College, a Master of Divinity degree from Gordon-Conwell Theological Seminary, and an MBA and a Doctorate in adult education from the University of South Dakota.

Espen J. Isaksen is currently an Associate Professor and teaches entrepreneurship and small business and small business management at the Bodø Graduate School of Business, Norway. He received his Doctorate in Economics from the Bodø Graduate School of Business in 2006. His current research interests include entrepreneurial intentions and actions as well as new small business performance.

Lars Kolvereid received his PhD in management from Henley Management College, UK in 1985. Prior to that he obtained his first degree in business from

Norway (1978) and his MBA from Wisconsin (1979). He has been employed by Bodø Graduate School of Business, Norway, since 1986. From 1986 to 1988 he was the associate dean, and from 1988 to 1990 he was the dean at the school. In 1993 he was appointed Professor of Entrepreneurship. Kolvereid has published more than 25 articles in refereed journals and has supervized 14 examined doctoral students. He is member of the editorial board of several academic journals, including *Entrepreneurship and Regional Development* and *Entrepreneurship Theory and Practice*.

Tatiana S. Manolova received her Doctorate of Business Administration from Boston University and is an Assistant Professor of Management at Bentley University, USA. Research and teaching interests include strategic management (competitive strategies for new and small companies), international entrepreneurship and management in transitional economies. Tatiana is the author of over 30 scholarly articles and book chapters. Recent publications appear in the *Journal of Business Venturing*, *Entrepreneurship Theory and Practice* and *The Academy of Management Learning and Education*. She is currently affiliated with the Panel Study of Entrepreneurial Dynamics, which investigates the new firm creation process, and with Diana International, which explores growth strategies of women business owners worldwide.

Erik Noyes is an Assistant Professor of Entrepreneurship at Babson College, USA, where he holds the Martin Tropp Term Chair. His research focuses on corporate entrepreneurship, corporate new venture creation and corporate innovation. Prior to joining Babson Professor Noyes was a senior consultant for a growth strategy and innovation consulting firm working with global companies such as Nokia, Hewlett-Packard, Motorola, BMW, Guidant and New Balance. His recent research examines the roles of networks in innovation, industry evolution and entrepreneurial opportunity recognition. He earned his BA in International Economic Relations from Brown University, an MBA from the University of New Hampshire and a Doctorate in Business Administration with a focus on Strategy from Boston University.

Hannes Ottósson is a PhD student at the University of Southern Denmark. He received his first degree in history (1996) and his MBA (2002) from the University of Iceland. His research interests include social capital, entrepreneur networks and the venture emergence process.

Einar Rasmussen received his PhD in 2006 and currently holds a Post Doctor position at Bodø Graduate School of Business, Norway. He has also been working as a researcher at the Norwegian University of Science and

Technology (NTNU) Entrepreneurship Center and is a visiting scholar at Nottingham University Business School and the University of Strathclyde Business School, UK. His main area of research is within academic entrepreneurship where he has been involved in several research and development projects regarding entrepreneurial activity at universities, such as studies of university spin-off venture formation processes, university support initiatives, entrepreneurship education and various types of government support mechanisms. He has published several articles in international journals.

Mark P. Rice, currently the Frederic C. Hamilton Professor for Free Enterprise at Babson College, USA, served as the Murata Dean of the F.W. Olin Graduate School of Business at Babson College from 2001–007. Professor Rice, who has been a director and chairman of the National Business Incubation Association, co-authored *Growing New Ventures – Creating New Jobs: Principles and Practices of Successful Business Incubation.* Based on his research in corporate innovation and entrepreneurship, he has co-authored numerous academic and practitioner publications, including *Radical Innovation: How Mature Companies Can Outsmart Upstarts.*

Beate Rotefoss is Associate Professor of Entrepreneurship at Bodø Graduate School of Business and senior adviser at The Centre of Innovation and Entrepreneurship in Bodø, Norway. She holds an MBA from Bodø Graduate School of Business (1998) and a PhD from Brunel University, UK (2001). Rotefoss's research interests are product development, regional innovation systems, strategy, the business start-up process, entrepreneurship among youths and entrepreneurship education.

Roger Sørheim is Professor in Technology Management at Trondheim Business School, Norway. The main part of his research is related to early-stage finance and commercialization of technology. Sørheim has published his work in a number of peer-reviewed journals such as the *Journal of Small Business Management, Venture Capital, Entrepreneurship and Regional Development, Family Business Review* and *Technovation.* Sørheim is one of the founders of the Norwegian University of Science and Technology's (NTNU) action-based entrepreneurship program 'NTNU School of Entrepreneurship' (http://www.iot.ntnu.no/nse). He currently holds part-time academic posts at NTNU and Bodø Graduate School of Business.

Ingebjørg Vestrum is employed as a researcher at Nordland Research Institute, Norway. She is currently writing a PhD at Bodø Graduate School of Business on community entrepreneurship. Her main research interests are within social and community entrepreneurship, rural communities and culture.

She is visiting the Hunter Centre of Entrepreneurship at the University of Strathclyde Business School in Glasgow, Scotland, in 2009–10.

Evgueni Vinogradov is a senior researcher at Nordland Research Institute, Bodø, Norway. He received his PhD from Bodø Graduate School of Business in 2008. His research interests include immigrant entrepreneurship, cognitive processes and the cultural context of entrepreneurship.

L. Øystein Widding's research field is within the commercialization of technology. Lately he has published papers related to entrepreneurs as knowledge managers, business angels, venture capital and spin-outs from universities. He is currently working as an Associate Professor at the Norwegian University of Science and Technology (NTNU) and at Bodø Graduate School of Business. Dr Widding is also a founder and coordinator of the NTNU School of Entrepreneurship, where the students are studying both an MSc in Technology and commercialization technology based business ideas.

Andrew Zacharakis is the John H. Muller, Jr Chair in Entrepreneurship and the Director of the Babson College Entrepreneurship Research Conference, USA. He previously served as Chair of the Entrepreneurship Department at Babson College and as Acting Director of the Arthur M. Blank Center for Entrepreneurship at Babson College. In addition, Zacharakis was the President of the Academy of Management, Entrepreneurship Division. Zacharakis's primary research area is the venture capital process. Zacharakis is the co-author of five books, *The Portable MBA in Entrepreneurship, Business Plans that Work, How to Raise Capital, Entrepreneurship, The Engine of Growth* and a textbook titled *Entrepreneurship.* He received a BS from the University of Colorado, an MBA from Indiana University and a PhD from the University of Colorado. Professor Zacharakis actively consults with entrepreneurs and small business start-ups. His professional experience includes positions with The Cambridge Companies (venture capital), IBM and Leisure Technologies.

Introduction

Candida G. Brush, Roger Sørheim, L. Øystein Widding and Lars Kolvereid

This book emerged from a series of research presentations held in 2007 and 2008 at the Norwegian University of Science and Technology (NTNU) and Babson College. Participants in the research presentations were from three schools, Babson College, NTNU and Bodø Graduate School of Business (Norway). All the researchers were active in entrepreneurship research, but approached the topic from a variety of disciplines including strategy, engineering, marketing, entrepreneurship, sociology, math/science and economics. The research presentations highlighted the approaches taken by entrepreneurs, challenges and factors influencing success across the life cycle of new ventures. We were intrigued by the similarities and differences between ventures in Norway and the USA and the idea for this book emerged.

Our purpose is to provide a cross-national comparison (USA and Norway) across the phases of venture growth; emergence, newness and growth. While comparing the USA and Norway may at first appear an unusual pairing, a comparison of the two countries from the Global Entrepreneurship Monitor (GEM) suggests that there are some similarities.

Overall, Norway has slightly more business start-up attempts than the other Scandinavian countries, but markedly lower than the USA (8.4 percent). Approximately 40 000 to 45 000 new businesses are registered in Norway each year, which corresponds to approximately 15 percent of the total business population (Spilling, 2006). However, each year an equivalent number of businesses close down. The USA reports approximately 627 200 new employer firms began operations in 2008, and 595 600 closed in 2008 (http://web.sba.gov/faqs/faqIndexAll.cfm?areaid=24). The GEM report for 2008 shows that the rate of entrepreneurial activity in the USA is around 10.8 percent (http://blogs.babson.edu/facultyblog/2009/11/13/public-policy-in-the-united-states-gem-2008-report/http).

Norway reports low rates of entrepreneurial intentions compared to other European countries and most of the start-up activity is carried out part time, suggesting that entrepreneurship may not be considered as a legitimate career path (Bosma et al., 2008). However, prevalence rate of entrepreneurial activity in 2008 was around 5 percent close to the USA which was 5.9 percent, although early stage activity lags the USA by more than 2 percent (Bosma et al., 2008).

The book is organized into four parts; context, emergence, newness and growth. These phases loosely follow the phases outlined in most of the life cycle literature (Greiner, 1972; Churchill and Lewis, 1983; Flamholtz, 1986). Although there is no agreement on the number of stages, most assume that there are contextual dimensions influencing the process, especially age, size and industry growth rate (Hanks et al., 1993).

The context refers to the policies, cultural, social and economic factors in the country environment. Emergence refers to the early nascent phase of a new venture, the time before sales and revenues are received (Gartner and Brush, 2006). Newness is the phase when the venture is working to gain sales, to manage early formation challenges and build stakeholders and customers. Growth is the phase when the firm is seeking additional resources, building the management team and expanding into new markets (Delmar et al., 2003). In this phase early stage financing is a crucial aspect as growth cannot occur without funding. We created a framework to guide this effort and it appears in Figure I.1. All chapters in this book have been peer reviewed by international experts in the same field.

PART I: CONTEXT

This part begins with a chapter by Noyes, Åmo and Allen that examines the conditions for entrepreneurship in the USA and Norway. The chapter provides

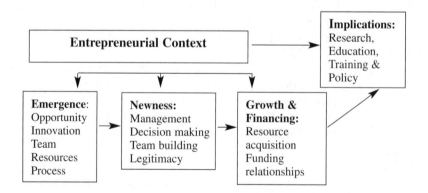

Figure I.1   Emergence, newness and growth

an overview of the US and Norwegian contexts using data from the 47 country GEM Study. The authors highlight macro information about rates of entrepreneurship in both countries. The chapter begins with a comparison of framework conditions for Norway and US demographic, geographic and economic differences. Even though there are similarities in GDP across the two countries, the total rates of entrepreneurial activity (TEA) vary in that Norway has a lower rate, and higher prevalence of male entrepreneurs. Comparisons by age, education, stage of business, motives and perceptions of the environment are included. The chapter concludes that even though the countries are similar, the framework conditions are quite different.

Chapter 2 by Rice and Habbershon investigates the context of entrepreneurship. The authors propose an input-output model that captures the flow of resources from the environment into a new venture. They describe the components of an entrepreneurship eco-system and operationalize this using the model of an incubator program. The incubator model reflects inputs from the community, to the companies and outputs into the community from the program. The model has two levels of context – first the incubator offers access to resources, advice and training, and it also serves as an intermediary between the community and the companies. The chapter concludes with implications for policy and education in Norway.

PART II: EMERGENCE

This part considers ventures in the nascent phase – before they have sales and revenues, while the venture is in the early formation (Gartner, 1985). Organizational emergence involves those events and activities before an organization becomes an organization, that is, organizational emergence involves those factors that lead to, and influence the creation and development of the organization. The value associated with the new reality is being discovered and exploited (Ronen, 1982). This process involves the entrepreneur's perception of opportunity structures, or gaps in the market, that are met by acquisition and the management of resources (land, labor and capital) and information networks (Glade, 1966). Leibenstein (1968) argues that entrepreneurs coordinate activities that involve different markets and that they are, in effect, an inter-market operator. Organizational formation is a dynamic process in which activities such as obtaining resources, developing products, hiring employees and seeking funds are undertaken at different times and in different orders. During emergence the entrepreneur(s) brings together resources, and engages in activities which will eventually distinguish the business as an entity that is separate from the individual(s) who began the firm (Reynolds and Miller, 1992; Carter et al., 1996).

In Chapter 3 Manolova, Edelman, Brush and Rotefoss compare nascent ventures in Norway with those in the USA. Their chapter empirically tests the Katz and Gartner (1988) framework that identifies core properties of emerging organizations: intentionality, resources, boundary and exchange. Using longitudinal data from Norway the authors test the composition and completeness of the properties on the likelihood of continued organizing. Their study finds that intentionality, boundary and exchange are necessary and sufficient for firm survival in the short term and that resources are necessary but not sufficient. Further, results show that entrepreneurs who engage in a larger number of start-up activities are more likely to continue the organizing effort in the short term and that initially engaging in a large number of activities is a good strategy for new ventures, but that there is a point where too many activities lead to diminishing returns.

The topic of commercialization of university research is considered in Chapter 4 by Rasmussen and Rice. The authors examine models for government support of university research in Norway. The authors examine approaches taken by universities to facilitate technology transfer, and consider initiatives based on benchmarking and experimenting. They discuss barriers and issues related to technology transfer and commercialization, and then investigate Norwegian initiatives developed to promote commercialization of university research. From this analysis Rasmussen and Rice propose a conceptual framework that articulates four models for ways government can promote the commercialization of university research. They conclude with implications for future policy programs.

In Chapter 5 Vestrum and Rasmussen investigate the emergence of a community venture in a longitudinal study. They explore aspects of legitimacy in the creation of two music festivals created in Norway. The festivals were designed to revitalize small rural communities. By investigating the early stages of the venture formation process over time, the authors explore how these community ventures gradually gained legitimacy. They make use of a novel theoretical framework that considers how nascent ventures can move beyond current stocks of resources. They explore the ways these ventures conformed and manipulated their internal and external environments. The chapter concludes with a description of legitimacy building strategies and implications for future research.

The final chapter in this part investigates industry incubators in Norway, and explores the link between open innovation policy and entrepreneurship. A central challenge for emerging firms is to gain access to resources and competences from which they can develop new products and services to be competitive. Industry incubators often assist in this process, using either open or closed models. Clausen, Rasmussen and Rice conduct a qualitative study of four industry incubators in Norway. They explore the role of the incubator management and their policies and the effects on the start-up firms. The chapter takes a societal perspective in understanding how policies affect the different actors in the incubator system (firms, universities, R&D institutes, government support systems). They conclude that policies can help to overcome challenges faced by start-up firms.

PART III: NEWNESS

This part investigates ventures in the newness phase, when the venture is working to gain sales, to manage early formation challenges and build stakeholders and customers (Gartner and Brush, 2006). This is the point where new venture is focused on surviving in the short term, and achieving performance in the longer run, although the organization may become 'stable' or decline. The direction of the venture is articulated through resource commitments and procedures for managing resource deployment are developed (Becker and Gordon, 1966; Dollinger, 1999). The individual human and social assets become increasingly institutionalized in the organization (Boeker, 1988; Shaver and Scott, 1991). The organization often faces liabilities of newness (Stinchombe, 1965).

This part begins with a chapter by Vinogradov and Elam that is rooted in entrepreneurial process theory (Shane, 2003). The authors address the research questions: (1) What are the key factors at various levels of analysis that differentiate immigrant entrepreneurs and their businesses from others? and (2) Do these factors matter more or less at various stages of the venture creation process? Vinogradov and Elam argue that selective migration and pre-migration experiences position immigrants in a unique way within their host countries and that the characteristics and resource sets of immigrant entrepreneurs differently influence the various stages of the venture creation process.

Erikson and George in Chaper 8 consider the decision-making disagreements and the influence on performance in venture capital backed firms in Norway. Based on information processing theory they develop hypotheses stating that task conflict is positively related to new venture performance, while process conflict is negatively related to new venture performance. Using a sample of 45 venture capital backed firms in Norway, they find support for their hypotheses.

In Chapter 9 Bjørnåli and Erikson focus on three factors which are expected to influence team member additions in academic spin-offs. These are board size, the number of outsiders on the board and board contribution to networking. In their sample of 95 academic spin-offs in Norway they found that board size and networking activity level facilitate the team number addition process, while the effect of the number of outsiders on the board had no significant effect.

The part ends with an analysis of design characteristics of firms associated with venture capital (VC) firms. In Chapter 10 Bjørnali, Sørheim and Erikson explore design characteristics associated with venture capital financed academic spin-off firms (ASO). In particular, they address the role of prior finance as well as management team and board design features. They analyse 106 firms using hierarchical logistic regression. They find that funding from seed capital funds and funding from industrial partners are design features associated with successful VC acquisitions. The presence of informal investors has a negative effect on subsequent VC financing. This is explained by the nature of the informal investors. They are often interlinked with other informal investors (and not to VCs). Further, this chapter extends our understanding of the role of the top management teams and boards in academic spin-offs by linking their design characteristics to VC financing and suggests that only team size and cognitive diversity among management team members are design features associated with VC acquisitions.

PART IV: GROWTH AND EARLY STAGE FINANCING

Growth is the phase when the firm is seeking additional resources, building the management team and expanding into new markets (Gartner and Brush, 2006). While not all firms choose to grow (Ginn and Sexton, 1990; Rosa et al., 1996; Wiklund et al., 2003) analysts suggest that some growth over time is desirable for continued survival (Delmar et al., 2003). A key aspect of growth is the ability to obtain early stage financing. Fast growing companies need cash to grow and the faster the growth, the greater the appetite for cash. As Churchill and Mullins (2001) have noted, there is a pace beyond which companies cannot fuel growth organically and must turn to external sources of cash flow – debt (whether it be permanent or semi-permanent), equity financing, owner and family financing or joint venturing are some of the more common solutions. This part includes chapters covering aspects of growth in new ventures such as venture capital acquisition, team management and effects of internationalization.

The relationship between the venture capitalist and the entrepreneur is investigated by Erikson and Zacharakis in Chapter 11. The chapter examines the effect of conflict upon confidence in partner cooperation. They demonstrate that conflict is harmful to the relationship and make three contributions. First, they find the entrepreneur perspective view of cognitive conflict as detrimental. Implications for investors and entrepreneurs are to be cautious in how they handle (good faith) disagreements, as they may turn into – often irreparable – affective conflicts. Second, they look at how process conflict within the dyad has an indirect negative effect through affective conflict component.

Finally, this chapter looks at how general intragroup conflict can transfer and lead to intergroup conflict.

Chapter 12 explores perceptions of the use of external funding by new business founders. Sørheim and Isaksen examine financial preferences and use of external funding among prospective and non-prospective employers in Norway. They find that prospective employers are more positive towards the use of external funding (both debt and equity). They also have been more active in the search for different types of external funding and also more successful in actually getting offers of external funding (debt and equity). At first sight, this chapter indicates that non-prospective employers follow a 'pecking order' reasoning. However Sørheim and Isaksen suggest that this rank of financial sources is primarily related to non-prospective employers' lack of growth aspirations. Prospective employers seem to adjust their perceptions and actual financial behavior to the actual situation of their business. Consequently, prospective employers perceive external funding (debt and equity) as the right means in order to achieve their goals.

The final chapter by Kolvereid, Isaksen and Ottósson presents a longitudinal study investigating the association between advice received by entrepreneurs during the new business start-up process and subsequent venture performance. In this chapter they investigate if advice has diminishing returns to scale. Entrepreneurship studies on diminishing returns are scarce and the purpose here is to contribute to this research, attempting to identify an optimal number of sources of advice. The results indicate a positive effect of advice on performance; however, utilizing more than six sources of advice has a negative effect on performance. Entrepreneurs should pay attention to the importance of the quantity and the quality of advice. Authorities may consider changing the focus of their initiatives to better reflect the findings reported in this chapter.

IMPLICATIONS

This book offers intriguing contributions with regard to the emergence and growth of knowledge-based firms in a developed economy like Norway. The book offers unique insights when it comes to direct and indirect efforts from the government in order to stimulate the formation of knowledge-based firms. The Norwegian efforts seem in many cases to be heavily influenced by experiences in prospering regions in the USA (like the Boston area and Silicon Valley). This is especially evident when it comes to stimulation of academic entrepreneurship. This can be traced back to the introduction of the Bayh-Dole Act in the USA. The subsequent success from leading research institutions in the USA in bringing new research findings to the marketplace has also inspired the development of efforts to increase the commercialization of technology-based firms in Norway. However, there is a growing awareness of the fact that facilitating the formation of knowledge-based firms in a prosperous US region is quite different from working in a more rural context as in Norway. This calls for other direct and indirect means, both when it comes to the development of infrastructure and schemes to support the emergence of knowledge-based firms financially. Rather, the findings from a Norwegian setting must be interpreted with caution and may not be directly transferable to a US setting. However, the US setting is also heterogeneous and findings from small developed countries in Europe may be more relevant to smaller US regions (and not to regions like Boston and Silicon Valley). These are important elements to take into account when carrying out comparative studies in the future. In all, we believe this book offers a significant and new cross-country comparison, as well as highlighting topics important to emergence and newness not previously researched.

REFERENCES

Becker, S.W. and G. Gordon (1966), 'An entrepreneurial theory of formal organizations, Part I: patterns of formal organizations', *Administrative Science Quarterly*, **11**, 315–44.

Boeker, W. (1988), 'Organizational origins: entrepreneurial and environmental imprinting at the time of founding', in G.R. Carroll (ed.), *Ecological Models of Organizations*, Cambridge, MA: Ballinger, pp. 33–51.

Bosma, N., Z. Acs, E. Autio, A. Coduras and J. Levie (2008), *Global Entrepreneurship Monitor, Executive Report*, Wellesley, MA: Babson College and Universidad de Desarollo.

Carter, N.M., W.B. Gartner and P.D. Reynolds (1996), 'Exploring start-up event sequences', *Journal of Business Venturing*, **11**(3), 151–66.

Churchill, N. and V. Lewis (1983), 'The five stages of small business growth', *Harvard Business Review*, **61**(3), 30–50.

Churchill, N. and J. Mullins (2001), 'How fast can your company afford to grow?', *Harvard Business Review*, **31**(4), 135–43.

Delmar, F., P. Davidsson and W. Gartner (2003), 'Arriving at the high-growth firm', *Journal of Business Venturing*, **18**(2), 189–216.

Dollinger, M.J. (1999), *Entrepreneurship: Strategies and Resources,* 2nd edn, Englewood Cliffs, NJ: Prentice Hall.

Flamholtz, E. (1986), *Managing the Transition from an Entrepreneurship to a Professionally Managed Firm*, San Francisco, CA: Jossey-Bass.

Gartner, W.B. (1985), 'A conceptual framework for describing the phenomenon of new venture creation', *Academy of Management Review*, **10**(4), 696–706.

Gartner, W. and C.G. Brush (2006), 'Entrepreneurship as organizing: emergence, newness and transformation', in T. Habbershon (ed.), *Praeger Perspectives on Entrepreneurship*, Vol. 3, Westport, CT: Praeger Publishers, pp. 1–20.

Ginn, C. and D. Sexton (1990), 'A comparison of personality type dimensions of the

Inc. 500 company founders with those of slower growth firms', *Journal of Business Venturing*, **5**(5), 313–26.

Glade, W. (1966), 'Approaches to a theory of entrepreneurial formation', *Explorations in Entrepreneurial History*, **4**, 245–59.

Greiner, L. (1972), 'Evolution and revolution as organizations grow', *Harvard Business Review*, **50**(4), 37–46.

Hanks, S., C. Watson, E. Jansen and G. Chandler (1993), 'Tightening the life-cycle construct: a taxonomic study of growth stage configurations in high-technology organizations', *Entrepreneurship Theory and Practice*, **18**(2), 5–29.

Katz, J. and W.B. Gartner (1988), 'Properties of emerging organizations', *Academy of Management Review*, **13**(3), 429–41.

Leibenstein, H. (1968), 'Entrepreneurship and development', *American Economic Review*, **58**(2), 72–83.

Reynolds, P.D. and B. Miller (1992), 'New firm gestation: conception, birth and implications for research', *Journal of Business Venturing*, **7**(5), 405–17.

Ronen, J. (ed.) (1982), *Entrepreneurship*, Lexington, MA: Lexington Books.

Rosa, P., S. Carter and D. Hamilton (1996), 'Gender as a determinant of small business performance: insights from a British study', *Small Business Economics*, **8**, 463–78.

Shane, S. (2003), *A General Theory of Entrepreneurship*, Cheltenham, UK and Northampton, MA, USA: Edward Elgar.

Shaver, K.G. and L.R. Scott (1991), 'Person, process, choice: the psychology of new venture creation', *Entrepreneurship Theory and Practice*, **16**(2), 23–47.

Spilling, O.R. (2006), 'Entreprenørskap i et dynamisk og strukturelt perspektiv', in O.R. Spilling (ed.), *Entreprenørskap på norsk*, 2nd edn, Bergen, Norway: Fagbokforlaget, pp. 73–96.

Stinchcombe, A.L. (1965), 'Social structure and organizations', in J.G. March (ed.), *Handbook of Organizations*, Chicago, IL: Rand McNally, pp. 142–93.

Wiklund, J., P. Davidsson and F. Delmar (2003), 'What do they think and feel about growth? An expectancy-value approach to small business managers: attitudes toward growth', *Entrepreneurship Theory and Practice*, **27**(3), 247–70.

PART I

Context

1. Entrepreneurship and conditions for entrepreneurs: Norway and the USA compared

Erik Noyes, Bjørn Willy Åmo and I. Elaine Allen

INTRODUCTION

In this chapter we compare total entrepreneurial activity in Norway and the USA using data from the Global Entrepreneurship Monitor (GEM). The two countries are contrasted with respect to national conditions including geographic, demographic, economic as well as stage and type of entrepreneurship. In addition, we distinguish projected growth and newness of technology in start-ups. Following this, we report on perceptions of entrepreneurs and perceptions of entrepreneurship in each country. When possible, statistical comparisons are made based on the 2001–08 GEM surveys from each country using chi-square statistics. The chapter provides a comparative introduction to entrepreneurial activity in both countries and an overview that connects and frames the chapters that follow.

FRAMEWORK CONDITIONS FOR ENTREPRENEURSHIP COMPARED

Geographic, Demographic and Economic Differences

Norway and the USA differ dramatically in terms of geography and demography as seen in Table 1.1. However, as shown, there are similarities in terms of the urban population percentage but more women are employed in Norway.

Broadly, key differences that complicate deeper comparisons include greater ethnic diversity and economic inequality in the USA. Norway offers a much more robust social safety net for all workers, including entrepreneurs, thus reducing the economic risks of new venture failure. Ethnically, Norwegians are much more homogeneous with a predominantly white

Table 1.1   Geographic and population differences between Norway and the USA

	USA	Norway	Unit
Land area	9 826 630	304 280	km²
Population	303 824 640	4 600 000	million
Territorial waters	664 707	145	km²
Exclusive economic zone	11 351 000	819 620	km²
Land boundary (Norway-North South distance)	12 034	2 500	km
Urban population	76.0	80.0	%
Women employment rate	59.0	70.0	%
Men employment rate	92.0	80.0	%

population. In contrast, the USA includes an increasingly diverse population of Blacks, Hispanics and Asians. In terms of expenditures by the government on social programs, the countries are quite similar with Norway spending more than 59 percent on social benefits and healthcare in 2007 (Statistics Norway, 2009). Comparatively, the USA spends 52 percent of its national budget on Social Security, Medicare, Medicaid and other safety net programs. However, the US government spent 21 percent of its budget on defense and security compared with less than 5 percent government spending in Norway in 2007.

The Norwegian economy features a combination of free market activity and government intervention. The government controls key areas, such as the petroleum sector, through large-scale state enterprises. The country has rich natural resources – petroleum, hydropower, fish, forests and minerals – but is highly dependent on the petroleum sector, which accounts for nearly half of exports and over 30 percent of state revenue. While Norway was previously the world's third largest gas exporter in the world, its position as an oil exporter has slipped to seventh largest as production has begun to decline. In anticipation of eventual declines in oil and gas production, Norway saves almost all state revenue from the petroleum sector in a sovereign wealth fund and part of these proceeds fund diversification and investment in expected future growth industries such as information technology and life sciences. After lackluster growth of less than 1.5 percent in 2002–03, GDP grew from 2.5 to 6.2 percent in 2004–07, partly due to higher oil prices. Growth fell to 2.3 percent in 2008 as a result of the slowing world economy and the drop in oil prices.

In contrast, the USA is a market-oriented economy where private individuals and business firms make most of the decisions and the federal and state governments buy needed goods and services predominantly in the private

Table 1.2   Number of patent applications per million inhabitants

	2001	2002	2003	2004	2005	2006	2007
Norway	263.46	259.59	236.37	248.70	247.23	246.53	259.71
USA	622.61	639.99	650.52	646.46	702.50	742.36	800.17

marketplace. US business firms enjoy greater flexibility than their counterparts in Europe and Asia with decisions to expand capital plant, to lay off surplus workers and to develop new products. At the same time, given the comparative flexibility, they often face higher barriers to enter foreign rivals' home markets abroad than foreign firms face entering US markets. US firms are at or near the forefront in technological advances, especially in computers and in medical, aerospace and military equipment; however, their advantage has narrowed since the end of World War II.

US firms are more likely to protect their technological investments by patenting them than are Norwegian firms. Table 1.2 shows this differential. For example, in the year 2007 Norwegians applied for 259.7 patents per million inhabitants while there were 800.2 patent applications from US citizens per million inhabitants in the same year.

Examining exports and the balance of trade, on a per capita basis, Norwegian citizens on average are more likely to be involved in export activity compared to their US counterparts as seen in Figures 1.1 and 1.2. Given the small size of their home market, Norwegian firms have to be more export oriented than those in the USA. As shown in Figure 1.2, the balance of trade has worsened recently in the USA while it has held steady over the same period in Norway.

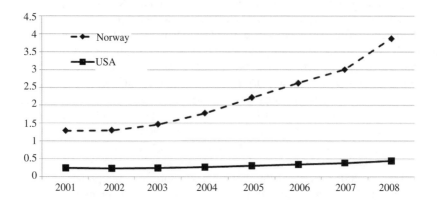

Figure 1.1   Exports per capita in $US millions per year

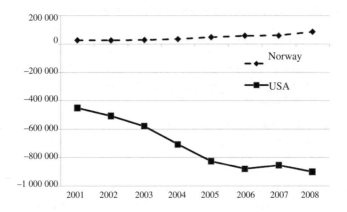

Figure 1.2   Balance of trade per capita in $US millions per year

Entrepreneurship Differences by Demographic Categories

Although GDP per capita is similar in both countries ($55 000 in Norway in 2008 compared with $48 000 in the USA) and among the highest in the world, Norway has a much lower rate of total entrepreneurial activity (TEA). Figure 1.3 indicates that these rates may be growing closer over time as the US TEA declines and Norway's TEA increases. The TEA rate is the proportion of people aged 18–64 who are involved in entrepreneurial activity as a nascent entrepreneur or as an owner-manager of a new business.

Using the most recent GEM data (Bosma et al., 2009), it is surprising that there are such wide and significant differences in the gender split of early-stage entrepreneurial activity between the USA and Norway – where 72 percent of entrepreneurs in Norway are male, but only 59.6 percent are male in the USA. The small percentage of entrepreneurs that are women is surprising because, as shown in previous studies of women's entrepreneurship using the GEM data (Allen et al., 2008), one consistently strong predictor of women's entrepreneurial activity is being employed and significantly more women in Norway are employed than in the USA.

The government in Norway has as an officially stated objective that women entrepreneurs should constitute 40 percent of all entrepreneurs in the country. However, the percentage of female entrepreneurs in the country is only 30.2 percent (2008), which is below the average for the GEM countries. Alsos and Kolvereid (2005) reviewed the empirical literature on entrepreneurship and gender in Norway and came up with the following explanations for the relatively low rate of entrepreneurship among women in the country: (1) women are less interested than men in becoming self-employed; (2) women perceive

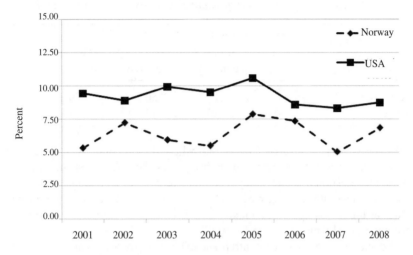

Figure 1.3   Total early stage entrepreneurial activity (TEA) rates in Norway and the USA from 2001–08

fewer business opportunities than men do; (3) more women than men lack the competence and skill required to start a business; and (4) among those who are interested in an entrepreneurial career, fewer women than men actually try to start a business. The Norwegian labor market is strongly segregated by gender and women and men are educated differently. As a result, their competence differs. Women in Norway have less experience in the private sector, and less management experience than men. Robust social benefits for women and families (for example, extended maternity leave) which offset potential lifestyle benefits of entrepreneurship may in part contribute to an explanation of this difference.

Examining other differences in entrepreneurial activity between Norway and the USA also shows some statistically significant differences (Table 1.3). The pattern of entrepreneurial activity by entrepreneur age shows significant

Table 1.3   Total early-stage entrepreneurial activity by age group

	% 18–24 years	% 25–34 years	% 35–44 years	% 45–54 years	% 55–64 years	% 65–98 years
Norway	17.70	24.80	24.80	19.10	5.70	7.80
USA	13.90	22.60	24.00	20.80	12.00	6.70

Table 1.4   Total early-stage entrepreneurial activity by education level

	% Some secondary	% Secondary degree	% Graduate experience
Norway	10.10	50.00	39.90
USA	13.30	42.50	44.20

differences only in the 55–64 age group where the rate in the USA is double that of Norway (12.0 percent versus 5.7 percent, $p < 0.05$). Again, there is reason to question if social policy factors, including more favorable conditions for retirement and retirees, may explain the decreased level of entrepreneurship for the 55–64 age group in Norway. However, this cannot be determined from the GEM data.

Education attainment and entrepreneurship activity are comparable at the lowest educational levels but markedly different for those with only a secondary degree education – with higher entrepreneurial activity in Norway – and slightly reversed for those with some graduate education (Table 1.4).

The relationship between household income and entrepreneurial activity is also different in Norway compared with the USA. In Norway entrepreneurs are more likely to be in the upper third of household income (38.7 percent) while in the USA they are more likely to be in the middle household income group (40.1 percent).

Country Comparisons by Stage and Type of Entrepreneurship

In the GEM data early-stage entrepreneurship is divided into two stages of entrepreneurial activity: nascent entrepreneurs who are planning to start a business in the next three months or who have started a business in the last three months; and baby business owners who own and manage a business that is between 3 and 42 months old. The USA had many more early-stage entrepreneurs through 2007 (–3 months pre-start to 3 months post-business start) but in 2008 the percentage of nascent entrepreneurs is almost identical in both countries. The reverse is true for baby business owners where there were significantly more of this type of entrepreneur in Norway until 2008 when they are almost identical (Table 1.5).

Motives for entrepreneurial activity are divided into two categories: opportunity motives when the entrepreneur is acting on a perceived business or economic opportunity; and necessity motives when the entrepreneur sees starting a business as a way to increase needed income or sees no economic opportunities in entering the workforce. Both countries have low levels of necessity

Table 1.5   Stage of entrepreneurial activity

		% 2001	% 2002	% 2003	% 2004	% 2005	% 2006	% 2007	% 2008
Norway	Nascent entrepreneur	61.40	60.90	53.00	55.70	46.30	54.40	62.10	56.80
	Baby business owner-manager	38.60	39.10	47.00	44.30	53.70	45.60	37.90	43.20
USA	Nascent entrepreneur	72.00	66.70	67.80	66.00	70.10	73.80	68.40	55.40
	Baby business owner-manager	28.00	33.30	32.20	34.00	29.90	26.20	31.60	44.60

Table 1.6   Motive for entrepreneurial activity

		% 2001	% 2002	% 2003	% 2004	% 2005	% 2006	% 2007	% 2008
Norway	Opportunity motive	92.10	89.30	90.90	86.10	89.90	95.30	87.80	85.00
	Necessity motive	2.20	3.10	9.10	11.90	9.40	3.90	6.70	7.10
	Other motive	5.80	7.60	0.00	2.00	0.70	0.80	5.60	7.90
USA	Opportunity motive	86.90	89.00	82.50	86.60	85.60	87.40	78.50	82.70
	Necessity motive	8.80	10.60	14.60	13.40	10.50	12.60	15.80	11.50
	Other motive	4.40	0.30	2.90	0.00	3.80	0.00	5.60	5.80

entrepreneurship; however, over the most recent three year period (2006–08) the percentage of necessity entrepreneurship in the USA has at times been double or triple that of Norway – showing a greater necessity motive in the USA (Table 1.6). This general relationship has held constant since data were initially collected in 2001.

Country Comparisons by Technology and Projected Growth

Similarities between the countries which shape entrepreneurial activity include great national wealth, a highly educated workforce, aggressive global trade and deep oil dependence (from a supplier perspective for Norway and a buyer perspective for the USA). However, the characteristics and projected growth of early-stage businesses in the USA and Norway are quite different.

Norwegian start-ups are significantly more likely ($p < 0.01$) to use the newest technology (14.4 percent in Norway versus 6.0 percent in the USA, $p < 0.01$) and, to a somewhat lesser extent, to believe that their businesses offer new product market combinations (25.7 percent in Norway versus 21.7 percent in the USA, $p < 0.05$).

In contrast, US entrepreneurs believe that their start-ups will grow faster and produce more jobs. Twenty-eight percent state that they expect to have more than ten employees and revenue growth over 50 percent in the next three years, higher than Norwegian entrepreneurs ($p < 0.05$). Norwegian start-ups are more likely to have more than one owner (55 percent versus 42 percent for US start-ups, $p < 0.05$). There is no statistically significant difference when examining the reported export intensity of new businesses (20 percent in Norway versus 18 percent in the USA expect at least 25 percent of the business to be outside the country). Only a small percentage of start-ups in both countries expect to create more than 19 jobs in the company within the next five years (0.8 percent and 1.9 percent in Norway and the USA, respectively).

Individual and Cultural Perceptions of Entrepreneurship

Importantly, individual perceptions about entrepreneurship – its risks and benefits – are different in Norway and the USA. Historically, fear of failure (that is, where individuals report that fear of failure would prevent one from starting a business) has been greater in Norway, although this trend has recently reversed (Bosma et al., 2009). In 2008 almost twice as many early-stage entrepreneurs in the USA believe that fear of failure would prevent them from starting a business (22.7 percent in the USA versus 11.9 percent in Norway; $p < 0.05$) (Table 1.7). This pattern shows a gradual reversal between the USA and Norway from 2001 to 2008.

Although entrepreneurs in Norway are more likely to report that they know an entrepreneur ($p < 0.01$), US citizens are more likely to report that they have the skill to start a business ($p < 0.05$). Significantly more Norwegians believe that there are good opportunities for starting a business in the next six months ($p < 0.01$) (Table 1.8).

Table 1.7   Fear of failure prevents a start-up effort in the USA and Norway from 2001–08

	% 2001	% 2002	% 2003	% 2004	% 2005	% 2006	% 2007	% 2008
Norway	15.00	26.50	17.00	13.40	18.40	14.30	14.70	11.90
USA	14.00	16.10	15.70	18.50	18.90	19.70	19.20	22.70

Table 1.8   Business knowledge and opportunities

	Knows a person who started a business in the past two years (%)	
	NO	YES
Norway	21.90	78.10
USA	39.70	60.30
	Sees good opportunities for starting a business in the next six months (%)	
Norway	29.50	70.50
USA	39.60	60.40
	Has the required knowledge/skills to start a business (%)	
Norway	15.60	84.40
USA	11.20	88.80

Comparisons between Norway and the USA on their perceptions of entrepreneurship as having higher status and good media coverage are significantly different. In Norway the entrepreneurs' perception of the status of entrepreneurs is lower than the perception of entrepreneurs by non-entrepreneurs (58.7 percent versus 54.0 percent, n.s.). In the USA entrepreneurs have significantly higher perception of the status of entrepreneurs than non-entrepreneurs (72.0 percent versus 59.4 percent, $p < 0.05$) and also significantly higher perception than entrepreneurs in Norway ($p < 0.01$).

CONCLUSIONS

Putting aside the current global recession, the 2008 GEM report cites continued rapid economic growth in the first years of the new millennium, low unemployment, labor shortages and favorable conditions for those who are currently employed as factors that likely weaken incentives for entrepreneurship in Norway. The report states, 'Norway scores lower than other western countries on a culture of promoting entrepreneurship, ability to innovate, opportunities for high growth firms, motivations for entrepreneurship in the population, government priority [of entrepreneurship] and dynamism in the home market' (Kolvereid et al., 2008, p. 5). The points noted above are consistent with the data presented in this chapter; however, there is a risk of overgeneralizing with respect to different types and stages of entrepreneurial activity.

In summary, although access to financial resources through state-owned and accumulated fuel wealth has improved considerably, total entrepreneurial activity in Norway is lower than in the USA. This, in part, may be explained by individual perceptions and socio-economic forces that dampen incentives to start a new business. Although both countries have similarities, the framework conditions for entrepreneurship are very different.

Policy actions and programs that will be successful in sparking and supporting greater entrepreneurship will vary depending on the national context. Norwegian entrepreneurship policy must take into account the perceived opportunity cost of starting a venture and consider the range of less risky opportunities available to individuals in a comparatively tight labor market. Although Norwegians are just as likely as individuals from the USA to report that they know an entrepreneur, there is the belief – and possible road block – among individuals in Norway that they are less likely to have the skill to start a business. This can potentially be offset by entrepreneurship training or correcting views about the varied skill requirements for entrepreneurship.

Although both countries face great pressure to be innovative, to spawn new ventures and to drive economic growth, Norway arguably has a greater challenge to diversify beyond its largely oil-related industry. Norway's enormous sovereign wealth can be both a blessing and a curse as it strives to stimulate innovation and new venture creation in the economy.

Due to the current global recession, US entrepreneurs face extreme challenges in raising capital and gaining access to credit. Broadly speaking, entrepreneurial capacity may outpace the national infrastructure to support entrepreneurial ventures and fund the expansion of wealth-creating new ventures. Moreover, opportunistic perceptions about the ease and benefits of entrepreneurship may be damped down by national problems with access to seed-stage and growth capital, despite an abundance of entrepreneurial talent. The strategic role for entrepreneurs in the USA is to drive entry into new sustainable industries that address national as well as global socio-economic problems such as pollution and resource depletion. Like Norwegian entrepreneurs, US entrepreneurs can help diversify the national economy to move away from oil dependence, a source of strategic tension, which affects political and economic security.

In summary, the histories and current conditions bearing on entrepreneurship are different for the two countries. While each country is looking to secure footholds in the high growth industries of the future, individual entrepreneurs are faced with very different national operating and social conditions.

REFERENCES

Allen, I.E., A. Elam, N. Langowitz and M. Dean (2008), *Global Entrepreneurship Monitor 2007 Report on Women and Entrepreneurship*, Babson Park, MA: Center for Women's Leadership at Babson College.

Alsos, H. and L. Kolvereid (2005), 'Entrepreneurship among women in Norway', in E.S. Hauge and P.A. Havnes (eds), *Women Entrepreneurs. Theory, Research and Policy Implications*, Kristiansand, Norway: Høgskoleforlaget, pp. 44–58.

Kolvereid, L., E. Bullvåg and B.J. Åmo (2008), *Global Entrepreneurship Monitor: 2007 Executive Report*, London and Babson Park, MA: London Business School and Babson College.

Statistics Norway (2009), http://www.ssb.no 20/10-2009 (accessed 13 March 2009).

2. The context for entrepreneurship

Mark P. Rice and Timothy Habbershon

The entrepreneur identifies an opportunity, assesses it – particularly with respect to the market, the competition and how the entrepreneur's offering might address the market need in a manner that differentiates it from competitors' offerings – conceives of a business model to pursue it, attracts resources and talent, and launches and builds the new venture. This entrepreneurial activity occurs within a particular context (Ucbasaran et al., 2001). Context does not have a singular or static meaning. Generally, context refers to environmental factors, societies and cultures, modes and organizations, communities, arenas, policies and structures. In order to fully understand the rich phenomenon that we refer to as entrepreneurship, we cannot constrain the definition of context, but rather we must identify the full range of contextual factors that interact with the entrepreneur and entrepreneurial process.[1]

CONTEXT AS AN INPUT-OUTPUT MODEL

Generally the entrepreneur does not start with all the elements for success fully assembled. The context in which the entrepreneur operates is the source from which the entrepreneur accesses or acquires the elements that enable the venture to build the capacity and to deliver value to its marketplace. Typically after a start-up and ramp up period of capacity building, the venture – if it is to survive and succeed – must achieve at least breakeven with respect to resources it accesses or acquires from within its context and the value it delivers to the stakeholders that provide those resources. The rates of acquisition and value delivery may vary over time, creating periods of decline, stability or growth in the venture. The context in which the entrepreneur chooses to start the endeavor significantly impacts the trajectory of these outcomes.

This idea of the flow of resources – the acquisition of resources by the entrepreneur and the delivery of value to the environment – is fundamental to the entrepreneurial process. It can be characterized as an input-output model. The external environment as well as the venture itself inputs various resources that are transformed through the entrepreneurial process into outputs that are delivered back to the external environment. Typically during the start-up phase of an entrepreneurial venture the resources acquired exceed the value of the products or services delivered by the venture to its customers. In the long run, however, the entrepreneur must establish a business model in which the value created equals or exceeds the resources consumed in order to achieve sustainability. The munificence of the context in which the entrepreneurial process operates can vary substantially, with munificence reflected in the quantity and quality of resources, as well as the relative ease with which they can be accessed. Because it is individual actors that engage in the process (for example, entrepreneurs, intermediaries, service providers, investors, early adopters and so on), the skill level of each of these actors also plays a critical role in determining the rate of entrepreneurial success. Referencing the skill levels of actors also speaks to the educational and support services associated with context and how they reciprocally function as an enhancer or detractor of inputs and outputs.

This input-output resource model is implicitly or explicitly evident in the descriptions and definitions of entrepreneurship. Schumpeter (1942) argued that entrepreneurship is creative destruction as resources are shifted to points of entrepreneurial value creation. Dynamic disequilibrium brought on by the entrepreneurial process, rather than equilibrium and optimization, is the norm of a healthy economy and the central reality of economic theory and practice (Drucker, 2002) and entrepreneurs are the driver of this disequilibrium as they search for change, respond to it and exploit it as an opportunity. Howard Stevenson proposed that entrepreneurship is the pursuit of opportunity beyond the tangible resources currently controlled (Stevenson et al., 1989). He emphasized that the entrepreneur must be adept at gaining access to and utilizing resources, rather than controlling and allocating them. The Timmons model (Timmons and Spinelli, 2003) operationalizes the entrepreneurial process by demonstrating how the interacting elements of the entrepreneur, resources and opportunity create the input-output system. Thus, the above macro to micro reflections on the concept of entrepreneurship and the allocation of resources further highlight the connections among the entrepreneur, the entrepreneurial process and the environmental context in which the entrepreneur operates. The entrepreneurial context is therefore a significant inhibitor or accelerator of the entrepreneurial process, depending upon the effectiveness and efficiency of the interactions in the input-output model.

IDENTIFYING CONTEXTUAL FACTORS

Contextual factors can be identified as a series of concentric circles ranging from global forces to national and regional infrastructures to cultural families and organizational forms. Though often interrelated, contextual factors can be viewed from an external and internal perspective (Zahra and Covin, 1995).

The external perspective comprises:

- global connectivity
- governmental infrastructure, public policy and regulations
- regional and national macroeconomic conditions
- regional and national education and support systems
- populations, cultures and societies of people
- communities, clusters and niches of organizations and services
- sophistication and readiness of customers
- outside sources and sophistication of risk capital for new ventures
- industry conditions, stage and globalization
- product and market life stage.

The internal perspective comprises:

- organizational forms and modes of doing business
- organizational processes, systems and structures
- business life cycle and stage of development
- organizational culture and mindset
- inside sources and sophistication of capital for corporate ventures
- stakeholder relationships and networks
- market channels and outlets
- entrepreneur and team experience.

AN ECOSYSTEM PERSPECTIVE

In order to explain how the contextual factors create an input-output model, a number of writers have recognized the concept of the entrepreneurship ecosystem at all economic levels – from micro to macro (Hamel, 2000; Zacharakis et al., 2003; Friedman, 2005). Zacharakis et al. (2003), for example, suggest that industries and sub-industry contexts could be characterized as an ecosystem with various relationships of interdependence. Aldrich and Martinez (2001) suggest that communities are a 'set of coevolving organizational populations' that are joined by ties of commensalism and symbiosis. They describe how new ventures can relate to populations that share the same niche by competing or cooperating (commensalism), or if they have different niches they can benefit from each other's presence (symbiosis). Recently, Fetters et al. (2010) have conducted case-based research into six longstanding university-based entrepreneurship ecosystems in the USA, Mexico, France and Singapore, exploring their evolution, system components and success factors. A common thread in ecosystem models is that different regions have characteristics that attract resources necessary for innovation and economic development and their characteristics vary from region to region. Thus, the characteristics of a certain entrepreneurial context may be more supportive of a certain kind of entrepreneurial activity, which in turn attracts entrepreneurs interested in that kind of entrepreneurial activity as well as the resources they need. The entrepreneurs and resources that are attracted to a region then become part of the ecosystem, leveraging and enhancing the original context. Lambkin and Day (1989) noted that there are a great variety of organizational forms and that some forms are more favored than others in certain environments. As in all ecosystem models, the organizational strategies and forms that the entrepreneur employs must match the ecological conditions if they are going to find an advantage within the ecosystem (Low and MacMillan, 1988).

The ecosystem model implies that context must be considered to be dynamic rather than static. An evolutionary approach has often been used to describe how the environment for entrepreneurs is constantly changing. Within this biological model new opportunities are created for expansion and founding of organizations as a result of environmental changes. These changes result in 'new resource sets' (Low and MacMillan, 1988) that are available within the entrepreneurial ecosystem. As entrepreneurs match their strategy with the evolving environment, they add new enterprises and further the overall economic progress of the ecosystem.

DELINEATING CONTEXTUAL CONTRIBUTIONS

In order to more fully understand the importance of context, we will continue to delineate some of the contributions that context makes to the entrepreneur and entrepreneurial process. We summarize these contributions within the following categories:

- supply of entrepreneurs
- sources of intellectual property
- conditions around failure
- extent of transaction costs
- rate of adoption
- effectiveness of service providers
- function of intermediaries
- availability of risk capital
- posture of public policy
- opportunities for training and education.

Though these categories are derived from our own in-depth field experience, a similar categorization was developed by Bruno and Tyebjee (1982) in their model of the entrepreneurial environment, which they developed based on a review of a dozen or so other researchers into the context for entrepreneurship. Their list of factors was analysed and categorized within two influences – resource availability and cost of doing business, which mirror two of our categories: availability of risk capital and extent of transaction costs.

SUPPLY OF ENTREPRENEURS

Context is critical to a region's supply of entrepreneurs. When there is an abundance of entrepreneurs in an area, they generate a high level of entrepreneurial energy as they interact, stimulate and challenge each other. This in turn creates demand for entrepreneurship supporters and intermediaries to provide resources that can support entrepreneurs. This is one of the reasons that the gap between entrepreneurial activity in US regions with highly evolved entrepreneurship ecosystems – like Silicon Valley and Boston's Route 128 – and entrepreneurial activity in other regions may grow wider over time. In a sense, the rich get richer. However, emerging entrepreneurial regions can take action to close the gap by:

- creating the infrastructure conditions that encourage entrepreneurs to move to their regions, or
- creating and supporting organizations and programs that develop local entrepreneurs.

To address the first category, in the USA a variety of context enhancing mechanisms have been adopted. For example, some regions have been successful at creating locally focused sources of risk capital such as angel networks and venture capital funds. (If the regions with a high concentration of entrepreneurs have an unfavorable ratio of supply of risk capital to demand, entrepreneurs might be motivated to move to regions with underutilized sources of risk capital.) In the Norwegian context, science parks were established throughout the 1990s adjacent to the larger research institutions in Norway, reflecting the perspective of the Norwegian government that it is particularly important to foster the creation of new research-based firms. In addition, technology transfer offices (TTOs) have been established at many universities in order to actively encourage spin-off firm formation.

The second category often includes business schools at local colleges and universities that develop entrepreneurship curricula and programs, incubators and small business development centers, entrepreneur networks and a wide variety of other economic development activities and organizations.

Trying to create an entrepreneurial ecosystem will simply be a financial black hole for its sponsors if there are not a sufficient number of entrepreneurs to take advantage of its resources. In addition, entrepreneurial skill is itself a key variable. Less skillful entrepreneurs will be inefficient in accessing the resources available within the ecosystem, while more skillful entrepreneurs will be efficient in leveraging the resources to accelerate the development of their ventures, thereby enhancing the probability of survival, the rate of growth and overall financial success. Hence, a mature ecosystem includes mechanisms that attract sophisticated entrepreneurs from outside and/or those that develop the sophistication of local entrepreneurs.

SOURCES OF INTELLECTUAL PROPERTY

For technology intensive entrepreneurial activity, sources of intellectual property (IP) may be a key variable to keep a steady flow of entrepreneurial output. Often, technological ventures are started by engineers or scientists who bring their IP with them. In these cases there is often the need for infrastructure and resources to turn it into a viable entrepreneurial endeavor. This process might include support for commercialization, the acquisition of additional technical talent to develop that IP further (which carries additional IP) or processes for licensing of IP to or from others. In other cases the entrepreneurial team is developing IP to which they have gained access. IP and/or technical talent are often acquired through universities that include engineering, science and/or medical schools, from government laboratories or through partnering relationships with large, technology intensive companies. Whether it is IP seeking an entrepreneurial team or an entrepreneurial team seeking IP, the systems, processes and structures for linking them are critical elements of the entrepreneurial ecosystem.

With a well-developed public university sector, Norway represents a rather typical case in Europe. As in many other European countries, Norwegian policy makers have in recent years adopted legislative initiatives and invested considerable funds to increase the commercialization of university research. This is particularly important with respect to enhancing the flow of IP, given the relatively low level of expenditures for research and development in the Norwegian industrial sector. By comparison, in the USA IP is generated from government, industry and university research laboratories.

CONDITIONS AROUND FAILURE

The national and regional contextual factors are critical to creating the conditions around entrepreneurial failure. Given the extensive number of failure factors implicit in the entrepreneurial process – lack of seed capital, poor delegation, ineffective team, lack of market knowledge, poor planning, competitor aggression and so on – entrepreneurs often must learn their way to success through failures. The USA has long been recognized for having a relatively entrepreneur friendly culture. The individual who takes risks, fails, learns from the failure, tries again and succeeds is highly regarded. The bankruptcy laws are designed to enable creditors, investors and entrepreneurs to settle up accounts when there is a business failure and to move forward. In many other countries risk taking and business failure carry a much heavier social stigma and/or legal penalty, hence people are discouraged from pursuing entrepreneurial opportunities. When potential entrepreneurs are inclined to pursue safe and stable employment in established companies, the entrepreneurial pipeline is constrained.

EXTENT OF TRANSACTION COSTS

Entrepreneurs are resource hungry. As they pursue the resources that they require for start-up and growth, inevitably they encounter transaction costs. In those regions where entrepreneurs must invest a relatively large amount of time, energy and current resources to overcoming barriers and systemic rigidities in order to leverage current resources into a larger and more complete resource pool, the probability of failure increases. Conversely, in regions that support fluidity and ease of access to resources, the probability of entrepreneurial success increases. Hamel (2000) suggested that the fluidity in the movement of entrepreneurial talent, IP and risk capital has made Silicon Valley the most successful entrepreneurial region in the world.

RATE OF ADOPTION

The adoption rate of new technologies, processes, products or services is often critical to the survival of the entrepreneurial venture. Entrepreneurs who are developing new products and services need to be able to test them with prospective customers. Entrepreneurial regions often evolve around the customer adoption mindset and capabilities. Similarly, a competitive industry drives companies to be alert to emerging innovations that have the potential to change the competitive landscape. If the competitors are relatively healthy from a financial perspective, they will be willing to invest resources in taking on the role of early adopters (Moore, 1991). The presence of early adopters can serve as an accelerator for the entrepreneur.

EFFECTIVENESS OF SERVICE PROVIDERS

The quantity and quality of service providers are important in determining the relative effectiveness of the entrepreneurial ecosystem. The service providers that are important to entrepreneurs include small business bankers, business attorneys, IP attorneys, accountants, marketing consultants, PR firms, HR consultants and search firms. These individuals and organizations provide services that the entrepreneur is often not prepared to deliver in-house. In some cases service providers will work on a pro bono basis or at a reduced rate, either to be seen as a good citizen of the community trying to develop a stronger economy or to promote long-term business development for their firms. Effective and committed service providers can be accelerators for entrepreneurs; ineffective and uncommitted service providers can be inexpensive financially but very expensive with respect to the time the entrepreneur must invest. In some cases the support organizations that are established to stimulate entrepreneurial activity in a given region also play an important role in accelerating the development of effective service providers (Rice, 1992; Rice and Abetti, 1993).

FUNCTION OF INTERMEDIARIES

Intermediaries play an important lubricating role in any context, increasing the fluidity with which people, IP and resources come together. Relatively mature entrepreneurial regions may have a ready supply of serial entrepreneurs. Nascent regions, in contrast, may have a limited supply of entrepreneurs in general and those that are present tend to be new to the game. Intermediaries can change the entrepreneurial context of a region. Intermediaries are the connectors and the boundary spanners in the entrepreneurial process. Their skills enhance the rate and intensity of linkages between entrepreneurs and resources and reduce the impact of systemic rigidities. They may also play an important training role, accelerating the rate at which nascent entrepreneurs increase sophistication with respect to resource acquisition and utilization skills (Rice, 2002). Intermediaries serve and support both entrepreneurs and 'know how experts' (Smilor and Gill, 1986) such as service providers discussed above.

Entrepreneurial intermediaries from the government and educational arenas generally serve a portfolio of ventures and seek to have a local, regional, national or international impact. At the local and regional levels in the USA programs designed to create a supportive entrepreneurial context include Small Business Development Centers (though they are sponsored by a national program), business incubators, science and technology parks, regional development councils, entrepreneur networks and a multitude of professional and trade associations. Many states have created programs to support entrepreneurial activity, such as the Massachusetts Technology Development Corporation, the Ben Franklin Partnership in Pennsylvania and the Centers for Advanced Technology in New York State. At the national level in the USA the Small Business Administration offers a variety of financing and assistance programs. Also the Small Business Innovative Research Act has provided significant support for technology and business development for technology based ventures.

In the Norwegian context, intermediaries may include technology transfer offices, science and technology parks, incubators, small business development centers, economic development agencies and private licensing firms. These intermediary organizations are to a large extent funded by public money and are designed to enhance the rate at which university spin-off ventures are established (see Chapter 4).

AVAILABILITY OF RISK CAPITAL

Some entrepreneurs start businesses that can achieve breakeven immediately, particularly if they are self-funding the start-up costs through sweat equity and/or investing their own capital. In start-ups with immediate strong cash flow and substantial assets, it may also be possible to secure debt financing from small business lenders, particularly if the entrepreneur is willing to pledge personal assets as collateral.

For those ventures that do not fit the self-funding capabilities model, the availability of risk capital is a critical success factor. Particularly in high potential ventures, the participation of equity investors is often necessary to cover the negative cash flows that occur during start-up and ramp up phases as the venture strives to achieve sustainability. In addition, risk capital may be important for supporting venture growth and competitiveness even after sustainability is achieved. The venture capital industry is well established in the USA and is emerging in other parts of the world; however it tends to be focused on the few highly entrepreneurial regions that provide attractive deal flow. In other regions that are striving to become more entrepreneurial, angel investors, angel investor networks and government-sponsored venture funds are critical for stimulating the growth of a local or regional entrepreneurship ecosystem.

As is the case for service providers and intermediaries, the sophistication of the providers of the risk capital is also a critical issue and is often dependent upon regional contextual factors. Sophisticated investors bring more than money to the table. They also add value through advising and mentoring the entrepreneurial team, and by utilizing their own networks to gain access for the venture to expertise, customers, suppliers, potential employees and other sources of financial support. Unsophisticated investors may increase the resource acquisition costs the entrepreneur must bear by providing too little value for the equity they take, thereby diminishing the prospects for entrepreneurial success.

In the Norwegian context, the government-sponsored program FORNY provides grants to research institutions, the commercialization actors and directly to commercialization projects. In addition, in the start-up phase Innovation Norway provides grants and the Industrial Corporation of Norway (SIVA) provides incubation services. Many research-based spin-off ventures are also able to take advantage of research and development tax deductions to leverage investment. As the new firms develop, additional cash flow is generated through the research and development contracts, seed funding and user driven research projects supported by Innovation Norway and the Research Council of Norway. The government provides loans with a risk reducing mechanism, while private investors provide equity capital to the funds. The goal of this scheme is to stimulate private investors to invest in early phases of a new venture development. In addition to the money invested it is also assumed that private investors will provide expertise to the new firms (see Chapter 4).

POSTURE OF PUBLIC POLICY

Public policy makers have a major impact on shaping the local, regional, state, national or international infrastructure and dynamics of the entrepreneurial context. At the local, regional and state levels public policy can stimulate the development of a variety of programs that establish and sustain the support infrastructure for the entrepreneurial ecosystem: incubators, regional entrepreneur networks, state-supported venture capital funds, economic development agencies, university-based research and research centers. At the national level public policy shapes commerce at a macro level in a wide variety of ways: bankruptcy laws, regulations defining processes, procedures and practices related to venture funding (both private equity and public offerings), laws governing disclosure and reporting requirements (for example, Sarbanes-Oxley), antitrust legislation, support for the research infrastructure (university, government and private sector) and education. Public policy may be designed to protect investors, to level the playing field, to protect workers (OSHA), to promote job creation, to create a specific social, political or economic capacity for the common good (defense, telecommunications, transportation, healthcare), and to make the country more competitive in the global marketplace. In many cases these public policy objectives are in conflict and hence can create a constraining environment for entrepreneurship. Inevitably, public policy can create new opportunities, accelerate or diminish existing economic activity, and deter or eliminate other forms of economic activity. It is, therefore, a critical contextual factor for entrepreneurship.

OPPORTUNITY FOR TRAINING AND EDUCATION

Training and education are key contextual influences, particularly for regions that are trying to develop nascent entrepreneurs. Entrepreneurs often affiliate with programs such as incubators, small business development centers and regional economic development organizations that offer periodic training programs intended to enhance the knowledge and skills of the entrepreneurs with respect to critical success factors they must address if they are ultimately going to be successful. Business plan competitions provide opportunities for entrepreneurial exploration and learning. In some cases entrepreneurs may start their ventures while they are working on a degree within an entrepreneurship program. For example, Babson College selects students each year for its Entrepreneurship Intensity Track, which supports students pursuing a venture start-up during the second half of the MBA program. These entrepreneurs are embedded in an ongoing training and education experience that is running in parallel with the launch of their entrepreneurial venture. Governments and university systems are often the prime movers in training and educational efforts.

OPERATIONALIZING A CONTEXTUAL MODEL

The context in which entrepreneurship occurs is often operationalized by establishing the processes, systems and organizational structures designed to stimulate and support entrepreneurial activity. One such example over the past 25 years is the business incubator. Incubators create a micro context in which entrepreneurship can be supported. They also serve as a catalyst for creating a macro context and for connecting incubating entrepreneurs to the macro context. Business incubation has expanded rapidly into a variety of industry sectors (high tech, services, arts and manufacturing) and into diverse settings (rural, inner city, industrial park and university campus). Once primarily the domain of stand-alone start-up ventures, business incubators now serve as vehicles for technology transfer and economic development for government, university and corporate research laboratories. The concept of incubation extends beyond the typical form taken by the 5000 incubators that are tracked by the National Business Incubation Association (NBIA). In fact the definition offered by the NBIA reinforces this observation. According to the NBIA (2009), 'Business incubation is a business support process that accelerates the successful development of start-up and fledgling companies by providing entrepreneurs with an array of targeted resources and services.' This definition can be applied to incubators that serve start-up ventures as well as to those in the corporate venture context. It can also occur in a community context, as suggested by Greene and Butler (1993), who compared the context for entrepreneurship provided by a traditional incubator to the context provided to entrepreneurs in the Pakistani community in Austin, Texas. They observed similarities in business advising, counseling and providing access to capital.

The traditional stand-alone incubator exemplifies the input-output model conceptually discussed earlier in this chapter. The input-output flow can be seen in Figure 2.1. It considers the relationship between entrepreneurial ventures and the external environment with the business incubator serving as both an intermediary and a context in which ventures can start, survive, grow and graduate (Rice and Matthews, 1995).

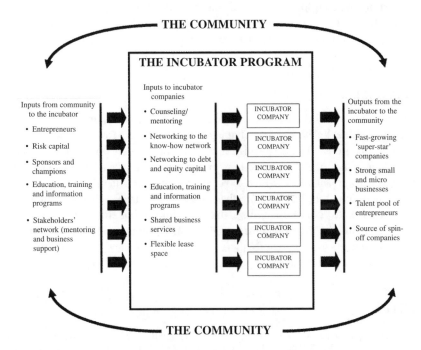

Figure 2.1   Input-output model of business incubation

There are actually two levels of context within this framework. First, the incubator itself offers (1) access to resources through shared facilities, equipment and services; (2) advising and counseling typically by the incubator staff and (3) training and education. Second, the incubator also serves as an intermediary between the incubator companies and the economic community in which the incubator resides, connecting its entrepreneurs to human and financial capital, external expertise through service providers, mentors, counselors and advisers available through partnering organizations and networks, and training and education through affiliation with educational and professional organizations.

The network within the incubator and the parallel networks it can access through its relationship with the community provide access to a variety of other resources, including potential suppliers and customers. In this sense, incubator companies and the economic community in which they reside are engaged in coproduction, in which both the producer of the ventures (the entrepreneur) and the consumer of the ventures and its outputs (products and services, jobs, return on investment), that is, the community, are engaged in the production process. The incubator, the resource networks and the know-how networks are thus the means through which the community engages with the entrepreneur in coproduction (Rice, 2002). The concept of the business incubator can, therefore, be generalized to the creation of a context, a system, a structure and a process for enhancing the start-up, survival, growth and success of ventures, which in turn can take a variety of forms.

SUMMARY

The interconnectedness of people, process and context is striking. Further, it is clear that context plays a role in shaping entrepreneurship from the most micro level to the global. Those organizations and individuals who are in positions to influence the context for entrepreneurship can opt to take a laissez-faire attitude or can proactively accelerate or inhibit entrepreneurship. These actors make decisions that reflect aims that range from narrow (that is, return on investment) to comprehensive (that is, improving lives worldwide). Understanding the gaps that entrepreneurs must overcome reveals opportunities for shapers of context to increase the rates of new venture start-up, survival, growth and success.

NOTE

1. This chapter builds on Mark P. Rice and Timothy G. Habbershon, 'Introduction', in Mark P. Rice and Timothy G. Habbershon (eds), *Entrepreneurship: The Engine of Growth – Volume 3*, Westport, CT: Praeger Publishers, 2007, pp. ix–xxv.

REFERENCES

Aldrich, H.E. and M.A. Martinez (2001), 'Many are called, but few are chosen: an evolutionary perspective for the study of entrepreneurship', *Entrepreneurship Theory and Practice*, **25**(4), 41–56.

Bruno, A.V. and T. Tyebjee (1982), 'The environment for entrepreneurship', in C.A. Kent, D.L. Sexton and K.H. Vesper (eds), *Encyclopedia of Entrepreneurship*, Englewood Cliffs, NJ: Prentice-Hall, pp. 288–315.

Drucker, Peter (2002), 'The discipline of innovation', *Harvard Business Review*, August, 95–102.

Fetters, M., M.P. Rice, P.G. Greene and J.S. Butler (eds) (2010), *The Development of University-based Entrepreneurship Ecosystems: Global Practices*, Cheltenham, UK and Northampton, MA, USA: Edward Elgar.

Friedman, T. (2005), *The World is Flat*, New York: Farrar, Straus and Giroux.

Greene, P.G. and J.S. Butler (1993), 'The ethnic community as a natural business incubator', *Journal of Business Research*, **36**(1), 51–8.

Hamel, G. (2000), 'Bringing Silicon Valley inside', *Harvard Business Review*, May, 70–84.

Lambkin, M. and G.S. Day (1989), 'Evolutionary processes in competitive markets', *Journal of Marketing*, **53**(3), 4–20.

Low, M.B. and I.C. MacMillan (1988), 'Entrepreneurship: past research and future challenges', *Journal of Management*, **14**(2), 139–61.

Moore, G. (1991), *Crossing the Chasm*, New York: Harper Business.

NBIA (2009), 'What is business incubation?', NBIA organization website, available at http://www.nbia.org/resource_library/what_is/ (accessed December 2009).

Rice, M. (1992), 'Building better businesses through the 3R program (3R = regular rigorous review)', Paper presented at the National Business Incubation Association Sixth Annual Conference, Austin, Texas.

Rice, M.P. (2002), 'Co-production of business assistance in business incubators: an exploratory study', *Journal of Business Venturing*, **17**(2), 163–87.

Rice, M.P. and P.A. Abetti (1993), 'A framework defining levels of intervention by managers of business incubators in new venture creation and development', *Frontiers of Entrepreneurship Research*, Babson Park, MA: Babson College, 102–16.

Rice, M.P. and J.B. Matthews (1995), *Growing New Ventures, Creating New Jobs: Principles and Practices of Successful Business Incubation*, Westport, CT: Greenwood Press.

Schumpeter, J. (1942), *Capitalism, Socialism and Democracy*, New York: Harper and Row.

Smilor, R.W. and M.D. Gill (1986), *The New Business Incubator: Linking Talent, Technology, Capital, and Know-how*, Lexington, MA: Lexington Books.

Stevenson, H.H., M. Roberts and H.I. Grousbeck (1989), *New Business Ventures and the Entrepreneur*, 3rd edn, Burr Ridge, IL: Richard D. Irwin.

Timmons, J.A. and S. Spinelli (2003), *New Venture Creation for the 21st century*, 7th edn, New York: McGraw-Hill.

Ucbasaran, D., P. Westhead and M. Wright (2001), 'The focus of entrepreneurial research: contextual and process issues', *Entrepreneurship Theory and Practice*, **25**(4), 57–80.

Zacharakis, A., D. Shepherd and J. Coombs (2003), 'The development of venture capital-backed internet companies: an ecosystem perspective', *Journal of Business Venturing*, **18**(2), 217–31.

Zahra, S. and J. Covin (1995), 'Contextual influences on the corporate entrepreneur-
ship-performance relationship: a longitudinal analysis', *Journal of Business
Venturing*, **10**(1), 43–58.

PART II

Emergence

3. The USA and Norway: empirical evidence on properties of emerging organizations

Tatiana S. Manolova, Linda F. Edelman, Candida G. Brush and Beate Rotefoss

INTRODUCTION

A central activity in entrepreneurship is the creation of new organizations (Gartner, 1985; Low and Abramson, 1997; Aldrich, 1999). Organizations are defined as goal directed, boundary maintaining activity systems that emerge when entrepreneurs take the initiative to engage in founding activities (McKelvey and Aldrich, 1983; Gartner, 1985). While organization theory examines the development of exchange relationships, acquisition of legitimacy (Aldrich, 1999) and mobilization of resources (Scott, 1987) in existing or established organizations, there is considerably less research investigating the ways in which new organizations emerge or come into being (McKelvey and Aldrich, 1983; Aldrich, 1999; Gartner, 2001).

Organizational formation is a dynamic process in which activities such as obtaining resources, developing products, hiring employees and seeking funds are undertaken at different times and in different orders (Gartner, 1985). Empirical studies find that more organizing activities improve survival chances (Carter et al., 1996; Lichtenstein et al., 2006), that new firm survival is enhanced when legitimacy building activities precede other types of organizing activities (Delmar and Shane, 2004) and that the concentration and timing of start-up activities impacts new firm formation (Lichtenstein et al., 2004).

These studies build on Katz and Gartner's (1988) well-regarded framework which explains organizational formation by outlining the properties of emerging organizations. Starting with the assumption that organizations emerge from the interaction between individuals and the environment, Katz and Gartner (1988) posit that four basic properties are central to organizational emergence. These properties are intentionality, the purposeful effort involved in organization emergence; resources, the tangible building blocks of an organization;

boundary, the creation of protected or formalized areas in which emergence occurs; and exchange, the crossing of boundaries to either secure inputs (for example, resources) or outputs of the organization. The authors argue that all four dimensions characterize a 'complete organization' (Katz and Gartner, 1988, p. 433).

Only a handful of studies have tested the four properties empirically (Reynolds and Miller, 1992; Reynolds and White, 1997; Chrisman, 1999). Recently, Brush et al. (2008) tested the framework in its entirety on a nationally representative sample of US nascent ventures. They found that all four properties are necessary for firm survival. Given that the USA has a fairly high rate of venture creation, resource access and positive perceptions of entrepreneurship (Bosma et al., 2008) it is of interest to explore whether or not the organizing process differs in another country context. This chapter builds on Brush et al. (2008) by exploring the four properties of emerging organizations in a different economic and institutional context: Norway. In many respects, Norway is similar to the USA given it is an innovation driven economy, has a relatively high gross national product (GNP), a well-educated workforce and a fairly high level of business start-up activity (Bosma et al., 2008). On the other hand, Norway has a comparatively small population, heavy contribution of the primary sector (agriculture, forestry, fishing, oil and gas extraction) to the economy, a lower rate of early-stage entrepreneurs and a much lower prevalence of high growth expectations (Bosma et al., 2008). Building on Delmar and Shane (2004) who examined the timing and influence of legitimizing activities on survival in a sample of Swedish firms, our work considers the extent to which the existence and completeness of organizational start-up properties influences the likelihood that the new venture will continue the organizing process.

CONTEXT OF THE STUDY

Norway is a small and relatively sparsely populated Scandinavian country, whose GNP per capita ranks among the highest in the world. North Sea oil and gas fields contribute significantly to the economy, representing more than one fifth of the total Norwegian GNP in 1998 (Statistics Norway, 2000). Norway boasts a highly educated workforce of about three million individuals. For the years 1993–98, the national unemployment rate was consistently under 6 percent. Finally, Norway has adopted a somewhat protective stance towards global integration, including continuing to vote against Norway's membership in the European Union.

One of the Norwegian government's goals is to ensure equal living conditions throughout the country through a public support system which includes the Norwegian Industrial and Regional Development Fund (SND), which in 2004 was reorganized, together with three other programs, into Innovation Norway. Government funding for start-ups, however, is the lowest among all OECD countries (Kolvereid, 2000).

Approximately 25 000–30 000 new businesses are registered in Norway each year, which corresponds to almost 10 percent of the total business population (Spilling, 1996). However, each year an equivalent number of businesses close down. Overall, Norway has slightly more business start-up attempts than the other Scandinavian countries (2.2 percent of the population in 1996 and 3.1 percent in 1997), but markedly lower than the USA (8.4 percent). Kolvereid (2000) found Norwegians report the lowest rate of entrepreneurial intentions compared to respondents in all other European countries in his study. Most of the start-up activity is carried out part time, suggesting that entrepreneurship may not be considered a legitimate career path (Bosma et al., 2008).

THEORY

Organizational Emergence and the Katz and Gartner (1988) Framework

While there is disagreement around the actual point at which an organization is formed, it is generally agreed that organizational emergence is the period in the life cycle of an organization when it is 'in creation'. During emergence the entrepreneur(s) brings together resources and engages in activities which will eventually distinguish the business as an entity that is separate from the founder (Reynolds and Miller, 1992; Carter et al., 1996). It is the 'territory between pre-organization and the new organization' and is defined by four basic properties: intentionality, resources, boundary and exchange (Katz and Gartner, 1988, p. 429). Each of the four emergent properties is discussed below.

Intentionality
Intentionality is 'an agent's seeking information that can be applied toward achieving the goal of creating a new organization' (Katz and Gartner, 1988, p. 431). Organizations are created by individual actors acting purposefully (Scott, 1987), and therefore it is the intentions of the entrepreneur(s) that lead to activities involved in creating an organization (Bird, 1988; Shook et al., 2003). For example, Kolvereid (1997) found support for the importance of entrepreneurial intentions to start-up success, and Krueger et al. (2000) studied two models of entrepreneurial intentionality finding that the decision to start a business often preceded scanning for an opportunity.

Resources

Resources are the building blocks of an organization. They include human and financial capital, property and equipment (Katz and Gartner, 1988, p. 432). These resources are then used, combined and coordinated into the production activities of the new organization (Penrose, 1957). The munificence or scarcity of resources in the environment, as well as their availability and specificity can affect firm survival (Becker and Gordon, 1966). Empirical studies find that different resource configurations influence new firm success, that firm resources interact with firm strategies and that entrepreneurs 'make do' with resources they have (Brush et al., 2001; Baker and Nelson, 2004).

Boundary

Boundary is the 'barrier condition between the organization and its environment' (Katz and Gartner, 1988, p. 432). It is the sometimes fuzzy space where the organization exerts some control over the resources in its environment. While not firmly demarcated, a boundary is often determined by social relations, time, legal and formal contracts as well as physical and spatial considerations (Scott, 1987). Boundaries may be formal, as in legal form, or informal, as in the case when the entrepreneur makes a conscious decision to found the business (Learned, 1992). Studies examining boundaries of new organizations find that in the early phases of organizational evolution structures, practices and boundaries varied widely, but tended to be informal and fluid (Bhave, 1994). Chrisman (1999) found that boundaries were created by nascent ventures early in their formation.

Exchange

Exchange refers to transactions that occur within or across the boundaries of organizations (Katz and Gartner, 1988, p. 432). The pattern of exchange usually involves resources or inputs that are transformed into outputs (Katz and Kahn, 1978). Exchanges are inherent in the social contract: employees or participants in the organization agree to perform certain work in exchange for pay, rights or privileges (Weick, 1979). Resources are acquired through an exchange process while goods and services are produced and exchanged across boundaries of the organization (Scott, 1987).

A significant number of studies have examined individual elements of the Katz and Gartner (1988) framework, or have used the framework as a conceptual anchor. However, only a few researchers have systematically studied the properties of emerging organizations. Reynolds and Miller (1992) examined the start-up process in new firms, finding variation in length and pattern of the process. Carter et al. (1996) examined the start-up activities of a cross-section of 71 nascent entrepreneurs finding that fledgling firms could be classified according to three activity profiles: started a business, gave up and still trying.

Chrisman (1999) examined three of the properties of emerging organizations in a study of Small Business Development Center clients. He found that 78 percent of respondents created organizational boundaries in their new ventures, that stocks of resources varied by geographic region and that intentions influenced the creation process. In a complete test of the Katz and Gartner (1988) framework, Kundu and Katz (2003) found that resources were significant predictors of exchange (their dependent variable), which they defined as exports. Finally, Brush et al. (2008) tested the entire Katz and Gartner (1988) framework using four years of data from the Panel Study of Entrepreneurial Dynamics I (PSED I). They found the four properties lead to a greater likelihood of firm survival and that the more activities in which a firm engaged, the greater the likelihood that the firm would not disband.

The next section develops hypotheses to test the basic tenets of the four properties framework on a Norwegian sample. Our goal is to add to the cumulative body of empirical evidence based on the Katz and Gartner (1988) framework by testing it in a non US environment, thus enhancing the ability to generalize from prior research.

HYPOTHESES

When nascent entrepreneurs gain control over resources and shape these into ongoing exchange relations, organizations coalesce as entities (Aldrich, 1999). Similarly, when intentions, resources, boundaries and exchange converge, the new venture assumes a life of its own (Welbourne and Andrews, 1996). Katz and Gartner (1988) note that not all four properties are brought together simultaneously in emerging organizations, but some aspects of these four properties must be present to identify the existence of an emerging new entity. Hence, the 'four properties characterize a complete organization' (Katz and Gartner, 1988, p. 388). In other words, the four properties of an emerging organization do not exist independently. Therefore:

Hypothesis 1: The four properties of emerging organizations are positively associated with the likelihood of continuing the organizing effort.

More specifically:

Hypothesis 1a: Intentionality is positively associated with the likelihood of continuing the organizing effort.

Hypothesis 1b: Resources are positively associated with the likelihood of continuing the organizing effort.

Hypothesis 1c: Boundary is positively associated with the likelihood of continuing the organizing effort.

Hypothesis 1d: Exchange is positively associated with the likelihood of continuing the organizing effort.

Due to the ambiguity that is inherent in the start-up process, new organizations face significant selection pressures (Reynolds and White, 1997). To mitigate this, fledgling firms seek to conform to standards, formalize operations and produce outcomes as a means to gain both sociopolitical and cognitive legitimacy (Aldrich, 1999). This suggests more visible evidence of organizational dimensions (for example, structure, resources, facilities and routines) would be better than less. Similarly, research shows that while there are many combinations of start-up activities, occurring in different orders, those nascent firms that carry out more activities are more likely to survive (Carter et al., 1996). Therefore, the more fully developed the resources, boundaries (or structural elements), exchange and intentions, the lower the likelihood of disbanding. Formally:

Hypothesis 2: Nascent ventures that manifest greater completeness of the four properties are more likely to continue the organizing effort.

Recently empirical work has moved beyond examining the existence of organizing activities to look at their timing (Lichtenstein et al., 2007; Brush et al., 2008). Should, for example, the nascent entrepreneur undertake a large number of organizing activities in a short period of time, or engage in those same activities in a more measured and continuous pace over a longer period of time? This type of decision involves the concentration of activities.

Given survival pressures, new ventures must move to overcome liabilities of newness and evolve into legitimate, ongoing organizations that are accepted by their stakeholders. This suggests that the faster the new venture engages in multiple organizing activities (a higher concentration of activities), the more likely the venture is to be perceived as viable (Aldrich, 1999). However, it also seems likely that too many organizing activities undertaken at the same time could overwhelm the nascent entrepreneur and, in the extreme, cause the abandonment of the organizing effort altogether. Therefore, there is a threshold effect with respect to the concentration of organizing activities in which the nascent entrepreneur must engage in enough activities to ensure legitimacy but not in so many activities as to be overwhelmed.[1] Formally,

Hypothesis 3: The likelihood to continue the organizing effort increases with the increase in the concentration of start-up activities, up to an optimal point, beyond which further increases in concentration decrease the likelihood of continuing the organizing effort.

METHODOLOGY

Sample

Data for the study come from a large representative sample of Norwegians 18 years or older, stratified by county. Consistent with prior research (Reynolds and Miller, 1992), the individuals contacted by MMI (a professional survey research institute in Norway), in their weekly 1996 CATI-bus telephone survey, were screened for nascent entrepreneurs of 18 years of age or older by asking two questions: (1) Are you today, alone or together with someone else, trying to start or acquire a business? and (2) Have you, alone or together with someone else, started or acquired a business during 1995 or so far in 1996? In total, 322 possible nascent entrepreneurs were identified (3.4 percent of the initial 9533 respondents) and were asked to provide their name and telephone number for further contact. Of the 322 respondents, 67 (20.8 percent) refused to participate in any further interviews. The names and telephone numbers of the 255 nascent entrepreneurs consenting to further interviews were purchased from MMI and were contacted immediately. Of these, 18 individuals (7.1 percent) were inaccessible, 27 (10.1 percent) did not identify themselves as nascent entrepreneurs and six respondents (2.4 percent) refused to participate, leaving a usable sample of 204 respondents.

Twelve months later, in February/March 1997, the 204 valid respondents were contacted again. Using a structured questionnaire, a telephone survey collected information about start-up activities and measured the self-perceived current status of their business. Fifteen of the 203 respondents (7.4 percent) in the valid sample could not be contacted. Hence, in 1997 data were gathered from 189 respondents. The third follow-up interviews were conducted in 1999 using the same questionnaire administered in 1997. A total of 145 (76.7 percent) of the 189 respondents were successfully contacted. The approximately 20 percent attrition rate in the Norwegian sample is consistent with prior longitudinal studies of nascent entrepreneurs in the USA (Brush et al., 2008), as well as in other Nordic countries (Delmar and Shane, 2003). There was no statistically significant non-response bias with regard to gender or region. Missing data in some of the categories rendered a usable sample size of 525 firm-year observations, for which we report the descriptive statistics and the results of the panel logistic regression models. For a more detailed account of the methodology, see Rotefoss and Kolvereid (2005).

Measures

This study utilizes nominal (binary and multinomial) measures. These measures were the same as those used previously in other PSED research (Carter et al., 2004) and, where possible, were operationalized as expressed in earlier work by Katz and Gartner (1988).

Start-up status

We used a self-reported categorical variable, indicating whether or not the start-up effort was, at the time of the initial and two follow-up interviews, still in the process of being established, abandoned or already established. Following Delmar and Shane (2003, 2004), we coded the second category (abandoned) as nascent venture disbanding (or failure). Over the four year course of the study, 12 percent of the nascent businesses had disbanded, and the remaining 88 percent had either reached an operating status or were continuing the organizing effort.

Properties of emerging organizations

We explored the four properties of emerging organizations: intentionality, resources, boundary and exchange, following the definitions provided by Katz and Gartner (1988, pp. 431–3). The dataset included questions on 20 founding activities, most of which followed Reynolds and Miller (1992) and Carter et al. (1996). Of these, three items (received private funding, received government funding and achieved positive net income) had over 50 percent missing values, and we had to exclude them from the analysis. We retained the remaining 17 items and classified them into the four properties of emerging organizations using expert opinions (for details on the classification approach, see Brush et al., 2008).

Intentionality

We followed Katz and Gartner's (1988) identification of purposeful actions for seeking information and taking action to start the venture using three binary variables. Nascent entrepreneurs reported whether or not they had developed a business plan, conducted market research to identify the business opportunity or started working full time for the nascent venture.

Resources

We measured resources according to Katz and Gartner (1988) and included human and financial capital, buildings and equipment. We used 11 dichotomous variables which indicated such things as whether or not nascent entrepreneurs had organized a start-up team, looked/bought/rented facilities or equipment, developed a product or service, saved money for the start-up, invested their own money in the start-up, asked for private/government funding, applied for a patent or hired employees.

Boundary
Boundary is the 'barrier condition between the organization and its environment' (Katz and Gartner, 1988, p. 432). Boundary was measured by using one self-reported binary item, indicating whether or not the entrepreneur had formed a legal entity.

Exchange
Exchange refers to cycles of transactions that occur across organizational boundaries (Katz and Gartner, 1988, p. 432). Exchange was measured by two dichotomous variables. Nascent entrepreneurs were asked to report whether or not they had started marketing or promotional efforts or received revenues from sales.

Property completeness
Property completeness was measured by summing up the counts across the four categories, ranging from 0 (no indication of any property of an emerging organization) to 17 (all 17 elements).

Property concentration
Temporal concentration was measured by the degree to which organizing activities were clustered together in time (Lichtenstein et al., 2007). To measure property concentration, we summed up the counts across the four categories at each wave of data collection (for example, 1996, 1997 and 1999), calculated the differences between 1996 and 1997 and between 1997 and 1999, and took the maximum value of the two differences. For example, the concentration for a nascent entrepreneur who engaged in six activities in 1996, seven activities in 1997, and nine activities in 1999 would equal max [(sum 1997 − sum 1996), (sum 1999 − sum 1997)] or max [1, 2] = 2. For another example, the concentration for a nascent entrepreneur who engaged in one activity in 1996, three activities in 1997 and eight activities in 1999 would equal max [2, 5] = 5.

Control variables
We controlled for entrepreneur, industry and year-specific effects. To account for the effect of a nascent entrepreneur's demographic characteristics and human capital, we included controls for gender, age and education. We also introduced five industry dummies and three year-specific dummy variables.

RESULTS

Descriptive Statistics

The nascent entrepreneurs in the sample were predominantly male (78 percent) and boasted high educational achievements, with over 37 percent having a college degree. The average age was 35.72 years, ranging between 18 and 69. The respondents contemplated entry into five industrial sectors, the most popular being business services (38 percent of the nascent entrepreneurial ventures), followed by consumer services (25 percent). Of note is the relatively high proportion of nascent ventures in primary sectors, such as agriculture and mining (14 percent). Twelve percent of the nascent businesses had disbanded during the time of the study.

The nascent businesses varied widely in the types of elements and completeness of emerging organizations' properties, with counts in the Boundary and Exchange categories generally higher than the counts in Intentionality and Resources. Thus, around 60 percent of the nascent ventures had formed a legal entity, started promotion or achieved first sale, but only one in three had conducted market research, one in four had developed a new product/service, and one in six had applied for a patent or a license. About two thirds of the respondents had invested their own money in the entrepreneurial initiatives. Overall, the nascent ventures had accumulated slightly over a third of the 17 property items we tracked in this study. Table 3.1 presents the descriptive statistics.[2]

Analytical Procedure

To model the likelihood of continuing the organizing effort, we implemented discrete time survival analysis, using the XTLOGIT procedure in STATA. Discrete time survival analysis concerns analysis of time-to-event data whenever survival times are grouped into discrete intervals of time (interval censoring) and can be fit using the maximum likelihood method. The estimation makes use of the property that the sample likelihood can be rewritten in a form identical to the likelihood for a binary dependent variable multiple regression model and applied to a specifically organized dataset of firm-year observations (Allison, 1984; StataCorp, 2007).

The –2 Log Likelihood ratio is a measure of how well the model fits the data. For individual independent variables, the OR (Odds Ratios) report exponentiated coefficients e^b rather than coefficients b and are more intuitively interpretable in terms of the increase/decrease in the odds of continuing the organizing effort. In addition, the χ^2 statistic tests the omnibus hypothesis that all regression coefficients are 0 (zero).

Table 3.1 Descriptive statistics

	N	Mean	SD	Min	Max
DEPENDENT VARIABLE					
Continue organizing	525	0.88	0.33	0	1
INDEPENDENT VARIABLES					
Intentionality					
Prepared business plan	525	0.49	0.50	0	1
Conducted market research	525	0.35	0.48	0	1
Devoted full time to business	524	0.37	0.48	0	1
Resources					
Organized start-up team	524	0.60	0.49	0	1
Looked for facilities/equipment	525	0.58	0.49	0	1
Bought facilities/equipment	525	0.49	0.50	0	1
Rented facilities/equipment	524	0.28	0.45	0	1
Developed product/service	525	0.25	0.43	0	1
Saved money	524	0.48	0.50	0	1
Invested money	523	0.64	0.48	0	1
Asked for private funding	524	0.44	0.50	0	1
Asked for government funding	523	0.39	0.49	0	1
Applied for patent/license	488	0.15	0.36	0	1
Hired employees	525	0.20	0.40	0	1
Boundary					
Formed legal entity	524	0.59	0.49	0	1

51

Table 3.1 Continued

	N	Mean	SD	Min	Max
Exchange					
Started sales promotion	524	0.56	0.50	0	1
Received first payment from sale	524	0.59	0.49	0	1
Property Completeness	591	6.60	4.05	0	15
Property Concentration	549	1.93	2.16	0	10
CONTROLS					
Consumer services	588	0.25	0.43	0	1
Business services	588	0.38	0.49	0	1
Transportation, utilities, communication	588	0.04	0.20	0	1
Manufacturing and construction	588	0.19	0.40	0	1
Agriculture and mining	588	0.14	0.34	0	1
Age	591	35.72	10.14	18	69
Gender: male	591	0.78	0.42	0	1
Level of education	591	2.14	0.76	1	3

Hypothesis Testing

Hypothesis 1 predicted that each of the four properties of nascent ventures affected the likelihood of continuing the organizing effort. As the interest here is in the joint significance of the items under each of the property categories, we specified four panel logistic regression models, one for each property category. Within each of the four models, we specified a chi-square (χ^2) test to check the probability that the regression coefficients under the corresponding property category are equal to zero (Allison, 1984).

The results from the testing of Hypothesis 1 are presented in Table 3.2 (Models 1–4). They suggest that the joint effects of intentionality, boundary and exchange items are significant, supporting Hypotheses 1a, 1c and 1d. The joint effect of the resource items failed to reach significance. Thus, Hypothesis 1b was not supported.

Among the individual organizing activities, both conducting market research and devoting full time to the new business in the Intentionality category significantly increased the odds of continuing the organizing effort. In the Resources category, buying or renting facilities and equipment, investing own money and hiring employees were also significantly and positively associated with the likelihood of continuing the organizing effort. Interestingly, saving money for the nascent venture had a significant negative effect. Those nascent entrepreneurs who had formed a legal entity, a Boundary item, had 62.61 the odds of continuing the organizing effort compared to those who had not formed a separate legal entity for the new business. Last, but not least, both items in the Exchange category (starting marketing and making a first sale) significantly increased the odds of continuing the organizing effort.

Hypothesis 2 predicted that property completeness will be positively associated with the continuation of the organizing effort. As results presented in Table 3.2 (Model 5) show, the accumulation of start-up activities significantly increases the odds of continuing the organizing effort, lending strong support for Hypothesis 2.

Hypothesis 3 predicted a curvilinear (inverted 'U') relationship between temporal concentration and the likelihood to continue the organizing effort. To test the hypothesis, we specified a regression model including concentration and its quadratic term. Results are presented in Table 3.2 (Model 6) and indicate that the linear term is positively and significantly associated with the likelihood to continue the organizing effort, whereas the quadratic term is in the expected direction and approaches significance ($p = 0.146$). Thus, Hypothesis 3 received partial support.

In sum, this study provides additional empirical evidence for the Katz and Gartner (1988) framework. The results from hypothesis testing showed the joint effects of intentionality, boundary and exchange items are significant, but

Table 3.2 *Logistic regression estimates on likelihood of continuing to organize: effect of property categories, completeness and concentration*

	MODEL 1 (n = 522)		MODEL 2 (n = 478)		MODEL 3 (n = 522)		MODEL 4 (n = 522)		MODEL 5 (n = 523)		MODEL 6 (n = 507)	
	OR	SE	OR	SE	OR	SE	OR	SE	OR	SE	OR	SE
Controls												
Year: 1996	**6.03****	3.65	**17.62****	17.62	**15.83*****	11.9	**10.41*****	7.49	**0.06*****	0.05	**7.63****	5.1
Year: 1997	0.62	0.34	0.37	0.28	2.41	1.37	0.37	0.23	**0.03*****	0.03	1.73	0.9
Year: 1999	0.12	0.27	**0.00***	0.00	0.13	0.24	**0.00****	0.00	**0.00***	0.01	**0.01***	0.01
Consumer services	1.28	2.67	**0.01**†	0.01	0.94	1.74	**0.01***	0.01	**0.03**†	0.05	0.06	0.13
Business services			**0.00**†	0.00			0.01	0.02	0.04	0.13	0.07	0.21
Transportation, utilities, communication												
Manufacturing and construction	0.72	1.57	**0.00**†	0.00	0.51	0.98	**0.00***	0.01	**0.03**†	0.06	0.05	0.11
Agriculture and mining	71.41	197.39			9.09	21.23						
Age	1.03	0.04	1.02	0.06	1.03	0.04	0.99	0.04	1.01	0.04	1.04	0.04
Gender: male	2.78	2.49	**10.96**†	15.67	2.49	1.97	**6.12**†	6.42	3.77	3.71	3.41	3.13
Level of education	0.68	0.37	1.22	0.95	0.57	0.28	0.88	0.53	0.69	0.40	0.68	0.38
Intentionality												
Prepared business plan	2.57	2.05										
Conducted market research	**5.42***	4.69										
Devoted full time to business	**45.26*****	54.05										
Resources												
Organized start-up team			0.87	0.92								
Looked for facilities/ equipment			0.45	0.46								

54

	(1)	(2)	(3)	(4)	(5)	(6)
Bought facilities/equipment	19.54†	29.81				
Rented facilities/equipment	33.65†	61.95				
Developed product/service	1.93	2.64				
Saved money	0.09†	0.11				
Invested money	31.24*	42.58				
Asked for private funding	0.26	0.34				
Asked for government funding	3.59	4.36				
Applied for patent/license	0.42	0.66				
Hired employees	121.25†	354.11				
Boundary						
Formed legal entity			62.61***	54.86		
Exchange						
Started sales promotion			10.04*	10.09		
Received first payment from sale			52.62***	51.85		
Property Completeness					2.21***	0.44
Property Concentration					4.38*	0.89
Property Concentration Squared					2.61	0.07
Regression Function						
Log likelihood	−134.93	−109.01	−128.11	−125.29	−126.16	−132.79
LR chi-square (*df*)	56.13*** (12)	75.79*** (20)	69.37*** (10)	75.44*** (11)	73.78*** (10)	
Tests of joint significance chi-square (*df*)	12.56**(3)	11.85(11)	22.29*** (1)	18.51*** (2)		43.23*** (11)

Note: † Significant at $p < 0.1$, *significant at $p < 0.05$, **significant at $p < 0.01$, ***significant at $p < 0.001$; figures in parentheses are the degrees of freedom in the regression function.

not resources. Further, the more complete the properties, the more likely organizing efforts will continue and after an initial cluster of activities is
performed, a steadier organizing effort may be more effective.

DISCUSSION

The objective of this inquiry is to validate the Katz and Gartner (1988) framework in the Norwegian context. Using longitudinal data on nascent organizations we empirically tested the four properties of emerging organizations,
intentionality, resources, boundary and exchange, and their effect on likelihood of continued organizing (Katz and Gartner, 1988). We then tested for
property completeness, following the logic that firms which engage in a
greater number of start-up activities are less likely to fail (Carter et al., 1996).
Finally, we tested for property concentration arguing that up to a point firms
which engage in more activities are likely to continue the organizing effort, but
that after the threshold is reached, there are diminished returns to engaging in
more organizing activities.

All Properties are Necessary for Continuing the Organizing Effort

Katz and Gartner (1988) argued that all four properties are necessary for
continuing the organizing effort. However, contrary to previous findings
(Brush et al., 2008) which found support for all four properties, in the
Norwegian sample we found that only intentionality, boundary and exchange
were significant, and that resources was not. Given previous work that argues
for the importance of resources for firm performance in a more mature small
firm context (Edelman et al., 2005), we were surprised that resources did not
play a more prominent role in the continuation of the start-up effort.

   To better understand this result, we referred to the definitions of each of the
four properties. We found that while intentionality is about information seeking, boundary is concerned with barriers between the fledging firm and the
environment and exchange is about transactions, resources are different in that
they are characterized as the building blocks of the new venture. From previous research we also know that while firms acquire some resources, new
ventures are typically resource constrained, and hence engage in bricolage and
other forms of behavior that allow them to leverage as many resources as
possible (Baker and Nelson, 2005). Therefore, we suggest that at least for new
ventures in the Norwegian context, in which a predominant number of new
ventures are in the agriculture (14 percent) and the manufacturing (20 percent)
sectors, resources are a necessary but not sufficient condition for continuation
of the start-up process. In other words, resources are necessary for the orga-

nizing effort to continue, but they are not enough to distinguish abandoned nascent ventures from those that choose to continue organizing.

Property Completeness

The second finding from this inquiry is that firms which engage in more activities are less likely to disband. This finding is consistent with Carter et al. (1996) as well as with Brush et al. (2008) and suggests that Norwegian nascent entrepreneurs who are actively engaged in the process of starting the venture are likely to end up with a viable new venture in the short run. As so many researchers have suggested, there is neither a set of magic properties, nor is there a particular sequence of activities that lead to the continuation of the start-up process (Carter et al., 1996; Brush et al., 2008). Instead the key to surviving the nascent phase is to engage in a number of properties, and by gaining momentum nascent entrepreneurs are likely to establish legitimacy and their firms are more likely to survive, at least in the short run.

Temporal Concentration of Property Accumulation

Finally we tested for the concentration of property accumulation, hypothesizing that new ventures need to engage in a number of organizing activities but that there is a threshold after which too many activities become overwhelming and lead to failure. Our finding of partial support in the Norwegian dataset challenges the previous literature, which found that a low concentration of organizing activities led to higher likelihood of new firm creation (Lichtenstein et al., 2007). One possible explanation for the difference between our finding and Lichtenstein et al.'s (2007) is that we looked at organizing activities in two time periods that were approximately one year apart, while Lichtenstein et al. (2007) used a much shorter one month window. Therefore, it seems likely that what could be overwhelming on a monthly basis, when spread out over 12 months is quite manageable. While Lichtenstein et al.'s (2007) findings support the old adage 'slow and steady wins the race', our findings suggest that in Norway nascent entrepreneurs need to gain start-up momentum, and, up to a point, one way to do this is to engage in a number of start-up activities.

IMPLICATIONS AND CONCLUSIONS

Using longitudinal data on nascent entrepreneurs this chapter empirically tests the effects of the four properties of emerging organizations – intentionality, resources, boundary and exchange – as identified by Katz and Gartner (1988) on the likelihood of continued organizing in Norway. Our findings suggest that intentionality, boundary and exchange are necessary and sufficient for firm survival in the short term and that resources are necessary but not sufficient. We also found that entrepreneurs who engage in a larger number of start-up activities are more likely to continue the organizing effort in the short term and that initially engaging in a large number of activities is a good strategy for new ventures, but that there is a point where too many activities lead to diminishing returns.

We do note a few limitations to our study. First, our sample is ten years old, but given the relative stability of entrepreneurial activity and the overall Norwegian economy, we have confidence that our results apply today. In addition, the choice of the underlying categories of the dependent variable is subject to debate. For example, Gartner and Carter (2003) consider four start-up status categories: operating, still trying, currently inactive and disbanded. Lichtenstein et al. (2004) collapse the currently inactive and disbanded categories into one and consider three categories: succeeded, ongoing and failed. Carter et al. (2004) consider operating and still active versus the other categories. As such, some might argue that a different categorization of groups might be more appropriate. However, we felt that more consistency would be achieved by building on research (Delmar and Shane, 2003, 2004) that analysed many of the same variables that we used.

Limitations aside, this chapter empirically examines the well-regarded Katz and Gartner (1988) framework of organizational emergence. Our findings provide validity for the original framework in a unique context of start-up ventures in Norway. In addition, our findings lend strong support to the dynamic nature of new venture emergence by suggesting that, up to a point, the more activities in which the entrepreneur is engaged, the more likely the continuation of the organizing effort. Organizational emergence plays a central role in the field of entrepreneurship, and empirically verifying the well-regarded Katz and Gartner (1988) framework in a non-US context adds to our understanding of this important process.

NOTES

1. In the natural sciences this argument is often referred to as 'the edge of chaos' (Langton, 1990).
2. The correlation matrix is not included because of space constraints and is available from the authors upon request.

REFERENCES

Aldrich, H. (1999), *Organizations Evolving*, Thousand Oaks, CA: Sage Publications.

Allison, P.D. (1984), *Event History Analysis: Regression Analysis for Longitudinal Event Data*, Beverly Hills, CA: Sage Publications.

Baker, T. and R. Nelson (2005), 'Creating something from nothing: resource construction through entrepreneurial bricolage', *Administrative Science Quarterly*, **50**, 329–36.

Becker, S.W. and G. Gordon (1966), 'An entrepreneurial theory of formal organizations Part I: patterns of formal organizations', *Administrative Science Quarterly*, **11**(3), 315–44.

Bhave, M. (1994), 'A process model of entrepreneurial venture creation', *Journal of Business Venturing*, **9**(3), 233–42.

Bird, B.J. (1988), 'Implementing entrepreneurial ideas: the case for intention', *Academy of Management Review*, **13**(3), 442–53.

Bosma, N., Z.J. Acs, E. Autio, A. Coduras and J. Levie (2008), *Global Entrepreneurship Monitor: 2008 Executive Report*, Wellesley, MA and Santiago, Chile: Babson College and Universidad del Desarrollo.

Brush, C.G., P.G. Greene and M.M. Hart (2001), 'From initial idea to unique advantage: the entrepreneurial challenge of constructing a resource base', *Academy of Management Executive*, **15**(1), 64–78.

Brush, C.G., T.S. Manolova and L.F. Edelman (2008), 'Properties of emerging organizations: an empirical test', *Journal of Business Venturing*, **23**(5), 547–66.

Carter, N.M., W.B. Gartner and P.D. Reynolds (1996), 'Exploring start-up event sequences', *Journal of Business Venturing*, **11**(3), 151–66.

Carter, N.M., W.B. Gartner and P.D. Reynolds (2004), 'Firm founding', in W.B. Gartner, K.G. Shaver, N.M. Carter and P.D. Reynolds (eds), *The Handbook of Entrepreneurial Dynamics: The Process of Organization Creation*, Newbury Park, CA: Sage Series, pp. 311–23.

Chrisman, J. (1999), 'The influence of outsider-generated knowledge resources on venture creation', *Journal of Small Business Management*, **37**(4), 42–58.

Delmar, F. and S. Shane (2003), 'Does business planning facilitate the development of new ventures?', *Strategic Management Journal*, **24**(12), 1165–85.

Delmar, F. and S. Shane (2004), 'Legitimizing first: organizing activities and the survival of new ventures', *Journal of Business Venturing*, **19**(3), 85–410.

Edelman, L.F., C.G. Brush and T.S. Manolova (2005), 'Co-alignment in the resource-performance relationship: strategy as mediator', *Journal of Business Venturing*, **20**(3), 359–83.

Gartner, W.B. (1985). 'A conceptual framework for describing the phenomenon of new venture creation', *Academy of Management Review*, **10**(4), 696–706.

Gartner, W.B. (2001), 'Is there an elephant in entrepreneurship: blind assumptions in theory development', *Entrepreneurship Theory and Practice*, **25**(4), 57–80.

Gartner, W.B. and N.M Carter (2003), 'Still trying after all these years: nascent entrepreneur "semi-survivor" bias in the panel study of entrepreneurial dynamics', paper presented at the Academy of Management Meetings, Seattle, Washington, August 2003.

Gartner, W.B., N.M. Carter and P.D. Reynolds (2004), 'Business start-up activities', in W.B. Gartner, N.M. Carter, K.G. Shaver and P.D. Reynolds (eds), *The Handbook of Entrepreneurial Dynamics: The Process of Organization Creation*, Newbury Park, CA: Sage Series, pp. 285–99.

Katz, D. and R. Kahn (1978), *The Social Psychology of Organizations*, New York: Wiley.

Katz, J. and W.B. Gartner (1988), 'Properties of emerging organizations', *Academy of Management Review*, **13**(3), 429–41.

Kolvereid, L. (1997), 'Organizational employment versus self-employment: reasons for career choice intentions', *Entrepreneurship Theory and Practice*, **20**, 23–31.

Kolvereid, L. (2000), 'Entreprenørskap i Norge', *Magma*, **1**, 40–48.

Krueger, N.F., M.D. Reilly and A.L. Carsrud (2000), 'Competing models of entrepreneurial intentions', *Journal of Business Venturing*, **15**(5/6), 411–32.

Kundu, S.K. and J. Katz (2003), 'Born-international SMEs: bi-level impacts of resources and intentions', *Small Business Economics*, **20**(1), 25–47.

Langton, C.G. (1990), 'Computation at the edge of chaos', *Physica D*, **42**, 12–37.

Learned, K. (1992), 'What happened before the organization? A model of organization formation', *Entrepreneurship Theory and Practice*, **17**(1), 39–48.

Lichtenstein, B.B., N.M. Carter, K. Dooley and W.B. Gartner (2004), 'Exploring the temporal dynamics of organizational emergence', paper presented at the Babson Entrepreneurship Research Conference, June 2004, Glasgow, Scotland.

Lichtenstein, B.B., K.J. Dooley and G.T. Lumpkin (2006), 'Measuring emergence in the dynamics of new venture creation', *Journal of Business Venturing*, **21**(2), 153–75.

Lichtenstein, B.B., N.M. Carter, K. Dooley and W.B. Gartner (2007), 'Complexity dynamics of nascent entrepreneurship', *Journal of Business Venturing*, **22**, 236–61.

Low, M. and M. Abramson (1997), 'Movements, bandwagons, and clones: industry evolution and the entrepreneurial process', *Journal of Business Venturing*, **12**(6), 435–58.

McKelvey, W. and H. Aldrich (1983), 'Populations, natural selection and applied organizational science', *Administrative Science Quarterly*, **28**(1), 101–28.

Penrose, E.T. (1957), *The Theory of Growth of the Firm*, New York: Wiley and Sons.

Reynolds, P.D. and B. Miller (1992), 'New firm gestation: conception, birth and implications for research', *Journal of Business Venturing*, **7**(5), 405–17.

Reynolds, P.D. and S.B. White (1997), *The Entrepreneurial Process: Economic Growth, Men, Women, and Minorities*, Westport, CT: Quorum Books.

Rotefoss, B. and L. Kolvereid (2005), 'Aspiring, nascent and fledgling entrepreneurs: an investigation of the business start-up process', *Entrepreneurship and Regional Development*, **17**, March, 109–27.

Scott, R. (1987), *Organizations: Rational, Natural and Open Systems*, 2nd edn, Englewood Cliffs, NJ: Prentice Hall.

Shook, C.L., R.L. Priem and J.E. McGee (2003), 'Venture creation and the enterprising individual: a review and synthesis', *Journal of Management*, **29**(3), 379–99.

Spilling, O.R. (1996), 'Regional variation of new firm formation: the Norwegian case', *Entrepreneurship and Regional Development*, **8**, 217–45.

StataCorp (2007), *STATA Survival Analysis and Epidemiological Table Reference Manual*, Release 10, College Station, TX: StataCorp LP.

Statistics Norway (2000), *Statistical Yearbook 2000*, Oslo: Ad Notam.

Weick, K. (1979), *The Social Psychology of Organizing*, Reading, MA: Addison Wesley.

Welbourne, T.M. and A.O. Andrews (1996), 'Predicting the performance of initial public offerings: should human resource management be in the equation', *Academy of Management Journal*, **34**(4), 891–919.

4. Models for government support to promote the commercialization of university research: lessons from Norway

Einar Rasmussen and Mark P. Rice

INTRODUCTION

It is a clear international trend that universities are expected to take on technology transfer and commercialization of research as a part of their mission in addition to teaching and research (Etzkowitz et al., 1998). This trend is partially induced by government policies and initiatives (Rasmussen et al., 2008) and many countries have numerous schemes that partly or fully are targeted to support the commercialization of publicly funded research (Feldman et al., 2002; Wright et al., 2007). European programs often seek to emulate the perceived US capacity for commercializing research results (Mustar et al., 2008). In the USA many universities and their Technology Transfer Offices (TTOs) take an active role in promoting research commercialization and national initiatives such as the SBIR program have successfully contributed to fostering academic entrepreneurship (Toole and Czarnitzki, 2007).

Apart from the fact that the number of government support programs and the resources invested in these has increased radically, there remains much work in integrating disparate practices into conceptual models that can lead to improved performance of these programs and improved return on investment of resources. Universities and countries vary enormously in their approaches to facilitate university technology transfer (Geuna and Muscio, 2009), and the initiatives are based on benchmarking and experimenting, rather than conceptual frameworks. In the next section we discuss key issues and barriers related to university technology transfer and commercialization. Then we present the Norwegian initiatives to promote commercialization of university research. Based on the Norwegian initiatives and the scholarly literature we outline a conceptual framework of four different models for how government can promote the commercialization of university research. Finally implications and conclusions are provided.

UNIVERSITY TECHNOLOGY TRANSFER AND COMMERCIALIZATION

What is University Technology Transfer?

Technology transfer is the application of information to use (Rogers, 2002) and may be defined as the process of developing practical applications from the results of scientific research. The term commercialization is also used to describe the technology transfer process. Commercialization is the conversion of an idea from research into a product or service for sale in the marketplace (Rogers, 2003). In the context of this chapter, technology transfer is the process through which the outputs of academic research are conveyed to those who make use of the research results. Indirectly, technology can be transferred through education and research-based teaching, through publication of articles, books and reports, through seminars and conferences as well as through informal contacts and researchers acting as consultants (Cohen et al., 2002). More directly, technology transfer may occur through contract research and industry collaboration and through licensing and the creation of new spin-off firms to exploit new technologies (Etzkowitz et al., 1998).

This chapter focuses on technology transfer of publicly funded university research in the form of commercialization projects where the university technology is transferred to potential users, such as when it is licensed to an existing firm or forms the basis for a new spin-off firm. Licensing and spin-off firm formation represent a relatively modest share of technology transfer from academic research, but can be an efficient way of transferring new knowledge and research findings from universities into application in industry and society. Commercialization of research makes available to the market new products, processes and services that may contribute to solving social, cultural or environmental challenges. Technology transfer is then seen as a way of communicating research results and thus a part of the research process. Commercialization may also be seen as an important mechanism for industry development. Success cases that have often been referred to are Silicon Valley in California and Cambridge in the UK where a considerable share of the local industry has emanated from local research institutions. Therefore, a significant potential might be realized if there exists a well-developed competence and infrastructure to support technology transfer through licensing and spin-offs.

Barriers to Technology Transfer

Even if a technology has characteristics which give it possible advantages in the market, it might not be utilized due to several reasons. Obstacles or barriers in the process of university technology transfer that must be overcome in order to create value include the following:

- Need for interdisciplinary cooperation. As noted by Rosenberg (1991), new innovations are increasingly interdisciplinary and close coopera-tion between a number of specialists is required to succeed.
- Lack of resources to support technology transfer. Technology transfer is more than knowledge transfer. Even if research results are published or instructed to students, this does not ensure that the technology is repli-cated or practised. People may not use what they know due to environ-mental factors such as lack of physical, financial, human or social resources (Rogers, 2003). Universities and government laboratories often have a shortage of risk capital and entrepreneurial talent necessary to accomplish technology transfer and commercialization.
- Communication gap between generators of intellectual property and adopters. There is often a communication gap between academics and potential adopters of the technology due to differences in expertise, motives, culture and language (Rogers, 2002). In order to understand scientific reports and to communicate with academics there is a need for specialized competence and infrastructure, which might not be present in industrial companies or other adopters. Likewise, academics may also lack awareness and understanding of business culture and the requirements of the commercialization process (Stankiewicz, 1994).
- Cultural bias against commercialization within the academic commu-nity. The term commercialization has traditionally evoked negative associations within many research departments because it signals that commercial interests are in focus. There are many examples of conflicts in the intersection between open research and commercial application (Blumenthal et al., 1997).
- Difficulty of converting tacit knowledge into explicit knowledge. The research process might generate a considerable share of tacit knowledge which cannot easily be converted to explicit knowledge, but instead may have to be transferred through personal interaction and learning over time (Jensen and Thursby, 2001).
- Necessity of acquiring protection for intellectual property before begin-ning commercialization. Intellectual property (IP) protection might be a critically important prerequisite for commercial interests to make investments in further development of a new technology, while open dissemination and publication are important to academics.
- Severity of risk and uncertainty. The innovation or technology might be so radical in nature that no existing companies are willing to undertake commercialization (Markham et al., 2002).

- The projected time to market and size of investment required to complete the commercialization process. University innovations are often embryonic in nature (Jensen and Thursby, 2001; Colyvas et al., 2002). There is considerable risk associated with commercialization of research results, and the time lag between a research result and a product or service introduced to the marketplace is often substantial. Thus, there are few economic incentives for single firms to invest in developing early-stage projects and established firms are mostly interested in the more fully developed technologies from universities (Thursby et al., 2001).

To sum up, the barriers and challenges identified above establish a gap between the generators of technology and the adopters of technology that needs to be addressed by institutions and policy makers seeking to increase the success rate for technology transfer and commercialization, thereby increasing economic and social impact.

Developing a Conceptual Model for Addressing the Barriers to Technology Transfer

The difficulty of transferring basic research into commercial products has been explored by many empirical studies. Key streams in the literature have looked at firm characteristics, university characteristics and channels of technology transfer (Agrawal, 2001). For instance, in the case of R&D cooperation between firms and research organizations, Mora-Valentin et al. (2004) highlighted success factors such as previous cooperative experience, partners' good reputation, clear definition of objectives, higher degree of institutionalization, greater proximity between partners, more commitment, better communication, higher levels of trust, lower level of conflict and greater dependence among partners. Most of these factors are difficult to address directly by government initiatives.

For policy makers, a key challenge is to find models that can lower the practical and cultural barriers in the intersection between academic research and commercial application. A frequent argument is that there exists a market failure in this particular phase of the research commercialization process (Salmenkaita and Salo, 2002). Tassey (2005) discussed the 'risk spike' occurring when a project moves from basic scientific research into technology research. In this phase both the technical risk and the market risk are high. Thus, the barriers to technology transfer can be conceptualized as a gap between academic research and commercial application. In the case of university spin-off ventures, Lockett et al. (2005) refer to the knowledge gaps and the finance gap encountered by these firms. Investors such as venture capital firms prefer that other actors take the initial investments and choose to invest in more mature projects with lower risks (Lockett et al., 2002). As reviewed above, the gap is also inherent in cultural factors. The aim of this chapter is to develop a conceptual framework that would enable policy makers and program managers to understand the types of initiatives and mechanisms governments can use to bridge the gap. In the next section the efforts made by the Norwegian government are presented.

THE CASE OF NORWAY

To explore how governments can promote the commercialization of research, we look at the development of government initiatives in Norway. With a well-developed public university sector, Norway represents a rather typical case in Europe. As in many other countries, the Norwegian policy makers have in recent years issued several legislative changes and spent considerable funds on initiatives to increase the commercialization of university research. Due to a relatively low level of industry R&D expenditure, the Norwegian government considers it to be particularly important to foster the creation of new research-based firms.

Government Instruments in Norway

The commercial application of research results has a long history in Norway, but the Norwegian government has not made any systematic efforts to increase the commercialization of research until recently. Over the last few years, the number of actors and the amount of resources used has increased dramatically. The first sporadic initiatives with support from one of the government agencies were started around some of the larger research institutions in the 1980s. Throughout the 1990s science parks were established adjacent to the larger research institutions in Norway with the aim of increasing the industrial application of commercially interesting research results. The government program FORNY was established in 1995 and has become the main instrument for supporting the commercialization of results from Norwegian research institutions receiving a steadily increased budget reaching NOK 59 million in 2002 and 145 million in 2008.[1] FORNY aimed to establish an infrastructure to lower the barriers towards commercialization at the research institutions and to professionalize the commercialization process. Commercialization was defined as a license to an existing firm or the start-up of a new firm.

Initially, the FORNY program worked exclusively through regional commercialization units that received an annual lump sum based on an application to the FORNY program. These units were often connected to science parks and acted as the operators of the program at regional level. Their assistance included the evaluation of an idea and its commercialization prospects, the implementation of a strategy with regard to IP, the addition of competence, the provision of commercial networks and access to financing. The initial experiences led to some changes from 2000. There was clearly a need for a stronger involvement from the research institutions and the funds were split in two: (1) the infrastructure funds for the research institutions and (2) the project funds that continued to be awarded to the commercialization units. From 2001 a new program plan outlined a new main goal for FORNY: 'to increase the value creation through commercializing knowledge-based business ideas with a high value creation potential'.[2]

From 2003 the universities were entitled ownership of intellectual property rights (IPR), which previously belonged to the individual researchers. As part of these legislative changes, the universities were assigned explicit responsibility for commercialization of research. The coordination from the Norwegian government has been limited and the universities have experimented with different solutions at the local level, often following the requirements from the FORNY program. The involvement by the universities was further strengthened in 2004 when they were allowed to apply for project funding directly without going through the commercialization units. The universities and several other public research institutions now established their own TTOs that partly took over the activities previously conducted by the science parks and many universities actively encouraged spin-off firm formation.

In 2008 FORNY provided financial support to 14 commercialization units, 7 universities/academic colleges, 18 R&D institutes, 5 university hospitals and 13 technical colleges. FORNY has four categories of schemes. The infrastructure fund seeks to increase the number of ideas developed in the research institutions, while the other schemes are aimed at specific projects in the idea development phase. As the projects develop into new ventures or move into existing ventures, a number of government support schemes become relevant. Table 4.1 provides an overview of these schemes.

An assessment of the portfolio of companies supported by FORNY grants from 1996 to 2007 (Borlaug et al., 2009) shows that 295 companies had started and 125 license agreements had been signed on the basis of technology developed in Norwegian research institutions. In 2008 about 200 of these firms still existed with a total turnover of about NOK 900 million and 700 employees. Most of these firms are small and only about 5 percent display patterns that make them likely to become high-growth firms. Thus, the direct results from the FORNY program are not impressive when measured in terms of value creation in spin-offs and licenses, while the indirect effects are more difficult to assess.

Table 4.1 Norwegian government support schemes relevant for the commercialization of university research

Scheme	Description	Usage
FORNY: idea generation and development of infrastructure (infrastructure funds)	The research institutions apply for funds to include commercialization as a part of their strategies, to increase the awareness and knowledge about patenting and commercialization and to stimulate the search for commercialization possibilities in the research activity. FORNY covers up to 50 percent of the total costs. FORNY also supports the establishment of university TTOs, cooperation between TTOs and other commercialization units, alignment of policies and rules at research institutions and part-funding of patenting costs.	Budget of NOK 27.4 million in 2008. Measured outcome includes the 500 conferences and seminars, 15 000 seminar participants, 672 potentially interesting research-based business ideas and 273 ideas actively pursued.
FORNY: commercialization funds	The commercialization units/TTOs receive a lump sum grant based on applications. The potential for commercialization at the institutions and the prior performance is considered when the funding decision is made. The funding decision for both infrastructure and commercialization funds are made by the FORNY secretary. Funds can be used to cover up to 50 percent of the costs of specific commercialization projects up to licensing or firm establishment, but not for product development.	Budget of NOK 47.8 million in 2008. Outcome includes 70 commercializations in 2008 (36 licenses and 34 start-ups).
FORNY: proof of concept funds	Grant awarded to specific projects to support technology development on the basis of panel evaluations of submitted applications. Application has to be submitted by an operator already receiving commercialization funds. The funds aim to strengthen the projects and lead to more successful commercializations.	Budget of NOK 46.5 million in 2008, 39 projects were supported in 2006.
FORNY: leave of absence grant	Grant to support researchers to commercialize an idea. Covers the cost of the employer for making 20 to 100 per cent of the researcher's position available to work on a commercialization project. Awarded to 16 projects in 2006.	Budget of NOK 6.5 million in 2008.

Table 4.1 Continued

Scheme	Description	Usage
The Research Council of Norway: User-driven research projects	Aim to trigger significant new R&D initiatives in Norwegian trade and industry. Many research-based new ventures use this type of funding for developing their technologies. Funding can only be awarded to established firms and covers only parts of the costs in the specified project (often 50 percent). Most relevant in later phases of the commercialization process.[a]	Almost 40 percent of FORNY supported firms also received R&D funding from the Research Council (Borlaug et al., 2009).
Tax deduction scheme (Skattefunn)	Aims to increase R&D and innovation effort in Norwegian industry. To qualify, a project has to be aimed at acquiring new knowledge, information or experiences that are relevant for developing new or improved products, services or production methods. The company can be reimbursed up to 20 percent of the expenses for the R&D activity in the form of tax deduction or a direct grant.[b] The level of reimbursement is higher when a research institution is involved. The reimbursement is based on fixed criteria and not dependent on the size of the budget allocated to the scheme.	Almost 80 percent of FORNY supported projects also make use of the tax deduction scheme (Borlaug et al., 2009).
Innovation Norway's start-up grants	Three specific schemes are particularly relevant. • Entrepreneur grant can be awarded to persons who are developing and starting their own firm, limited to NOK 400 000. • Incubator grant is for establishing new firms based on advanced knowledge or technology with prospects of reaching a large international market, limited to NOK 800 000 over a two year period for start-ups located in an incubator. • Grant for developing technology projects covers personal expenses for one person and traveling costs during the idea development project.	Close to 60 percent of FORNY supported projects make use of start-up grants (Borlaug et al., 2009).

Research and development contracts (IFU/OFU)	Aim to stimulate innovations based on new product development projects in collaboration between a supplier and a customer within the public sector (OFU) or industry (IFU). The requirement of collaboration with a customer strengthens the market focus of the projects.	Close to 40 percent of FORNY supported firms make use of this scheme (Borlaug et al., 2009).
Seed capital funds	Joint funds between the government and private investors. The government provides loans with a risk reducing mechanism, while private investors provide equity capital to the funds. The goal is to stimulate private investors to invest in early phases of new venture development. It is also assumed that private investors will provide competence to the new firms.[c]	The first seed capital funds were established in 1997 and a new round of seed capital funds were set up in 2006 with a total public capital of NOK 667 million in four funds.
SIVA	Government agency that makes investments in infrastructure for innovation in all parts of Norway. Part-owner in many local and regional innovation enterprises and science parks, including eight science parks connected to the largest research institutions in Norway and 18 incubators where most have a relation to universities or university colleges.[d]	An assessment of nine incubators revealed that 40 out of 109 companies in these incubators had their origin in research institutions.

Notes:

[a] As referenced above, this pattern is similar to the phased funding model under the SBIR and STTR programs in the USA.

[b] There is a similar incentive program in the USA, the federal research and experimentation tax credit, which provides a 20 percent credit on selected research expenditures. Several states offer similar research credit incentives as well.

[c] This program is conceptually similar to the Small Business Investment Company (SBIC) program administered by the US Small Business Administration.

[d] In the early stages of the development of incubators in the USA, the federal Economic Development Agency (EDA) played a leadership role. Subsequently state and local economic development agencies became more actively involved in the development of incubators and other organizational resources supporting new business development, though EDA has continued its involvement on a more limited basis.

DISCUSSION: FOUR MODELS FOR RESEARCH COMMERCIALIZATION SUPPORT

This section discusses the Norwegian efforts and outlines a conceptual framework for how governments can support the commercialization of university research. Conceptually, four different models can be identified where each has a distinct logic for how to bridge the gap between academic research and commercial application. First, significant effort has been made to close the gap from the university side by developing competence, infrastructure and incentives for academics and research institutions to become more involved in the commercialization process. Second, a number of initiatives are aimed at industry and commercial actors to increase their willingness to become involved in science-based projects. Thus, it is possible for the gap to be closed through actions taken from either side, essentially extending the traditional roles of these actors into the gap. However, since frequently those actions either do not occur or are insufficient, a third model is found in the establishment of inter-mediators such as TTOs and commercialization units (science parks). The rationale is that engagement of a third party with special competencies and resources in collaboration with the technology generator and the technology adopter can increase the odds of closing the gap. The fourth model used by the Norwegian support schemes is to provide support directly to specific commercialization projects, rather than to universities, industry or intermediators. In the following each of the four models is discussed.

Extending the University Role

The first model is to extend the role of academic research. In this way the university and the researchers take an active role in developing the inventions and technologies further in order to make them more interesting to commercial partners. In Norway the FORNY program has actively supported initiatives to change culture and develop a commercialization infrastructure at the universities. Still, commercialization was not seen as an issue of high priority until 2003 when new legislations turned the universities into IPR owners and required them to take a more active role. From being an external activity managed by actors that were both located and funded outside the university, technology transfer and commercialization has become prioritized within the universities and research groups and most institutions have included commercialization in their strategies. Moreover, the universities have increasingly become more involved in the operation of TTOs. It seems clear that this has resulted in a stronger awareness about commercialization among the scientific staff.

Typical government programs aiming to expand academic research towards industry are related to changing attitudes. They increase awareness and train-ing to create a supportive culture and competence inside the universities. Also informal efforts to legitimize such activity within the university are important. In total, a significant share of government initiatives, particularly policy changes, are directed towards extending the university role. Terms such as academic entrepreneurship and entrepreneurial universities are based on this conception of a more active role for universities in commercialization.

The Norwegian efforts follow an international trend that can be traced back to the introduction of the 1980 Bayh-Dole Act in the USA. This Act trans-ferred the ownership of IP to the universities, and contemporary policy changes stressed the expectations that the universities could contribute more directly to industrial development (Stevens, 2004). The subsequent success in the USA in bringing new research findings to the marketplace has, however, inspired legislative changes in many countries all over the world (Mowery et al., 2004). The logic is to give the universities incentives to support and to build an infrastructure for the commercialization of research. Still, this is a long-term effort that requires continuous work to maintain the awareness and reach out to new researchers, and the awareness still varies significantly among different research groups.

Facilitating Industry and Investor Interest

The second model implies that the gap can be narrowed down from the market side by making the development of early-stage research-based technology more attractive for industry, entrepreneurs and investors. Many of the Norwegian support schemes provide funding to incentivize commercial actors. The research and development contracts and the tax deduction scheme are not specifically developed for the commercialization of university research, but evaluations show that these schemes are actively used to develop university technologies (Borlaug et al., 2009).

One way governments have induced interest from commercial partners is by providing financial incentives, such as tax deductions and capital injection in privately managed seed and venture capital funds (Wright et al., 2006). Government can also support technology transfer by making grants to commercialization projects which are contingent on matching investment commitments from private investors or industry partners (Rasmussen, 2008). The Norwegian efforts have relied on more general initiatives to promote R&D effort and the development of high technology firms, but have not made any particular effort to connect science-based ventures to investors. Thus, the connection to investors is low and the spin-offs in the FORNY portfolio strug-gle to get equity capital from private sources, while public funding, from the R&D tax deduction scheme, for example, is at a much higher level.

The access to finance and commercial partners, such as venture capital, is seen as one of the major challenges to commercialization projects (Lockett et al., 2002). Some of the Norwegian support actors have developed good networks with investors and industrial partners, while there is still room for improving this relation at most universities.[3] Involving these partners early in the development projects is sometimes crucial to getting these actors to invest in the projects in later stages. Involving investors and industrial partners in early phases may also provide access to small-scale funding, competence, equipment and an arena for testing the product or service on potential customers. Finding such partners requires the existence of a well-developed industry or investment community, which may be difficult depending on the type of technology and regional conditions. With the exception of the seed capital scheme, there are relatively few initiatives to stimulate interest from private investors in Norway.

Supporting the Development and Engagement of Intermediators

The third model is to support the development and engagement of intermediators who can connect research-based technologies and adopters. Intermediators may include TTOs, science and technology parks, incubators, small business development centers, economic development agencies and private licensing firms. One or more such intermediator organizations can be found in connection with almost every university. The FORNY program initially relied on an intermediator model where the responsibility for the commercialization of research results was placed within actors such as science parks located outside the universities. From 2004, however, intermediators became more integrated with the universities. The largest research institutions have established their own TTO. In cities with medium-sized universities the TTOs are composed of a shared infrastructure in collaboration with the university, the university hospital and research institutes in the region. International experience shows that it might be necessary that some TTOs build strong competence in specific technology areas and that good networks and contacts between the TTOs can provide access to this competence for commercialization projects at other institutions as well (Geuna and Muscio, 2009).

The introduction of an intermediator reduces the need for technology generators and adopters to extend their roles beyond their current competencies and instead fills the gap with individuals and organizations that are skilled at boundary spanning. As a result there are two much smaller gaps that must be bridged – the gap between the technology generator and the intermediator, and the gap between the intermediator and the technology adopter. To work with technology transfer in the intersection between the university and industry demands a thorough understanding of both the academic and the business sectors. The technology transfer function within universities is increasingly seen as a job which requires a particular type of boundary spanning skills (Lockett and Wright, 2005; Rasmussen, 2008). Due to the young infrastructure in Norway, this competence is in short supply.

In Norway the intermediary organizations are to a large extent funded by public money and focus primarily on creating spin-off ventures and licensing. Thus, their role as technology transfer agents is relatively narrow and may lead to a priority of formalized technology transfer (that is, patented inventions) and hamper the dynamics of direct interaction between academics and the commercial sector. The US model of operating TTOs aiming to secure a share of economic revenue from commercialization successes is increasingly criticized (Rasmussen, 2006; Litan et al., 2007). This does not mean that the TTOs cannot have a significant mission in the academic system as a link between the academic and the business community. Many universities do not operate their technology transfer programs with an underlying profit motive (Trune and Goslin, 1998), but rather as a part of their societal mission.

Supporting Specific Commercialization Projects

As a fourth model, the gap can be mitigated by direct support to the specific commercialization projects. This model differs from the other three as the aim is not to induce systemic changes by changing institutional structures or building competence and networks that are better able to handle the commercialization process. Rather, these initiatives act at the micro level or project level. A common scheme found in many countries is the provision of development grants or so-called proof-of-concept funds to verify the industrial applicability of the research-based invention (Rasmussen, 2008). Often, a second round of funding is available if an investor or industrial partner is committed to the project. A reported challenge of such proof-of-concept grants is to make sure that the funding is used for commercialization activities, and not for further research.

Most schemes of this type provide the commercialization projects with funding, while there are also examples where the schemes add other resources to the project such as physical infrastructure and soft support in the form of mentoring, training and networking (Rasmussen et al., 2008). The focus on soft support is increasing and is related to an increased emphasis on skills and competence, not only financial and physical resources. The Norwegian leave of absence scheme seems to be unique as it makes it possible for university researchers to spend time on commercialization projects. In other countries there are examples where government schemes support mentors and consultants who contribute with their experience and networks to the spin-off projects (Rasmussen et al., 2008).

IMPLICATIONS

Technology transfer is a complex activity in which it is difficult to identify conceptual models that are generally applicable across different national and university contexts. The challenge of creating effective mechanisms to transfer new technologies into application can be seen as a challenge to bridge the gap between academic research and commercial application. This chapter outlined four conceptual models to bridge this gap. In Norway these four models have developed over time, from an initially strong reliance on the intermediators, to a gradually stronger focus on involving the universities, and an increasing number of schemes targeted at specific commercialization projects. To increase the interest of industry actors have not been a primary target of the research commercialization schemes, but empirical data show that the commercialization projects make use of a number of different schemes set up to promote industry R&D.

The government efforts have extended the role of Norwegian universities to include a responsibility for commercial application of the research results. The effects of this change have not materialized in an increased number of high-growth spin-off firms, but rather have created a more formalized system for commercialization of research. Critics worry that an overly strong focus on commercialization may have a negative impact on the academic system of open science and drain resources from basic science (Nelson, 2004). For example, in Norway issues related to ownership, revenue distribution and handling of IPR have become an issue high on the agenda of Norwegian universities and policy makers. A current discussion is whether the universities as a general rule should retain ownership of any IPR and sell licenses to users, or if they should be willing to sell the IPR. Unclear IPR ownership can lead to problems during the commercialization process and in the collaboration with industry, but studies indicate that IPR protection by patenting may have a negative effect on the diffusion of scientific knowledge (Murray and Stern, 2007).

Successful initiatives often emerge bottom-up from individuals and institutions at the local level, rather than top-down as a result of government intervention (Goldfarb and Henrekson, 2002; Rasmussen, 2008). Many of the Norwegian initiatives are partly developed by experimentation and in collaboration with the actors at a local level. As the infrastructure is becoming more developed at institutional and regional levels, the need for government instruments is changing. Thus, to develop new initiatives and to be well connected with the current needs at the operational level is particularly important for developing efficient policy initiatives.

The Norwegian policy to increase the commercialization of research is mainly based on a rationale to foster industry development. In other countries the goal of commercialization also includes terms like social wellbeing (Langford et al., 2006). For example, the research council for health research in Canada defines the role of commercialization as benefiting Canadians through 'improved health, more effective services and products, and a strengthened health care system' (Rasmussen, 2008, p. 515). Other US programs supporting innovation, for example, the Partnership for Innovation grants from the National Science Foundation, include social as well as economic objectives and metrics. To achieve this the universities may play an important role, as contributing to social wellbeing is a part of the general mission of the universities. The use of quantitative measures (number of patents, licenses, spin-off firms, revenue generated and so on) is somewhat problematic. A too narrow focus on short-term indicators could be misinterpreted and could under-represent positive outcomes with respect to achieving social and economic benefits from research. There are challenges related to goal formulation and assessment of the results from the commercialization of research, as the impacts of such a complex array of initiatives are extremely difficult to measure. Thus, an important challenge is to develop more relevant output metrics for measuring the performance of government initiatives.

CONCLUSION

In spite of the numerous studies of different outputs from universities, such as patents, licensing agreements and spin-off ventures, there is limited knowledge about how to promote the commercialization of research. Despite the research that has been conducted to date, there is still much to learn about the diversity of university initiatives designed to promote technology transfer in support of social and economic development. In this chapter we have proposed a conceptual framework to discuss how government initiatives can promote the commercialization of university research. We are not able to conclude that any of the four models are superior to the others, rather they appear as complementary. Together they provide a framework for discussing the objectives and possible strengths and weaknesses of different government initiatives and for assessing the policy mix.

NOTES

1. 1 EUR is about 8 NOK and 1 USD is about 6 NOK.
2. The FORNY program has goals that are similar to those of the Small Business Innovative Research and the Small Business Technology Transfer programs in the USA, though the FORNY program engages the support of institutions directly and the researchers/entrepreneurs indirectly, whereas the reverse is the case in the USA.

3. In the USA university-based technology business incubators, entrepreneurship centers, action learning project courses and outreach programs have been particularly effective in broadening and strengthening networks connecting the university and business communities. They have also increased the competence of a new generation of technologists in boundary spanning.

REFERENCES

Agrawal, A. (2001), 'University-to-industry knowledge transfer: literature review and unanswered questions', *International Journal of Management Reviews*, **3**(4), 285–302.

Blumenthal, D., E.G. Campbell, M.S. Anderson, N. Causino and K.S. Louis (1997), 'Withholding research results in academic life science – evidence from a national survey of faculty', *Journal of the American Medical Association*, **277**(15), 1224–8.

Borlaug, S.B., L. Grünfeld, M. Gulbrandsen, E. Rasmussen, L. Rønning, O.R. Spilling and E. Vinogradov (2009), *Between Entrepreneurship and Technology Transfer: Evaluation of the FORNY Programme*, Oslo: NIFU STEP.

Cohen, W.M., R.R. Nelson and J.P. Walsh (2002), 'Links and impacts: the influence of public research on industrial R&D', *Management Science*, **48**(1), 1–23.

Colyvas, J., M. Crow, A. Gelijns et al. (2002), 'How do university inventions get into practice?', *Management Science*, **48**(1), 61–72.

Etzkowitz, H., A. Webster and P. Healey (1998), *Capitalizing Knowledge – New Intersections of Industry and Academia*, Albany NY: State University of New York Press.

Feldman, M.P., A.N. Link and D.S. Siegel (2002), *The Economics of Science and Technology: An Overview of Initiatives to Foster Innovation, Entrepreneurship, and Economic Growth*, Boston, MA: Kluwer Academic Publishers.

Geuna, A. and A. Muscio (2009), 'The governance of university knowledge transfer: a critical review of the literature', *Minerva*, **47**(1), 93–114.

Goldfarb, B. and M. Henrekson (2002), 'Bottom-up versus top-down policies towards the commercialization of university intellectual property', *Research Policy*, **32**(4), 639–58.

Jensen, R. and M. Thursby (2001), 'Proofs and prototypes for sale: the licensing of university inventions', *American Economic Review*, **91**(1), 240–59.

Langford, C.H., J. Hall, P. Josty, S. Matos and A. Jacobson (2006), 'Indicators and outcomes of Canadian university research: proxies becoming goals?', *Research Policy*, **35**(10), 1586–98.

Litan, R.E., L. Mithell and E.J. Reedy (2007), *Commercializing University Innovations: A Better Way*, Cambridge, MA: National Bureau of Economic Research.

Lockett, A. and M. Wright (2005), 'Resources, capabilities, risk capital and the creation of university spin-out companies', *Research Policy*, **34**(7), 1043–57.

Lockett, A., G. Murray and M. Wright (2002), 'Do UK venture capitalists still have a bias against investment in new technology firms', *Research Policy*, **31**(6), 1009–30.

Lockett, A., D. Siegel, M. Wright and M.D. Ensley (2005), 'The creation of spin-off firms at public research institutions: managerial and policy implications', *Research Policy*, **34**(7), 981–93.

Markham, S.K., A.I. Kingon, R.J. Lewis and M. Zapata III (2002), 'The university's role in creating radically new products', *International Journal of Technology Transfer and Commercialisation*, **1**(1/2), 163–72.

Mora-Valentin, E.M., A. Montoro-Sanchez and L.A. Guerras-Martin (2004), 'Determining factors in the success of R&D cooperative agreements between firms and research organizations', *Research Policy*, **33**(1), 17–40.

Mowery, D.C., R.R. Nelson, B.N. Sampat and A.A. Ziedonis (2004), *Ivory Tower and Industrial Innovation: University-Industry Technology Transfer Before and After the Bayh-Dole Act in the United States*, Stanford, CA: Stanford Business Books.

Murray, F. and S. Stern (2007), 'Do formal intellectual property rights hinder the free flow of scientific knowledge? An empirical test of the anti-commons hypothesis', *Journal of Economic Behavior and Organization*, **63**(4), 648–87.

Mustar, P., M. Wright and B. Clarysse (2008), 'University spin-off firms: lessons from ten years of experience in Europe', *Science and Public Policy*, **35**(2), 67–80.

Nelson, R. (2004), 'The market economy, and the scientific commons', *Research Policy*, **33**(3), 455–71.

Rasmussen, E. (2006), 'Two models for university technology transfer operation: patent agency and 2g', *International Journal of Technology Transfer and Commercialisation*, **5**(4), 291–307.

Rasmussen, E. (2008), 'Government instruments to support the commercialization of university research: lessons from Canada', *Technovation*, **28**, August, 506–17.

Rasmussen, E., O.J. Borch and R. Sørheim (2008), 'University entrepreneurship and government support schemes', in A. Fayolle and P. Kyrö (eds), *The Dynamics between Entrepreneurship, Environment and Education*, Cheltenham, UK and Northampton, MA, USA: Edward Elgar, pp. 105–30.

Rogers, E.M. (2002), 'The nature of technology transfer', *Science Communication*, **23**(3), 323–41.

Rogers, E.M. (2003), *Diffusion of Innovations*, 5th edn, New York: Free Press.

Rosenberg, N. (1991), 'Critical issues in science policy research', *Science and Public Policy*, **18**(6), 335–46.

Salmenkaita, J.-P. and A. Salo (2002), 'Rationales for government interventions in the commercialization of new technologies', *Technology Analysis and Strategic Management*, **14**(2), 183–200.

Stankiewicz, R. (1994), 'Spin-off companies from universities', *Science and Public Policy*, **21**(2), 99–107.

Stevens, A.J. (2004), 'The enactment of Bayh-Dole', *Journal of Technology Transfer*, **29**(1), 93–9.

Tassey, G. (2005), 'Underinvestment in public good technologies', *Journal of Technology Transfer*, **30**(1/2), 89–113.

Thursby, J.G., R. Jensen and M.C. Thursby (2001), 'Objectives, characteristics and outcomes of university licensing: a survey of major U.S. universities', *Journal of Technology Transfer*, **26**(1/2), 59–72.

Toole, A.A. and D. Czarnitzki (2007), 'Biomedical academic entrepreneurship through the SBIR program', *Journal of Economic Behavior and Organization*, **63**(4), 716–38.

Trune, D.R. and L.N. Goslin (1998), 'University technology transfer programs: a profit/loss analysis', *Technological Forecasting and Social Change*, **57**(3), 197–204.

Wright, M., A. Lockett, B. Clarysse and M. Binks (2006), 'University spin-out companies and venture capital', *Research Policy*, **35**(4), 481–501.
Wright, M., B. Clarysse, P. Mustar and A. Lockett (2007), *Academic Entrepreneurship in Europe*, Cheltenham, UK and Northampton, MA, USA: Edward Elgar.

5. A longitudinal study of community venture emergence through legitimacy building

Ingebjørg Vestrum and Einar Rasmussen

INTRODUCTION

While most entrepreneurship studies have looked at the emergence of new commercial ventures, this study keys into the start-up process of non-profit community ventures (CVs). CVs seek to create social values for their community and are likely to stimulate social and cultural life, increase business development and possibly strengthen the identity of communities. CVs contribute to revitalizing communities hit by structural change, which are experiencing economic stagnation or decline or are facing the challenge of depopulation (Johannisson, 1990; Johnstone and Lionais, 2004). Most communities have numerous organizations aiming to solve social and societal problems and create welfare. Still, this important type of organizational creation is vastly under-researched in previous entrepreneurship studies (Mair and Martí, 2006; Peredo and McLean, 2006).

One of the greatest challenges for entrepreneurs is that they lack the legitimacy needed for resource providers to believe their nascent venture is proper. The legitimacy perspective has added important contributions to the commercial entrepreneurship literature (Zimmerman and Zeitz, 2002; Tornikoski and Newbert, 2007). Legitimacy is seen as a resource needed to get access to other critical resources for a new venture (Lounsbury and Glynn, 2001; Zimmerman and Zeitz, 2002). The issue of gaining legitimacy has not been addressed in the community entrepreneurship literature. This chapter aims to build theory through an exploratory study designed to answer the following research question: how do nascent CVs build legitimacy?

We propose that gaining legitimacy is relevant for emerging CVs in particular. CVs are not driven by a profit motive, nor is their success measured in terms of the profit they generate (Austin et al., 2006; Haugh, 2007). Thus, CVs need to legitimate their role towards stakeholders and often convince resource providers to accept non-financial gains in exchange for resources. Moreover,

CVs are dependent on the local community for access to a range of resources and need to create engagement within the local community to reach their goals of meeting local community needs (Peredo and Chrisman, 2006; Haugh, 2007).

The understanding of the process of gaining legitimacy is typically deduced retrospectively (Zimmerman and Zeitz, 2002), as it is difficult to get access to data from the earliest phases of legitimacy building. We resolve this challenge by conducting a longitudinal case study of the start-up process of two music festivals aiming to revitalize small rural communities in Norway. By investigating the early stages of the venture formation process longitudinally, from when the initial idea is conceived until the venture has achieved its social goal, we show how the CVs gradually gained legitimacy. Building on a legitimacy perspective, our study makes use of a novel theoretical framework that takes into account how nascent CVs can move beyond their current stocks of resources.

This chapter proceeds as follows. The next section outlines the theoretical foundation. The third section presents the methodological approach. In the fourth section the cases of developing a jazz camp festival and a rock music festival within two rural communities are presented. The fifth section analyses the findings using a legitimacy framework. Finally, conclusions and implications are provided.

THEORETICAL FOUNDATION

Community Entrepreneurship

Most entrepreneurship research has investigated the creation of CVs aiming to create personal wealth and economic values for shareholders. Recently, considerable interest has been devoted to social entrepreneurship, defined as entrepreneurial activities creating social and other non-economic values (Dees, 2001; Mair and Martí, 2006; Sharir and Lerner, 2006). Community entrepreneurship can be seen as a sub-category of social entrepreneurship where the social value creation is related to a specific community context. Community entrepreneurship is the process of recognizing and pursuing of opportunities resulting in a CV that creates social values for a local community (Peredo and Chrisman, 2006; Haugh, 2007). The social values might be to change a negative image in a regional and national context as well as to re-establish pride in communities (Johannisson, 1990). Examples of CVs are sports or cultural events (Haugh and Pardy, 1999), museums (Borch et al., 2008), business networks (Johannisson, 1990; Johnstone and Lionais, 2004) and job creation organizations (Lotz, 1989).

Prior studies have looked at both non-profit and for-profit CVs. Peredo and McLean (2006) argue that social ventures range from non-profits with exclusively social goals to for-profits where social goals are subordinate to profit-making activities. The inclusion of for-profits in the definition of CVs blurred the differences between CVs and commercial business ventures. To distinguish community entrepreneurship from commercial entrepreneurship, this study focuses on the creation of non-profit CVs. This means that any economic surplus is reinvested in the venture to increase the social value creation rather than distributed to the owners or shareholders (Austin et al., 2006; Sharir and Lerner, 2006; Shaw and Carter, 2007). Non-profit ventures are not synonymous with CVs unless their goal is to create social values for a local community.

The local community context plays a key role in the CV literature. A community can be explained as an 'aggregation of people that is defined ... by shared geographical location, generally accompanied by collective culture and/or ethnicity and potentially by other shared relational characteristic(s)' (Peredo and Chrisman, 2006, p. 315). A community may be defined by political boundaries such as a village or a municipality. Examples of communities being studied in the community entrepreneurship literature are depleted communities (Johannisson, 1990; Johnstone and Lionais, 2004), rural communities (Haugh, 2007) and impoverished communities (Peredo and Chrisman, 2006). Peredo and Chrisman (2006) argued that a community acts corporately as both entrepreneur and enterprise in pursuit of the common good. In other words, the community is not merely a context but becomes a key participant in the initiation and development of the nascent CV. In addition, the resources needed are likely to reside within a large number of stakeholders within the community context (Johannisson, 1990; Haugh, 2007). Haugh (2007) studied the creation of five CVs in rural communities and found that in the creation of CVs, competing ideas become filtered into one idea that gains the most support.

CVs are non-profits and often need to rely on non-economic exchange because the economic value they create is not sufficient to pay for the resources they use (Dees, 2001). As a consequence, gaining legitimacy becomes critical to obtaining resources for the emerging CV.

Strategies to Gain Access to Legitimacy

Legitimacy refers to 'a generalized perception or assumption that the actions of an entity are desirable, proper or appropriate within some socially constructed system of norms, beliefs, and definitions' (Suchman, 1995. p. 574). Legitimacy is an instrumental resource necessary to acquire other resources from the environment (Zimmerman and Zeitz, 2002). CVs as well as new ventures in general need to search actively for legitimacy to be perceived as proper among resource providers (Lounsbury and Glynn, 2001; Zimmerman and Zeitz, 2002; Tornikoski and Newbert, 2007).

The literature has highlighted four strategies that new ventures can use to gain legitimacy. The first strategy, to conform, is a relatively passive strategy where the venture changes itself to acquire legitimacy by adapting to the demands and expectations in the environment (Suchman, 1995). The second strategy, to select, is more proactive than to conform (Suchman, 1995; Zimmerman and Zeitz, 2002). A venture can select an environment that does not demand any changes of the venture. Third, to manipulate, is an even more proactive strategy than to select and is necessary for new ventures that need to manipulate the environment to believe that it is proper (Suchman, 1995; Zimmerman and Zeitz, 2002). Fourth, to create, is a strategy which involves creating something new in the environment, for example, a new product, service and/or practice that might change the environment (Zimmerman and Zeitz, 2002).

Tornikoski and Newbert (2007) found that to manipulate the environment was more important than to conform to norms and expectations in the environment for the creation of a new venture. A new venture might employ individuals with characteristics that increase the venture's credibility or develop networks with external actors that already have obtained legitimacy (Rao et al., 2008). In this way, the nascent venture acquires legitimacy from actors in the environment.

METHODOLOGY

A qualitative case study methodology was used to explore how two nascent CVs within two rural communities in Norway gained legitimacy. The case studies offered rich context-related information about the communities (Flyvbjerg, 2006; Johns, 2006) and made it possible to collect data at different levels in the process (Eisenhardt, 1989). A longitudinal approach was warranted to capture the changes over time and reduce problems of retrospective biases (Pettigrew, 1990).

Case Selection

Rural communities are frequently studied in the community entrepreneurship literature (Johannisson, 1990; Haugh, 2007). To demarcate the context is easier within a rural area compared to an urban area and the legitimacy building process is more transparent because the individuals in a rural community are more visible. Both CVs in our study emerged within rural communities with sparse populations facing the challenge of depopulation. Together with an open culture and a rather transparent Norwegian society, the rural context has contributed to good availability of data for this study.

The empirical setting is the numerous cultural festivals that have been established in Norway since the 1980s. A cultural festival is an event usually arranged over a short time period with regular intervals, often over one weekend or week, once a year. Cultural festivals vary in size and scope and are most frequently connected to a music genre. Although there are examples of for-profit festivals, this study focuses on non-profit festivals aiming to create new activities and social values for the community. Several studies have shown the economic, social and cultural impact of cultural festivals on local communities (Delamere, 2001; Gursoy et al., 2004).

The time frame of the study begins from when the idea was conceived until the festivals had sustained their operation as a positive contribution to the rural community, indicating that the festivals had built needed legitimacy. We approached the first case when the CV was about one year old and still in a very early phase of development. The second case was chosen to replicate the findings from the first case (Yin, 2003) and had been organized for four years when we started to collect data. We followed the cases for three years and one year, respectively.

Data Collection

Data were collected between 2006 and 2008 using a wide range of sources to facilitate data triangulation. Secondary data were collected by reviewing email communication, web pages, newspapers and other written documents. Primary data were gathered through interviews with the community entrepreneurs and other key actors in the process, as shown in Table 5.1. Narrative interviewing was used to obtain data from the entire entrepreneurial process by asking the interviewees to tell the story from the first time they heard about the emerging CV until the present day.

The interviews were conducted in the home of the informants, at their work or at the festival arena. Key actors were interviewed several times and asked to tell the narrative about the activities since the previous interview. A total of 26 interviews were conducted with nine persons from each festival. The interviews lasted from half an hour to three hours. We used interview protocol with questions about the resource acquisition process to get information that the interviewees did not tell in their narratives.

Participant observations from both festivals supplement the data. In the first case one of the researchers was an observer during the five-day festival event. The following year the researcher participated as a voluntary staff member and the last year she was a visitor at the festival. At the second festival the

Table 5.1　Persons interviewed (number of interviews in parentheses)

	The Groove Valley (TGV)	Skiippagurra festival (SKI)
Community entrepreneur (CE)	CE: The founder of TGV (4 and emails)	CE: Booking, festival leader No. 3 (2)
Members of the entrepreneurial team (M)	M1: Music responsible (1) M2: Public administration (3) M3: First camp host (emails) M4: Second camp host (1) M5: Technician responsible (1)	M1: Leader of the public project (0) M2: Festival leader No. 1 (2) M3: Festival leader No. 2 (1) M4: The landowner (1) M5: Board leader (1)
Local government (G) Volunteers (V)	G1: The mayor (2) V1: Community central (emails) V2: Technical assistant No. 1 (1) V3: Technical assistant No. 2 (1) V4: Organizer at the school (1)	G1: The mayor (1) V1: Media spokesperson from Skiippagurra (1) V2: Safety and guard responsible (1)
Support (S)	S1: Regional jazz center (emails)	S1: Leader of regional business park (1)
Number of interviews	15	11
Observations, meetings and events	Participated at the festival (3) Participated at meetings (6)	Participated at the festival (1) Participated at meetings (1)

researcher participated as a voluntary staff member during the two-day festival event. The observations were open-ended to achieve the greatest understanding of the festivals; however, the researcher focused on acquiring information about which resources and actors were involved in the festival and why. After each day the researcher made notes about the observations. Being in the field allowed the researcher to develop personal contacts which made it easier to gain trust among the interviewees and discover new informants. The observations and narrative interviewing made it possible to collect data close to real time and to gain a thorough understanding of the process. In order to avoid confirmatory biases, one of the authors did not participate in data collection.

Data Analysis

The collected data provided narrative accounts of the process (Pentland, 1999) and factual descriptions of context, actors and events from a large number of sources. The interviews were recorded and transcribed as part of the data analysis process. The interview transcripts and other material were read and reread as data were collected; emerging themes were refined and checked through repeat interviews with the main players (Yin, 2003). The views of the different respondents within each case were also compared. To analyse the process we wrote the narrative of the resource acquisition process and searched for structures in the narratives (Pentland, 1999). Legitimacy emerged from the data as very important to access resources. The data were categorized to identify the specific strategies used to obtain legitimacy and the categories then compared with the legitimacy literature. The conclusions were reached in a discussion between both authors.

THE CV CASES

The Groove Valley (TGV)

TGV is an annual jazz music festival arranged over five days in August every year since 2005. TGV is organized as a meeting place where amateurs join workshops and clinics where they are instructed and get a chance to play with professional musicians. There are also lectures open for visitors. During the festival the amateurs and professionals play outdoor concerts, jam sessions in the local pub, concerts in a concert hall and concerts in an art gallery. In addition, camp activities such as sightseeing, caving, sea rafting and night fishing in the river are offered.

As a result of TGV, the small community with 1200 inhabitants has attracted much positive attention from both regional and national media. For instance, a national newspaper had a two-page article with the headline 'The jazz camp in Beiarn. Jazz success in a green valley'. The attention has resulted in a more positive image of the community among the inhabitants and beyond. TGV has resulted in new cultural activities such as local jazz groups, more regular concerts around the year and higher quality in the municipal music school. TGV also has a positive effect on business life amongst the shops, the pub, the local art gallery and the landowners of the fishing river, all generating income from the new visitors and activities.

The Skiippagurra Festival (SKI)

SKI is a two-day rock festival arranged one weekend in July every year since 2003. At the festival international and national rock artists and groups perform outdoor concerts on a river beach. The festival is pervaded by Baltic music and the Sami traditions and music plays the key role. There is also a course for children to learn the chanting songs of the Sami people, and youths from different places in Europe are instructed by professional musicians to perform a concert. In addition, activities such as sand castle competition, volleyball competition and horse riding are offered.

The Skiippagurra village attracted negative media attention nationwide during the 1990s because of social problems taking place at the local camp ground. The community of 3000 inhabitants struggled to change this reputation even many years after the social problems ceased. The festival has successfully changed the media focus on the Skiippagurra village both regionally and nationally. Today the youth in this part of the country associate the community with a 'cool festival' and the local youths are again proud of being from the Skiippagurra village. In addition, SKI has had a positive effect on local business life.

FINDINGS: STRATEGIES FOR GAINING LEGITIMACY

The case studies illustrate the need for creating legitimacy both within the rural community (the internal environment) and outside the rural community (the external environment) to acquire resources. The festivals needed many volunteers within the local community to work as guards, to sell tickets and food, to take care of the artists, build the scene and to tidy up during and after the festival. They also needed legitimacy among local businesses to arrange accommodation, food and nature experiences below the market price. Moreover, the CVs needed to be perceived as proper to get access to financial support from the local government and local firms. They also needed to receive resources (for example, artists, sponsoring, scene and sound technique and visitors) from the external environment. Thus, both festivals needed legitimacy within the music industry, regional and national sponsors and others to receive resources below the market price.

The legitimacy literature refers to four strategies for acquiring legitimacy – select, conform to, manipulate and create the environment (Suchman, 1995; Zimmerman and Zeitz, 2002). The strategy of selecting the environment was less relevant for the CVs because they aimed to create values for a specific community and could not choose another context. Moreover, the strategy of creating the environment could be seen as a result of the entrepreneurial process, rather than a strategy to obtain legitimacy because the goal of the CVs was to change the local communities. Compared to the legitimacy literature our study found that the emerging CVs used only conform to and manipulate the environment as strategies to gain legitimacy. The strategies differed, however, depending on whether the CV sought legitimacy in the internal or the external environment. Thus, we revealed four strategies to gain legitimacy for new CVs: conforming to the internal environment, conforming to the external environment, manipulating the internal environment and manipulating the external environment.

Gaining Legitimacy by Conforming to the Internal Environment

In our cases the internal conforming strategy was evident when the CVs used legitimacy held by other individuals or organizations in the rural community and when they conformed to the demands from internal resource providers. For instance, the entrepreneurs of both CVs were from outside the community and asked the local government to become the owner and financially responsible party of the CV. In this way the festivals immediately got access to legitimacy. By becoming a part of the local government, however, the ventures conformed to the bureaucratic-decision making processes and the goal of rural development.

SKI had some problems with getting access to resources in the local community as it met opposition from the Skiippagurra village where the social problems had taken place. The entrepreneur responded by including individuals from the community in the CV team to create ownership for the idea. The headmaster of the municipal culture school for children (M2) was invited to join the CV. 'It was accepted that he became the festival leader, because he had a well-known name' (CE; as listed in Table 5.1). In addition, a young girl from the Skiippagurra village became the festival's press spokesperson and the owner of the festival arena became involved in the organization.

Both CVs were innovative and met skepticism or low participation in the rural community. As a result, the entrepreneurs combined their innovative ideas with traditions in the community and conformed to the demands of potential resource providers. The CE of TGV combined his innovative jazz music idea with an idea of a sports base camp activity for youths that already existed in the community. In addition, the local government convinced the CE to include more well-known artists at the festival to engage a larger part of the community. SKI also offered nature-based activities and sports activities which built upon existing activities in the community as well as including the Sami music and traditions to gain legitimacy.

Gaining Legitimacy by Conforming to the External Environment

The strategy of conforming to the external environment was evident when the CVs used legitimacy that belonged to other individuals or organizations in the external environment and when the CVs conformed to demands from external resource providers. As an example, TGV recruited an internationally known jazz artist living in the regional center (M1) to the festival organization. The inclusion of M1 provided legitimacy that was highly useful in accessing international jazz musicians; however, the CV needed to conform to the expectations and standards of the music industry demanded by M1.

SKI did not include anyone with legitimacy in the external environment, but did create networks with external organizations. Their legitimacy in the music industry increased significantly when they received sponsorship from the Norwegian Culture Council in the second year of operation. They received several congratulatory telephone calls from artist managers asking if they wanted to book with them. This was in sharp contrast to the first year when the CE felt that the artist managers were laughing at the Skiippagurra name. Similarly, the CE in TGV used a positive response he had received from the regional jazz center (S1) to establish legitimacy in the external environment: 'we will refer to the Jazz centre when we present the project for potential collaboration partners, otherwise it will be impossible to show seriousness in the work from our side' (CE email).

Both festivals were formed according to demands in the external environment. SKI was conscious of showing the Sami culture at the festival in order to receive support from the Sami assembly. TGV included one day with concerts to receive sponsorship from the Norwegian Culture Council.

Gaining Legitimacy by Manipulating the Internal Environment

The entrepreneurs of both CVs had high musical ambitions for the festivals and needed to manipulate the potential resource providers in the local community to gain their trust. To manipulate the environment was more complicated and took a longer time than to conform. The strategy of manipulating the internal environment was done by using legitimacy acquired from conforming to the external environment and through the use of communication and media.

To legitimate the quality of the music part, the TGV entrepreneur sent the positive email he had received from the regional Jazz center (S1) to organizations in the rural community. The SKI entrepreneur used the legitimacy gained by conforming to the demands of the Norwegian Culture Council to manipulate the internal environment: 'I have argued much in the board and among key persons ... . If we ask that band to come, the other band will not be here, and then the Norwegian Culture Council will not give us money' (CE). This means that the CVs could build on legitimacy gained in the external environment to manipulate the internal environment.

Both festivals arranged open meetings with the inhabitants to talk about their festival idea and to persuade them to believe in the idea. This was especially important for SKI which met opposition in the local community. In addition, the first festival leader (M2) went from house to house to tell about the festival. The CVs worked much with the media to gain trust in the community.

The local businesses saw the benefits of the publicity of TGV in regional and national media and increased their sponsorship each year; the local government continued their support as well. The attitude towards the CV in the Skiippagurra village became more positive when the inhabitants saw the new and more optimistic view of the Skiippagurra name in the media.

Gaining Legitimacy by Manipulating the External Environment

The strategy of manipulating the external environment was achieved by using legitimacy acquired from conforming to the internal environment and through communication and media. Both festivals promoted the rural community with the external music industry to legitimate their location and to get the artists below the market price. The entrepreneurs promoted the nature-based experiences such as fjord fishing, salmon fishing and caving to the artists. After some years both festivals had created good reputations within the music industry and the artists bragged about the festivals highly. Thus, the festivals could receive artists for only a fraction of the price the bands usually charged. The CE in TGV legitimized the jazz music for external visitors by combining it with nature-based activities. M2 from the public administration explained: 'the one who had the caving, she had people who said that they came to listen to jazz, but they had not come if it had not been for the announcing of other adventures'.

The media was used to promote the festivals among external sponsors and visitors. The choice of jazz as the music genre and the concept of amateurs and professional musicians meeting to play together in the rural setting made TGV unique. This attracted media attention and positive publicity about the rural community. SKI got the festival published on national television (TV2).

CONCLUSIONS AND IMPLICATIONS

This chapter has identified four legitimacy building strategies for CVs: to conform to the internal environment, to conform to the external environment, to manipulate the internal environment and to manipulate the external environment.When conforming to the environment, the CVs adapted to existing traditions, demands and resources in order to gain legitimacy. In contrast, the manipulation strategy created changes in the environment and is crucial for CVs aiming to create something new for the rural community.

Because the emerging CVs are non-profits and the exchange for most of the resources is non-monetary, legitimacy seems to be especially important for the development of CVs. The involvement from the inhabitants in a rural local community has been highlighted in earlier studies of CVs (Peredo and

Chrisman, 2006; Haugh, 2007). Our study extends the literature by illustrating that CVs do not emerge isolated in the local community as they need resources from the external environment as well. This implies that further studies on community entrepreneurship should distinguish between the internal and external environment.

By using a longitudinal approach, this study shows the dynamics of the legitimacy building process. Early in the start-up process the emerging ventures needed to build legitimacy through conforming to the environment before they managed to manipulate the environment. The external and internal legitimacy was built in an iterative process, making it possible for the venture to leverage internal legitimacy into external legitimacy and vice versa. In other words, if an external resource provider believes that the venture has broad support within the local community, it will be more confident in engaging in the venture. The local community will also be more confident if they perceive that the venture is credible among external stakeholders.

This study shows how the inclusion of new individuals in the CV organization creates legitimacy for the nascent venture. Each individual has goals and ideas for the CV, and the more individuals from the community are involved, the more the CV becomes embedded in the community. In cases where most of the inhabitants are active in the development of the CV, the local community is defined as both the entrepreneur and the venture (Peredo and Chrisman, 2006). This study extends the literature (Mair and Martí, 2006; Peredo and Chrisman, 2006) by showing how the strategies of gaining legitimacy works as a driving force to embed the CVs in the structures of the local community. In addition, this study increases the understanding of how the CVs are created through a process in which different ideas become filtered into one which obtains the most support (Haugh, 2007).

The cases in our study occurred in a national context with a well-developed welfare system and a strong public sector. The results in this study might also be relevant in other contexts where the public sector is not so strong. Depopulation is a problem for many rural communities and CVs can be important tools to create social values and increase the communities' attractiveness. To gain legitimacy becomes crucial and the division into internal and external contexts is relevant. To create more robust results, however, more cases from different contexts are needed.

REFERENCES

Austin, J., H. Stevenson and J. Wei-Skillern (2006), 'Social and commercial entrepreneurship: same, different, or both?', *Entrepreneurship Theory and Practice*, **30**(1), 1–22.

Borch, O.J., A. Førde, L. Rønning, I.K. Vestrum and G.A. Alsos (2008), 'Resource configuration and creative practices of community entrepreneurs', *Journal of Enterprising Communities: People and Places in the Global Economy*, **2**(2), 100–23.

Dees, J.G. (2001), 'The Meaning of "Social Entrepreneurship"', Kauffman Center for Entrepreneurial Leadership, available at http://cdi.mecon.gov.ar/biblio/docelec/dp4012.pdf.

Delamere, T.A. (2001), 'Development of a scale to measure resident attitudes toward the social impacts of community festivals, Part II: verification of the scale', *Event Management*, **7**, 25–38.

Eisenhardt, K.M. (1989), 'Building theories from case-study research', *Academy of Management Review*, **14**(4), 532–50.

Flyvbjerg, B. (2006), 'Five misunderstandings about case-study research', *Qualitative Inquiry*, **12**(2), 219–45.

Gursoy, D., K. Kim and M. Uysal (2004), 'Perceived impacts of festivals and special events by organizers: an extension and validation', *Tourism Management*, **25**(2), 171–81.

Haugh, H. (2007), 'Community-led social venture creation', *Entrepreneurship Theory and Practice*, **31**(2), 161–82.

Haugh, H.M. and W. Pardy (1999), 'Community entrepreneurship in north east Scotland', *International Journal of Entrepreneurial Behaviour and Research*, **5**(4), 163–72.

Johannisson, B. (1990), 'Community entrepreneurship – cases and conceptualization', *Entrepreneurship and Regional Development*, **2**, 71–88.

Johns, G. (2006), 'The essential impact of context on organizational behavior', *Academy of Management Review*, **31**(2), 386–408.

Johnstone, H. and D. Lionais (2004), 'Depleted communities and community business entrepreneurship: revaluing space through place', *Entrepreneurship and Regional Development*, **16**(3), 217–33.

Lotz, J. (1989), 'Community entrepreneurs', *Community Development Journal*, **24**(1), 62–6.

Lounsbury, M. and M.A. Glynn (2001), 'Cultural entrepreneurship: stories, legitimacy, and the acquisition of resources', *Strategic Management Journal*, **22**(6–7), 545–64.

Mair, J. and I. Martí (2006), 'Social entrepreneurship research: a source of explanation, prediction, and delight', *Journal of World Business*, **41**(1), 36–44.

Pentland, B.T. (1999), 'Building process theory with narrative: from description to explanation', *Academy of Management Review*, **24**(4), 711–24.

Peredo, A.M. and J.J. Chrisman (2006), 'Toward a theory of community-based enterprise', *Academy of Management Review*, **31**(2), 309–28.

Peredo, A.M. and M. McLean (2006), 'Social entrepreneurship: a critical review of the concept', *Journal of World Business*, **41**(1), 56–65.

Pettigrew, A. (1990), 'Longitudinal field research on change: theory and practice', *Organization Science*, **1**(3), 267–92.

Rao, R.S., R.K. Chandy and J.C. Prabhu (2008), 'The fruits of legitimacy: why some new ventures gain more from innovation than others', *Journal of Marketing*, **72**(4), 58–75.

Sharir, M. and M. Lerner (2006), 'Gauging the success of social ventures initiated by individual social entrepreneurs', *Journal of World Business*, **41**(1), 6–20.

Shaw, E. and S. Carter (2007), 'Social entrepreneurship: theoretical antecedents and empirical analysis of entrepreneurial processes and outcomes', *Journal of Small Business and Enterprise Development*, **14**, 418–34.

Suchman, M.C. (1995), 'Managing legitimacy: strategic and institutional approaches', *Academy of Management Review*, **20**(3), 571–610.

Tornikoski, E.T. and S.L. Newbert (2007), 'Exploring the determinants of organizational emergence: a legitimacy perspective', *Journal of Business Venturing*, **22**(2), 311–35.

Yin, R.K. (2003), *Case Study Research: Design and Methods*, 3rd edn, Thousand Oaks, CA: Sage.

Zimmerman, M.A. and G.J. Zeitz (2002), 'Beyond survival: achieving new venture growth by building legitimacy', *Academy of Management Review*, **27**(3), 414–31.

6. The link between open innovation policy and entrepreneurship: the case of industry incubators in Norway

Tommy Høyvarde Clausen, Einar Rasmussen and Mark P. Rice

INTRODUCTION

A central challenge for emerging firms is to access resources and to get access to a diverse competence and skill base from which they can develop new products and services that will enable them to compete with other firms (Aldrich, 1999). Emerging firms also lack working ties to suppliers, customers and other external resource providers, causing them to face a 'liability of newness' (Stinchcombe, 1965). Whereas new firms lack resources in general, established incumbent firms often face resource abundance as they often generate and make new technologies and resources that may, or may not, be compatible with their existing strategy (Burgelman, 1983). Recent organizational theory suggests that older and established firms face a 'liability of senescence' where they accumulate durable features, such as precedents, political coalitions and taken for granted understandings that constrain collective behavior and force firm strategy towards exploitation of known alternatives (Hannan, 1998). Empirical research has confirmed that incumbent firms possess technologies that are economically valuable, but which the firms have chosen not to exploit (Rivette and Kline, 1999).

We argue that policy may have a role in addressing and connecting (1) new firms searching for valuable external resources and (2) incumbent firms possessing – but not exploiting – valuable resources. Policies addressing these issues may differ from traditional neoclassical technology policies which are based upon the premise of market failures that recommend policymakers to subsidize internal research and development (R&D) within firms. In contrast to market failure based policies, we argue that policymakers may use the Open Innovation (OI) model (Chesbrough, 2003; Chesbrough et al., 2006) as a framework when designing policies that link resource seeking start-ups with external resources and exploit and commercialize the resources of resource abundant large firms.

The reason we put forth the OI model as a potentially relevant alternative for policymaking is that this model is considered to be the antithesis of a model of innovation where internal R&D is celebrated and where knowledge spillovers between firms are considered to be a damaging side effect of innovative activity within firms (Chesbrough, 2003; Chesbrough et al., 2006). By promoting knowledge spillovers between firms, the OI model may be particularly efficient to promote entrepreneurship (Audretsch et al., 2005). Although the OI model offers a contrasting view of the innovation process, the policy foundation of the OI model has not been examined nor developed (Chesbrough et al., 2006). This chapter aims to develop the policy rationale behind the OI model. Our analysis is based upon an evaluation of a public program where ideas from the OI model were central (but not recognized as OI). We subsequently seek to identify and derive key OI policy practices that emerge from our study.

CLOSED AND OPEN MODELS OF INNOVATION AND THEIR POLICY IMPLICATIONS

OI has recently been promoted as a new paradigm for understanding the nature, emergence and diffusion of innovation in industry (Chesbrough, 2003). According to the author that first coined the term, OI is 'the use of purposive inflows and outflows of knowledge to accelerate internal innovation, and expand markets for external use of innovation' (Chesbrough, 2006b, p. 1). OI is the antithesis of a traditional or closed model of innovation where internal R&D is the main driver of innovation and value creation at the firm level (Chesbrough, 2003). In the closed model external sources of knowledge have little use and almost no commercial value. In contrast, OI is a paradigm assuming that firms can and should use external ideas, as well as internal ideas, in order to advance the pace of industrial innovation (Chesbrough, 2006b).

Conceptual ambiguity surrounds the concept of OI however. Although this may be expected from an aspiring theory of innovation (Dodgeson et al., 2006), researchers need to address several issues in order to established OI as a new paradigm for industrial innovation (Chesbrough, 2006a; Dodgson et al., 2006). In this chapter we focus on the relationship between OI and innovation policy.

The closed innovation model builds on the premise of market failures (Nelson, 1959; Arrow, 1962; Hall, 2002). According to the classical market failure argument, firms will not invest enough in R&D because the benefits of innovative activities cannot be fully reaped due to incomplete appropriability and knowledge spillovers between firms (Nelson, 1959; Arrow, 1962). Hence, by subsidizing innovative activity, technology programs and policymakers can reduce the appropriability problems faced by R&D active firms. A large theoretical and empirical literature has accordingly argued that firms face insufficient incentives to invest in R&D from the viewpoint of society (Hall, 2002). The closed innovation model therefore builds on a theoretical literature that recommends policymakers to support internal R&D within private firms. In addition, the closed innovation model highlights that society, and not only firms, can benefit from pursuing policies associated with subsidizing internal R&D. This view of innovation differs from the OI model where innovations do not automatically spill over to competitors without costs and effort. Knowledge spillovers are instead encouraged, relevant external knowledge sources are hard to identify and managing such knowledge is a key process in the open approach to innovation. In contrast to the closed innovation model, the OI model does not offer clear policy advice.

The OI model has also put private firms in the center of analysis and focused attention towards how private firms can profit from sourcing of external technology and knowledge. What remains to be discussed within the OI model is whether and how society can benefit from pursing OI. In order to contribute to the development of the policy foundation of the OI model, we draw attention to an industry incubator program where theoretical ideas from the OI model were central.

INDUSTRY INCUBATORS IN NORWAY

Our empirical case is a publicly cosponsored industry incubator program aiming to commercialize new ideas, innovations and spin-off firms from traditional manufacturing firms. The industry incubator program is set up around established industrial firms operating in traditional industries in 14 smaller towns in Norway. These industrial firms are typically major employers in their communities. There are 22 such firms in the program, referred to as 'mother companies' as each of them hosts and sponsors an incubator. The mother companies are located in a regional context that has offered regional advantages in areas such as ship building, energy intensive processing industry, oil and gas and fisheries. Most firms have strong engineering divisions and are the most important knowledge institutions in the region. The firms operate in industries that Norway has excelled in for the last 40–50 years. Due to increasing globalization, including low cost competition from Asia and Eastern Europe, many of the mother companies have faced particular challenges in relation to moving into more upstream activities such as high technology engineering and specialized industrial production based on flexibility and innovation.

Most of the mother companies in the incubator program are caught in a structural inertia trap. On the one hand, they need to change in the direction of more high tech specialized production and engineering. This strategy involves shedding many employees with large industrial experience and relevant knowledge that do not fit into the strategic priority areas of the mother companies. On the other hand, these mother companies have little prior history with entrepreneurship and large-scale organizational change. At the policy level this structural inertia trap has some important challenges: (1) how to preserve and retain relevant industrial knowledge (embodied in workers losing their jobs) within the region and (2) how to transform this relevant industrial knowledge into new industrial activity.

With the aim of promoting entrepreneurship and industrial development within these firms and within their regions, private-public partnerships in the form of an industry incubator have been established. The industry incubator is set up as a joint venture between the government agency for industry development (SIVA) and one or several mother companies at each location.

METHOD AND DATA

To get an in-depth understanding of how the industry incubators contribute to innovation and entrepreneurship, and whether and how the industry incubator program illuminates the policy side of OI, we combined qualitative and quantitative methods. Qualitative data were collected through visits to four incubators, and interviews with five incubator managers, three mother companies and seven start-up firms that were or had been connected to the industry incubators. To examine whether the knowledge gained through the interviews could be generalized to the population of incubator managers, incubator firms and mother companies an email survey was distributed to the CEOs of all 22 mother companies (response rate 77 percent), to all 101 CEOs of the start-up firms in the industry incubators (including product development projects within the mother companies) (response rate 47 percent), and to the CEOs/incubator managers in all of the 14 industry incubators (response rate 100 percent).

Questionnaire items in our surveys to the three sets of respondents were based upon qualitative insights from the interviews. In addition, we consulted prior research on incubators (Rice, 2002; Hackett and Dilts, 2004). The survey data are of an exploratory nature and will not be used to test hypotheses using econometric analysis as this would require the presence of some kind of OI policy theory. Variables and questions in the three surveys are analysed descriptively as the aim in this chapter is rather to help develop the policy rationale of the OI model. It is in this regard important to examine whether and to what extent policies pursued by the industry incubators have beneficial effects.

Using public funds to increase the level of innovation and the pace of technological progress in the economy is not a straightforward task (Mytelka and Smith, 2002). Efficient use of public funds to support innovation and commercialization of technology in industry requires that public resources do not simply replace activities that firms would have financed in the absence of a policy intervention (David and Hall, 2000). Public funds should instead come in addition to what firms would have spent on innovation without the public program. Additionality, defined as the extent to which public funds complement private funds or efforts is thus an important requirement when using public resources to stimulate technological progress in industry (Buisseret et al., 1995).

Additionality is usually examined in economics by comparing a group of subsidized firms (treatment group) to a group of non-subsidized firms (the control group). The difference in average scores between the two groups on some performance indicators (for example, R&D spending) is used to approximate the causal effect of the policy intervention. Such methods will provide an unbiased estimate of the effect of public policies if the control and treatment groups are identical, with the exception that the latter group receives policy support. Because of the early stage involvement in projects and the multiple outcomes pursued by the industry incubators, it is extremely hard to find two such similar groups of firms, or to fully control for their differences in an econometric framework. We avoided such difficulties by using the counterfactual scenario where respondents were asked to assess 'what would have happened if there was no government sponsored industry incubator program' (Rye, 2002). The main reason for our methodological approach is that we could not identify meaningful control groups for our three sets of respondents (incubates, incubator managers and mother companies).

FINDINGS: IDENTIFYING OI POLICY PRACTICES AND ASSESSING THEIR ADDITIONALITY

The goal of the industry incubators is to recruit ideas and entrepreneurs both within the mother companies and from other sources. The outcome of the incubator activity is defined to materialize at three levels: first, by stimulating innovation and entrepreneurship in the form of new ventures, either as spin-offs from the mother companies or as independent start-up firms; second, by stimulating innovation in the mother companies, primarily in the form of developing internal product development projects; and third, by stimulating innovation more generally in society, especially through stimulating innovation and entrepreneurship locally where the industry incubators are located.

The industry incubators in our study were actively searching for potential ideas within the mother companies as well as serving as a door-opener for external entrepreneurs seeking access to the resources within these firms. In many cases the incubators matched ideas and technology within the mother companies with entrepreneurs and management teams from outside the mother companies. Furthermore, the mother companies were in possession of resources such as financing, production equipment, market knowledge and legitimacy that the nascent incubator ventures in our program were able to access. Hence, most start-ups commercialized knowledge and resources contained within large industrial firms.

For instance, some of the start-ups that we interviewed were not spin-offs from the large manufacturing companies, but they were nevertheless given access to relevant resources and knowledge within the mother companies in order to help advance their competitiveness and market success. After an idea search initiated by the incubator, a firm providing high quality industrial painting services was started. The start-up was supported by the incubator's mother company, which had performed this service in-house but now became the largest customer. The new firm provided better quality and a more flexible solution for the mother company, but was also highly welcomed by other local firms that earlier had to go out of town for this service. The industry incubators identified ideas that did not fit internally in the industry firm, but could be commercialized through establishing a new venture. In one case the incubator assisted an internal engineering division that was closed down by the mother company to spin-off as an independent firm. The new firm has grown from initially 19 to nearly 100 employees in a few years. We also found examples where external ideas that increased the firm's competitiveness were obtained from external sources and developed in the incubator context.

The case studies and interviews conducted proved to be highly valuable for our endeavor to identify what may be key OI policy practices. In addition, no prior study has attempted to outline how incubators fit within the OI paradigm. The findings from the interviews and case studies suggest that the OI policies in association with the industry incubators are hands-on towards knowledge transfer processes: (1) the incubators and incubator managers connected ideas, entrepreneurs, management teams and mother companies based on their own knowledge, networks and expertise and (2) they managed the process from business idea to a potential high growth entrepreneurial venture. Thus, using a an OI model, process and organizational design, such as that embodied in an industry incubator, may facilitate access to and transfer of knowledge and resources between firms.

The incubators in the policy program had quite recently been established (between four and one year old), so it is still early to assess the output, but from the overall figures they seem quite successful. According to the incubator managers, the 14 incubators in the program have worked with 560 business ideas. In addition, they have been involved in assessing 64 ideas within the mother companies that have resulted in 29 new product development projects within these firms. The 47 firms and product development projects that responded to our survey (47 percent of the population) reported a total of 405 employees and NOK 255 million (about USD 45 million) in revenue in 2007. These numbers are relatively high considering that only one third of the firms in our sample consider themselves to be in a regular operation or a growth phase, while two thirds are in an idea or early operation phase. The industry incubators have received a total of NOK 48 million in funding over the four year period, from the government agency SIVA (14.5 million), other public sources (12 million) and the mother companies (21 million).

To further examine the role of the incubators and their policies, we asked the incubator firms about the role of the incubator for developing their business. This was done to examine the additionality of the industry incubator program, which is a vital assessment when using public funds and resources to support firms (David and Hall, 2000). To examine this we asked the incubator firms a series of questions where they assessed 'what would have happened to their firm in absence of the industry incubator'. Such questions are typically used in policy evaluation where the goal is to examine additionality (Rye, 2002). In an overall assessment from incubator firms, 10 of 45 respondents claimed that their project or firm would not have been started without the incubator. Eighteen respondents claimed that the incubator had increased the scale of their business activity, ten respondents reported that the incubator had increased the speed of development and seven respondents claimed that the incubator had no effect. Based on these results it seems like most nascent ventures in our sample would not have been established without assistance from the industry incubator. Hence, the industry incubators have been able to initiate and support transfer of knowledge and ideas from the mother companies to society that would not have been the case without the industry incubators. These self-reported data suggest that the incubators play an important role for most projects and that the additionality of the incubators is significant.

Moreover, we sought to investigate the specific contributions of the incubators in more detail. As reported in Table 6.1, the same question was asked to both the projects/firms and to the incubator managers to see whether they had the same views on the incubator's role. It should be noted that the answers are not directly comparable as the incubator managers provided an overall assessment of all projects in their incubator, while the projects/firms reported on their specific cases. The answers were consistent, however, as our two types of respondents reported the contribution to the initiation of the project/firm as most important, while the contribution to technology development was least important.

Table 6.1   Role of the incubator assessed by project/start-up and by
incubator manager (Likert 7 point scale)

Question: Please assess the role of the incubator for the initiation and further development of your firm/project (1 = no contribution, 7 = very large contribution)	Projects/ start-up firms	Incubator manager
	Average score	Average score
Contributed to the initiation of the project/firm	4.6	5.4
Contributed to access critical resources for the project/firm	4.6	5.0
Contributed to increase the development speed of the project/firm	4.5	5.0
Contributed to identify business opportunities for the project/firm	4.4	5.2
Contributed to develop the market aspects of the project/firm	3.9	4.7
Contributed to develop the technological aspects of the project/firm	2.9	3.5
N	45	9

The results in Table 6.1 are very much in line with an OI model where the incubators seem to play an important role by initiating processes and access-ing resources, while their specific contributions to develop the technological aspects of the idea are more modest. It thus appears that the incubators and their activities are able to connect resource seeking start-up firms with exter-nal resources, and are able to help commercialize and develop unexploited technology and resources within the mother companies.

To further assess the specific contributions from the incubators we asked the projects/firms to rate their satisfaction with the services offered by the incubator. As a validity check the mother companies were asked the same questions, but the scores are not fully comparable because the mother compa-nies provide an overall assessment, while the responses for the projects/firms are specific to their cases. Based on our interviews we identified the most common incubator services and the satisfaction with each are listed in Table 6.2. Only the answers from respondents that confirmed that they used the specific service are included.

The assessment of incubator services shows that the role as a network actor is a very important part of the incubator's role. General roles related to

Table 6.2 Assessment of the services delivered by the incubator (Likert 7 point scale)

Question: How satisfied are you with the services delivered by the incubator in the following areas: (1 = very unsatisfied, 7 = very satisfied)	Incubator project/firm	Mother company
	Average score	Average score
Network (e.g. access to researchers, institutes and industry)	5.3	5.4
Business development (e.g. assistance with business plan, budgeting)	5.2	5.4
Monitoring (e.g. coaching, mentor services, define and reach milestones)	4.9	5.2
Financing (e.g. contacts to seed and venture capital firms, banks, government support schemes)	4.9	4.9
Equipment and technical assistance (e.g. office space, internet access, technical equipment and advice)	4.9	5.0
Organizational development (e.g. recruiting, management)	4.7	5.1
Market development (e.g. customer relations and marketing)	4.5	4.5
Legal advice (e.g. intellectual property rights assistance)	3.6	4.1
N	17–43	11–17

networking, business development and monitoring score higher than more specific services related to legal assistance, market development and organizational development. The assessments made by the projects/firms are confirmed by the responses from the mother companies.

DISCUSSION

The aim of this chapter has been to help develop the policy foundation of the OI model. Our research strategy has been to empirically examine an industry incubator program with public and private funding in which ideas from the OI model were central but not explicitly recognized. Results from the case studies suggest that the OI policies are hands-on and pursue, connect and develop policy practices. In our case studies this materialized in the following ways: (1) resource seeking start-up firms were actively matched with external resources; (2) incubator managers ran internal product development projects within the mother companies; (3) start-up firms were given access to resources from the mother companies where the incubator acted as a door-opener and (4) the incubator helped commercialize some of the unexploited technologies and resources of the mother companies by facilitating spin-off activity and providing access to resources within the mother companies for external entrepreneurs.

The OI policy practices identified above stand out in contrast to technology policies based upon the premise of neoclassical market failures for two reasons. First, neoclassical technology policies recommend subsidizing internal R&D within firms (Hall, 2002). However, offering internal R&D subsidies to the mother companies in our study would not have ensured the commercialization of non-exploited technology and resources. Second, neoclassical market failure policies assume that R&D and technology will flow freely and without costs among economic actors. The empirical data we have collected (surveys and interviews) suggest that such knowledge transfer does not happen automatically and that such knowledge transfer processes need to be managed actively. Helping start-up and established firms to overcome the liabilities of newness and senescence (Stinchcombe, 1965; Hannan, 1998) may thus be a policy practice that is distinct to the OI model.

An issue that remains to be addressed is the societal influence and importance of the policies pursued by the industry incubators. Hence, it is important to examine the additionality of the OI policy practices identified in this chapter. Our case studies and interviews suggest that the knowledge and resources that were transferred from the mother companies to society would not have been commercialized by the mother companies themselves or transferred to society in the form of entrepreneurial new ventures in the absence of the incubator program. Survey evidence further suggests that most of the start-up ventures in our sample would not have been established without the industry incubator program. Incubator managers, CEOs of start-up firms and CEOs of the mother companies all agree that the program had high additionality in relation to entrepreneurship and spin-off activity from the large industrial firms. Even though a minority of the projects involving the incubators were product development projects within the mother companies, the incubators and incubator managers provided valuable management expertise and project leadership. In the majority of cases these product development projects would not have been initiated without the incubator program. The CEOs of the mother companies all deem the incubators to have high additionality also in this regard. Hence, active transfer of knowledge between economic actors that would not have taken place without the policy intervention may be a type of additionality that is distinct to the OI model.

CONCLUSION

This chapter takes a societal perspective on OI, rather than an internal corporate perspective. This is important because the policy side of the OI model has not been addressed nor developed (Chesbrough et al., 2006). Based on our study of a publicly cosponsored industry incubator program, we argue that OI policies connect different types of industrial actors (small and large firms, universities, R&D institutes and government support actors) that without the policy intervention would not have been connected. Such policies have knowledge transfer as an important aim because it is recognized that knowledge sources relevant for industrial innovation do not simply diffuse freely among industrial actors (Von Hippel, 1988). Furthermore, OI policies manage and develop industrial projects in order to commercialize technology that would not have been commercialized without the policy intervention. Such policies have an active and hands-on approach. An important social goal of both the connect and the manage and develop part of OI policies is to preserve and retain knowledge that has an economic value to society but which large corporations themselves choose not to commercialize or to exploit, and from which resource seeking start-up firms may benefit. Our study suggests that these activities may be key OI policy practices.

A significant share of the knowledge transfer processes and entrepreneurial activities identified in this study would not have taken place without the involvement of the incubators; or they would not have happened in the same time frame or at the same scale. As such, our empirical example suggests that OI policies can support significant additionality in relation to knowledge transfer and commercialization of resources and technology. The social value of the OI policies pursued by the industry incubators is not more private internal R&D (as would be the performance criteria within the closed innovation model), but rather that unused but economically valuable resources and technology are transferred, managed and put into new productive means and applications.

An important implication that emerges from our study is that incubators may facilitate knowledge spillovers from large companies to society by promoting OI. An interesting parallel to the role of the industry incubators for the large manufacturing companies and incubates in our study is the role attributed to Technology Transfer Offices (TTOs) within a university and an academic entrepreneurship context (Carlsson and Fridh, 2002). Whereas there is extensive literature on the role of the TTO for the commercialization of academic science and basic technology from universities to society in the form of academic spin-offs, we are not aware of studies that have looked at whether and how publicly supported incubators can commercialize some of the unused (but still economically valuable) technology and resources within large firms.

Our study suggests that the economic value of this technology is significant, may help resource seeking start-up firms to assemble critical external resources and may even help major companies to transform themselves.

Although our study has been done within the Norwegian context, we believe that the basic relationships described between incubators, large firms and start-up firms, and the outcomes of the interactions between these actors, can provide implications for how OI policies can be designed and promoted in other countries, such as the USA. Although country context is important, the overall majority of start-up firms face the liability of newness in most countries (Stinchcombe, 1965), while many established incumbent firms face the liability of senescence (Hannan, 1998). OI policies may help firms to overcome these two liabilities.

REFERENCES

Aldrich, H. (1999), *Organizations Evolving*, Thousand Oaks, CA: Sage Publications.
Arrow, K.J. (1962), 'Economic welfare and the allocation of resources for invention', in R. Nelson (ed.), *The Rate and Direction of Inventive Activity*, Princeton, NJ: Princeton University Press, pp. 609–25.
Audretsch, D., M. Keilbach and E. Lehmann (2005), 'The knowledge spillover theory of entrepreneurship and technological diffusion', in G.D. Libecap (ed.), *University Entrepreneurship and Technology Transfer: Process, Design, and Intellectual Property*, Oxford: Elsevier, pp. 69–91.
Buisseret, T.J., H.M. Cameron and L. Georghiou (1995), 'What difference does it make – additionality in the public support of R-and-D in large firms', *International Journal of Technology Management*, **10**(4-6), 587–600.
Burgelman, R. (1983), 'A process model for internal corporate venturing in the diversified major firm', *Administrative Science Quarterly*, **28**(3), 223–44.
Carlsson, B. and A.C. Fridh (2002), 'Technology transfer in United States universities – a survey and statistical analysis', *Journal of Evolutionary Economics*, **12**(1–2), 199–232.
Chesbrough, H.W. (2003), *Open Innovation: The New Imperative for Creating and Profiting from Technology*, Boston, MA: Harvard Business School Press.
Chesbrough, H. (2006a), 'New puzzles and new findings', in H. Chesbrough, W. Vanhaverbeke and J. West (eds), *Open Innovation: Researching a New Paradigm*, Oxford: Oxford University Press, pp. 15–34.
Chesbrough, H. (2006b), 'Open innovation: a new paradigm for understanding industrial innovation', in H. Chesbrough, W. Vanhaverbeke and J. West (eds), *Open Innovation: Researching A New Paradigm*, Oxford: Oxford University Press, pp. 1–12.
Chesbrough, H.W., W. Vanhaverbeke and J. West (2006), *Open Innovation: Researching a New Paradigm*, Oxford: Oxford University Press.
David, P.A. and B.H. Hall (2000), 'Heart of darkness: modeling public-private funding interactions inside the R&D black box', *Research Policy*, **29**(9), 1165–83.
Dodgeson, M., D. Gann and A. Salter (2006), 'The role of technology in the shift towards open innovation: the case of Procter & Gamble', *R&D Management*, **36**, 333–46.

Hackett, S.M. and D.M. Dilts (2004), 'A systematic review of business incubation research', *Journal of Technology Transfer*, **29**(1), 55–82.

Hall, B.H. (2002), 'The financing of research and development', *Oxford Review of Economic Policy*, **18**(1), 35–51.

Hannan, M.T. (1998), 'Rethinking age dependence in organizational mortality: logical formalizations', *American Journal of Sociology*, **104**(1), 126–64.

Mytelka, L.K. and K. Smith (2002), 'Policy learning and innovation theory: an interactive and co-evolving process', *Research Policy*, **31**(8–9), 1467–79.

Nelson, R.R. (1959), 'The simple economics of basic scientific research', *Journal of Political Economy*, **67**, 297–306.

Rice, M.P. (2002), 'Co-production of business assistance in business incubators – an exploratory study', *Journal of Business Venturing*, **17**(2), 163–87.

Rivette, K.G. and D. Kline (1999), 'Discovering new value in intellectual property', *Harvard Business Review*, January–February, 54–66.

Rye, M. (2002), 'Evaluating the impact of public support on commercial research and development projects: are verbal reports of additionality reliable?', *Evaluation*, **8**(2), 227–48.

Stinchcombe, A.L. (1965), 'Social structure and organizations', in J.G. March (ed.), *Handbook of Organizations*, Chicago: Rand McNally, pp. 153–93.

Von Hippel, E. (1988), *The Sources of Innovation*, Oxford: Oxford University Press.

PART III

Newness

7. A process model of venture creation by immigrant entrepreneurs

Evgueni Vinogradov and Amanda Elam

INTRODUCTION

Over the past three decades immigrant entrepreneurship has gained significant attention among scholars who study self-employment, entrepreneurship and small business management. After examining over 1700 academic sources, Rath and Kloosterman (2003, p. 4) concluded that 'immigrant entrepreneurship ... has become a kind of growth sector itself'. This interest is driven by the understanding that both ethnic societies and host countries benefit from the rise of immigrant entrepreneurship (Wadhwa et al., 2008). Although it is still unclear under what conditions immigrants and their host countries benefit from business ownership, there is little doubt that this kind of activity significantly affects every society. As such, a more profound understanding of the phenomenon of immigrant entrepreneurship is warranted.

Immigrant entrepreneurship studies consider a broad range of topics varying from early entrepreneurial intentions to the intergenerational succession of well-established firms. The breadth of this research has identified several distinct factors influencing immigrant experiences and outcomes in entrepreneurship, defined broadly herein as the creation of new ventures from self- employment to high potential start-ups. These distinct immigrant factors include ethnic networks and resources, relationships with family and friends in both host countries and countries of origin and the role of cultural and language differences on the creation and growth of entrepreneurial ventures (Rath and Kloosterman, 2003).

Despite the advances in research on the key factors distinguishing immigrant entrepreneurship from other forms, the research in this area has remained disconnected from recent advances in general entrepreneurship theory. Process views of the venture creation process, for example, have driven significant advances in research on entrepreneurship (Reynolds and White, 1997; Shane and Venkataraman, 2000; Sarasvathy, 2001; Shane, 2004; Baker et al., 2005; Reynolds et al., 2005). The purpose of this chapter is to establish connections between findings on immigrant entrepreneurship and recent advances in general theories of venture creation. We focus on two key research questions. First, what are the key factors at various levels of analysis that differentiate immigrant entrepreneurs and their businesses from their mainstream counterparts? Second, do these key factors matter more or less at various stages of the venture creation process?

As a result of this investigation, we develop a process model of immigrant entrepreneurship which we believe will help advance comparative research on immigrant entrepreneurship. We pose two key arguments – first, that selective migration and pre-migration experiences position immigrants in unique ways within their host countries; and second, that the characteristics and resource sets that define the positions of immigrants in their new found contexts influence these individuals, or groups, differently at various stages of the entrepreneurship process.

THEORETICAL APPROACHES TO IMMIGRANT ENTREPRENEURSHIP

Any theoretical discussion of immigrant entrepreneurship requires the clarification of two key constructs: entrepreneurship and immigrant entrepreneurship. In this chapter we explicitly adopt a broad and active definition of entrepreneurship. Following Gartner (1985), we define entrepreneurship as a venture creation process – that is, planning, organizing and establishing new organizations (Gartner, 1985). Furthermore, we adopt a broad, if sometimes controversial, definition of entrepreneurship as including a range of new ventures from basic self-employment models to team-based models of high potential ventures. Additionally, theoretical discussions in academic journals often confound the terms 'ethnic', 'minority' and 'immigrant' as interchangeable descriptors for entrepreneurial activities of non-majority individuals (Greene, 1997; Chaganti and Greene, 2002). In our view these terms hold different meanings in relation to venture creation.

Minority entrepreneurs, for example, are business owners who are not of the majority population and represent statistical minorities (Chaganti and Greene, 2002). As a further complication the term minority is based on crosscutting descriptors like race, ethnicity and gender. Also, the term minority typically describes a statistical minority within the overarching social landscape and not necessarily within the subpopulation of interest, as a statistical minority among a defined subpopulation of entrepreneurs. To illustrate, while immigrants are typically statistical minorities in most national contexts, as a social group, they tend to be over-represented among entrepreneurs and tend to be comprised of males (a statistical majority marker among entrepreneurs, but not in national population) and people of strong ethnicity (a statistical minority marker among both entrepreneurs and national population). What characterizes minority entrepreneurs, then, are factors that relate specifically to the experience of being a statistical minority.

In contrast to the objective statistical definition of minority entrepreneurs, ethnic entrepreneurs are typically operationalized by self-report measures (Wilson et al., 2004). The reason for this is that ethnicity denotes a level of personal involvement in an ethnic community (Chaganti and Greene, 2002). In this sense, an ethnic business is 'a business whose proprietor has a distinctive group attachment by virtue of self definition or ascriptions by others' (Aldrich and Waldinger, 1990, p. 113). Ethnicity and immigrant status tend to be confounded in the study of entrepreneurship following the assumption that all immigrants identify with, and participate regularly in, a community of others with whom they share a common cultural background. Indeed, Waldinger, et al. (1990, p. 3) define ethnic entrepreneurship as 'a set of connections and regular patterns of interaction among people sharing common national background or migration experiences' (Waldinger et al., 1990, p. 3). To clarify, the factors that set ethnicity apart from immigrant status are the level of personal identification and regular interaction patterns within ethnic communities, not migration experiences or statistical representation.

Immigrant entrepreneurs can, and often do, share characteristics with other statistical minorities and ethnic groups. Still there are distinct differences that set immigrants apart from this group. We define immigrant entrepreneurs as individuals who are recent arrivals in the host country and engage in a business start-up. As such, immigrants may or may not be statistical minorities in the host country (for example, English-speaking males of mainly European descent who migrate to the USA) and immigrants may or may not identify with their ethnic heritage. Beyond the cross-cutting labels of minority and ethnic, the factors that distinguish immigrants from the rest of the population are the experiences and resource advantages and disadvantages that are derived from actual migration experiences. Among these factors are linguistic disadvantage (Marlow, 1992; Johnson, 2000), legal status (Barrett et al., 2002), and shared historical memories and migration experience (Basu and Altinay, 2002). In particular, we are interested in the concept of transnationalism which is rooted in the migration experience (Tong et al., 2003) and which defines a clear set of advantages for immigrant entrepreneurs and others who accumulate migratory experiences and use the resulting experience and social ties to their advantage in the venture creation process (Terjesen and Elam, 2009).

THEORIES OF IMMIGRANT ENTREPRENEURSHIP

Existing theories on immigrant entrepreneurship tend to highlight the importance of a variety of factors as sources of advantage and disadvantage for immigrant entrepreneurs. Bonacich (1973), for one, famously proposed a rather dim view of immigrant entrepreneurship, indicating that immigrants tend to face a large amount of hostility, discrimination and blocked mobility in host countries. As a result, she argued, immigrant entrepreneurs tend to hold very marginal positions in society as 'ethnic middlemen' serving elite members of the host society, avoiding assimilation and finding refuge in self-isolation and high levels of ethnic solidarity. While this theory may describe some subset of immigrant entrepreneurs, it obscures the agency and strategic advantages exploited by many immigrant entrepreneurs in the pursuit of identified market opportunities or inefficiencies.

In fact, other scholars have challenged this rather dismal view of the oppressed and marginalized immigrant entrepreneur with a view focused on the advantages that ethnic culture and community may confer on the immigrant entrepreneur. Drawing on a thesis of cultural advantage, a few scholars have argued that some groups of immigrant entrepreneurs draw considerable advantages from ethnic networks. For example, ethnic cultural values, like a strong work ethic, may predispose some groups of immigrant entrepreneurs towards entrepreneurship and market success (Weber, 1958; Light, 1984). Certainly the migration decision represents a definite selection effect resulting in the migration of individuals or groups with particular sets of psychological and cultural resources, such as a sense of adventure, self-sacrifice and a willingness to work hard. In a more immediate sense, Portes and Zhou (1992) argued that immigrants from close ethnic communities are able to acquire critical resources (including money, knowledge, labor, customer referrals and so on) and are provided with strong incentives to act.

In an effort to reconcile the contrast between the hostile environment and resource advantages, scholars have pointed out that the observed rates and patterns of immigrant entrepreneurship are, in fact, a result of both individual level factors and macroenvironmental contexts. Waldinger et al. (1990), for example, proposed that immigrant entrepreneurship is really a result of the interaction between opportunity structures and group characteristics. Kloosterman and Van Der Leun (1999) improved upon this interactive model of local and macro context to argue that immigrant entrepreneurship represents the dynamic interplay between social, economic and institutional contexts at multiple levels of analysis from neighborhood and city locales to national environments.

While some attention has been paid to modeling immigrant entrepreneurship across levels of analysis with special attention to the ways cross-level factors interact, we find the existing models to be too static. In other words, existing models fail to consider that various sets of factors at the micro, macro and interactional level of analysis may vary across stages of start-up activity. In order to generate better knowledge about immigrant entrepreneurship, a dynamic or process-based, multilevel model of immigrant entrepreneurship is required.

To summarize our objectives in this chapter, we seek to develop a theoretical view of immigrant entrepreneurship that accomplishes a number of goals. First, we consider the importance of a dynamic and interactive perspective on immigrant entrepreneurship. Second, we focus on explaining the causal factors or antecedents at multiple levels of analysis and across time that may help to explain the variation in observed rates and patterns of venture creation among immigrant groups and across countries as well as between immigrant and non-immigrant entrepreneurs. And finally, we look to the field of general entrepreneurship research to provide the basis of a process model of venture creation that allows for the likelihood that key factors at varying levels of analysis matter at different points in the venture creation process.

ENTREPRENEURIAL PROCESS THEORY

Process views of entrepreneurship emerged in response to calls for multilevel models of entrepreneurial activity, that is, theoretical models of the integration of factors across levels of analysis and the ways in which they drive entrepreneurship. In 1991 Reynolds observed a troubling divide in entrepreneurship research. He argued that research on traits and contexts in entrepreneurship studies had reached a dead end and future efforts must focus on the intersection between traits and contexts. For Reynolds (1991), this meant focusing on the processes that characterize entrepreneurship – the intersection between entrepreneurial action at the micro level and the material, social and cultural environment or the macro level context. A few years later and based on earlier work by Venkataraman (1997), Shane and Venkataraman (2000) introduced the concept of the 'individual-opportunity nexus', proposing that opportunities are discovered, evaluated and exploited by alert individuals. With this advance in general entrepreneurship theory, the authors drew attention to both the micro-macro interactions and the stages of entrepreneurship that result. This was an important step in the development of entrepreneurship theory and one that has brought widespread inspiration to entrepreneurship researchers.

More recently, Shane (2004) expanded the process view of this individual-opportunity nexus model. Essentially, he further specified the entrepreneurial process view, especially in terms of the characteristics of opportunities, the individuals who discover and exploit them, the process of resource acquisition and organization, and the strategies used to exploit and protect the profits from those efforts. In short, Shane (2004) identified seven stages in the entrepreneurial process: (1) existence of opportunities, (2) discovery of opportunities,

(3) decision to exploit opportunities, (4) resource acquisition, (5) development of entrepreneurial strategy, (6) organizing process and (7) performance.

Importantly, Shane's (2004) process perspective is rooted in Kirznerian economic theory (Kirzner, 1985) and generally referred to as a market process or entrepreneurial discovery perspective. As such, Shane's process model is founded upon assumptions about the pre-existence of market opportunities and the alertness of particular individuals to these opportunities. Opportunities are defined as solutions to market inefficiencies, as opposed to technologies that disrupt markets. Hence, because markets never reach full efficiency or equilibrium, opportunities always exist. At the individual level alertness is derived from both cognitive differences and information asymmetries.

While this entrepreneurial discovery perspective has proved to be very inspiring in the entrepreneurship research community, there are some important shortcomings that we must acknowledge. First, Shane's model assumes a linear movement through the various stages. Sarasvathy (2001), for example, argues that individuals do not move in especially rational or goal directed fashion through the start-up process. Not only does she not articulate a view of the stages of the venture creation process in her effectuation theory, but she also tends to focus exclusively on the decision-making aspect (or lack thereof) of the venture creation process. Likewise, Baker and Nelson's (2005) bricolage theory focuses on the resource mobilization aspect of the venture creation process, also introducing a sense of randomness to the way in which individuals are likely to navigate the process.

Second, the model is undersocialized (Baker et al., 2005) in that the importance of national context and social/cultural embeddedness for both the individuals and the opportunities was completely overlooked. As a solution, Baker et al. (2005) proposed an antecedent category to the process – comparative, discovery, evaluation, exploitation (CDEE) – arguing that the opportunity structures can vary significantly across sociopolitical and economic contexts. On this point, Elam's (2008) work showed that, while differences in opportunities can vary significantly across levels of national development, the biggest differences between countries may emerge from the distribution of individuals across the opportunity structure, particularly in relation to perceptions and access to resources.

Third, Shane's model underplayed the importance of psychological factors. De Carolis and Saparito (2006) addressed this point by highlighting the importance of both external/institutional and internal/psychological factors. Missing in their formulation, however, was the important connection between individual level and macro level factors in the entrepreneurial process. Earlier work by Harper (2003) did a much better job unpacking the interaction between psychological factors and macro level cultural/institutional factors in ways that influence entrepreneurial behavior.

Despite the limitations inherent in Shane's (2004) process framework, we find it to be a useful heuristic model for our theory development. The integration of a well-specified process model with a multilevel view of immigrant entrepreneurship is our central aim in this chapter. In the next section we summarize our multilevel, process view of immigrant entrepreneurship and discuss how various levels of factors are likely to influence immigrant entrepreneurship at various stages of the entrepreneurial process.

A PROCESS MODEL OF IMMIGRANT ENTREPRENEURSHIP

Early on in this chapter we specified two key questions as central to our theoretical approach to immigrant entrepreneurship: (1) What types of factors differentiate immigrant entrepreneurship from other forms at varying levels of analysis? and (2) How do those differences influence how immigrants navigate the entrepreneurship process? In response, we propose that the factors that differentiate immigrant entrepreneurs from other entrepreneurs are rooted largely in the pre-migration and migration experiences of immigrant entrepreneurs, as well as in possible selection effects that arise from the actual migration event itself. In this section we discuss how these distinctions influence immigrant entrepreneurship throughout the entrepreneurship process. Given space constraints, we restrict our discussion to the first four stages of Shane's (2004) framework – existence, discovery, decision to exploit and resource acquisition.

Based on the analysis of existing theories and relevant empirical evidence we argue that immigrants may differ from native entrepreneurs in several ways. Immigrant specific traits influence the entrepreneurial process as summarized in Figure 7.1.

At the macro level host country laws and regulations can make certain opportunities inaccessible to immigrants (link 1). Positive consumer discrimination (which emanates from the implementation of government procurement programs or private preferences for dealing with immigrant entrepreneurs) opens opportunities that are available only for immigrants (link 2). Liability of foreignness expressed in insufficient language abilities and general unfamiliarity with the host country context hinders acquisition of information critical for discovering mainstream entrepreneurial opportunities (link 3).

At the group level ethnic culture affects the decision to exploit entrepreneurial opportunities in two ways. First, in accordance with the aggregative psychological trait approach, some ethnic cultures reinforce independence, need for achievement, internal locus of control and other psychological traits that encourage entrepreneurial behavior. Individuals embedded in such

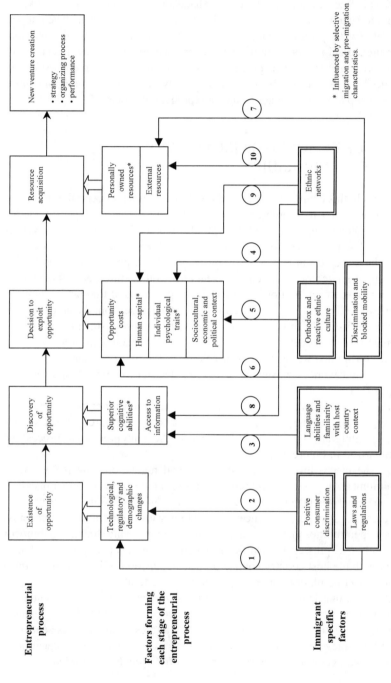

Figure 7.1   A process model of immigrant entrepreneurship

cultures are relatively likely to exploit entrepreneurial opportunities (link 4). Second, within certain cultural contexts entrepreneurs may be more socially accepted gaining higher status and respect from co-ethnics. Such ethnic cultures stimulate individual entrepreneurs to make a positive decision considering exploitation of entrepreneurial opportunities (link 5).

Discrimination and blocked mobility on the general labor market lowers the opportunity costs for potential entrepreneurs. In the absence of alternative ways to improve their economic and social position, immigrants are likely to decide to exploit even marginally profitable entrepreneurial opportunities (link 6). On the other hand, discrimination hinders immigrants from acquiring loans from the mainstream sources that impose additional limitations on the resource pool necessary to exploit an opportunity (link 7).

Ethnic networks of immigrants shape the entrepreneurial process in several ways. First, specific knowledge about co-ethnic consumer preferences and home country specific knowledge allows immigrants to discover the entrepreneurial opportunities hidden from natives (link 8). Second, social capital acquired through ethnic networks creates additional entrepreneurship specific human capital primarily in the form of relevant training. This specific human capital provides confidence necessary to make a positive decision considering exploitation of entrepreneurial opportunities (link 9). Finally, resources critical for establishing a business may be acquired from co-ethnics (link 10). Pre-migration characteristics of immigrants and selectivity of migration influence the critical stages of the entrepreneurial process.

Existence of Opportunities

The existence of entrepreneurial opportunities is a key source of debate in entrepreneurship studies. Following Schumpeter (1934), many scholars argue that opportunities result from innovations that disrupt the marketplace. Whereas other scholars like Shane (2004) follow Kirzner (1985), arguing that opportunities always exist insofar as markets are always imperfect and market inefficiencies provide opportunities. Markets are dynamic contexts where change is constant. Opportunities arise from change and growth. Consequently, while innovations may drive changes and growth processes, not all opportunities result in innovation. In fact, most innovations are incremental and only disruptive upon reflection. As such, it is reasonable to assume that market inefficiencies are always present and that once identified constitute entrepreneurial opportunities. With that general position in mind, the factors that define the existence of opportunities exist largely at a macro level. In fact, Shane (2004) identified three categories of entrepreneurial opportunities: technological, political/regulatory and social/demographic. These macro factors, he argued, define the types of opportunities available. We argue that these factors also define the types of opportunities available to specific groups, like immigrants.

In terms of technology (that is, tools/systems that change the relationship to the physical environment or geography), opportunities can be created or blocked for immigrants. Historically, many countries have relied on immigrant labor to perform agricultural, manual and service work. As host countries become more developed, relying more heavily on industrialized technologies for everyday living, skill and educational requirements have increased. These trends create opportunities for immigrants who gain access to higher education and training in host countries, but also may reduce the opportunities available to low-skilled immigrants and impose barriers to occupational mobility. In reverse, the opportunities for highly educated and skilled immigrants in developing countries may also exist depending on the state of technological development and the inefficiencies that can be identified and exploited.

Political/regulatory factors can also create or block opportunities for immigrant entrepreneurs. Immigrants face legal restrictions in many countries (Magatti and Quassoli, 2003; Peberdy and Rogerson, 2003; Wilpert, 2003). While legal status issues for new immigrants can often be resolved over time as they become legally established, sometimes they face ethnic or racial restrictions that limit opportunities. Historically, government policies enforced by laws and regulations, such as the Chinese Exclusion Act of 1882 in the USA, have directly prohibited immigrants to occupy certain positions, at least for some restricted period after migration (Wong, 1998). On the other hand, government policies can provide special advantages to immigrant entrepreneurs. In the USA, for example, government procurement programs promote businesses owned by minorities, creating for them opportunities unavailable to mainstream entrepreneurs. Such instruments of governmental support are also associated with 'positive discrimination' and are a subject for political debates (Cormack and Niessen, 2002).

As for social and demographic changes, consumer preferences for particular types of services or products can create or ban opportunities for immigrants. According to the mixed embeddedness perspective, accessibility is one of the dimensions of opportunity structure that is critical for understanding the process of insertion and social mobility of immigrant entrepreneurs (Waldinger et al., 1990; Kloosterman and Rath, 2001). For example, some opportunities easily accessible for natives may be unavailable for immigrants when special permissions or educational qualifications that can only be acquired in the country of settlement are required in order to start a business.

Additionally, discriminatory rules or cultural practices prescribing immigrants to settle in particular areas may influence the availability of business opportunities. Also, demographic shifts like the growing Hispanic market in the USA increase opportunities within ethnic niche markets and may contribute to a broader consumer interest in particular ethnic products and services. Driven by solidarity, co-ethnics may buy products from immigrants even when comparable products are available from native sellers. In this way co-ethnics create opportunities for immigrant entrepreneurs which are not available for natives.

Insofar as the existence of opportunities are defined primarily by macro level trends and structures, the pre-migration and migration experiences, along with other individual level factors, hold little influence beyond a fit with the social and economic landscape. The individual level factors and consequently the interactional factors begin in the discovery phase of the entrepreneurship process.

Discovery of Opportunities

In Shane's (2004) formulation there are two key factors in the discovery of opportunities—alertness and information asymmetries. Discovery, in this sense, is very much an individual level phenomenon for Shane. Psychological characteristics, for example, alertness and information asymmetries contribute to the likelihood of discovering opportunities. In fact, we suspect that many immigrants hold a unique advantage in terms of alertness over native entrepreneurs, if some likely disadvantages in terms of information asymmetries. At the macro level we see that cultural stereotypes and consumer preferences influence both the alertness and information available to immigrant entrepreneurs compared to others. Informal institutions such as cultural beliefs and ideals can influence the types of opportunities to which certain groups of individuals are alert and can constrain or enable access to information about business opportunities.

With regard to psychological aspects, Shane (2004) argued that opportunities have an objective component, but that the discovery of opportunities requires a sort of subjective creativity as opposed to a purely rational optimization oriented analysis. In this view the process of opportunity discovery is cognitive and, therefore, only individuals, not groups of people, discover entrepreneurial opportunities. Prior entrepreneurial experience seems to improve an individual's ability to identify opportunities within a given information pool. Those immigrants coming from the countries with relatively broad involvement of population in entrepreneurial activities may, therefore, be better equipped for identifying business opportunities (Cobas, 1986; Yuengert, 1995; Ekberg and Hammarstedt, 1999; Hammarstedt, 2001). Additionally, immigrants may be more confident in their own human capital and ability to succeed in a new, uncertain environment, if not more averse to risk than non-immigrants (Clark and Drinkwater, 1998; Levie, 2007).

Some people discover opportunities where others cannot because they have better access to information. An individual's prior life experience, social networks and systematic search for relevant data are the sources of information that facilitate the discovery of opportunities. Of course, relevant information regarding market opportunities is not equally distributed between immigrants and natives. Many new immigrants face limitations to the discovery of opportunities because of language barriers and a lack of familiarity with the culture and formal institutions in their host country. These factors are especially limiting for immigrants looking for opportunities in mainstream markets. Problems regarding understanding of the legislation and regulations, as well as lack of knowledge about the local market, were reported among the main hurdles faced by immigrant entrepreneurs in Norway (Enger et al., 1992). Moreover, experience which allows immigrants to spot opportunities in the host country are not always easily transferable across borders (Razin and Scheinberg, 2001).

That said, many immigrants possess knowledge about ethnic goods and services and the needs of co-ethnics in host countries, allowing them to identify the relevant opportunities which are hidden from the mainstream entrepreneurs. For example, pre-migration experience and deep knowledge about their home countries provide relative advantages for immigrants when looking for opportunities for international trade. It may explain why many immigrants are involved in import/export and other transnational activities. Intensive communication to co-ethnics provides immigrants with information on the opportunities which are not readily available for outsiders – for example, the best industries to enter, pricing, technology and business methods (Chotigeat et al., 1991). Business information delivered by co-ethnics is often highly credible in the context of mutual trust. In some cases ethnic chauvinism encourages immigrants to deliver important messages solely to co-ethnics, avoiding sharing important information with members of other ethnic groups (Light et al., 1993).

Decision to Exploit

As with discovery, individual psychological factors are also important for the decision to exploit an opportunity, particularly in the context of the calculation of opportunity costs and expected gains that underlie any decision to start a business (Shane, 2004). Research has shown that while psychological factors are the strongest predictors of the decision to start a business, those factors are further shaped by human capital and more macro level sociocultural factors (Shane, 2004; Elam, 2008).

There are two sources of cultural factors likely to influence immigrant entrepreneurship. There are the basic values brought from the country of origin and the values picked up in the host country (Light, 1980; Yoon, 1991).

In this way, cultural values and psychological propensities for venture creation can be picked up in pre-migration experiences, through selective migration processes, and from host country communities, ethnic and otherwise.

Pre-migration experiences may include exposure to values, beliefs and experiences that are more closely linked to the decision to exploit an entrepreneurial opportunity. Numerous studies on relationships between national culture and entrepreneurship have been conducted at the population level. Certain characteristics such as individualism, autonomy, high power distance and high internal locus of control have been associated with entrepreneurial behavior (Davidsson and Wiklund, 1997; Hayton et al., 2002; Elam, 2008).

Selective migration processes may also cull individuals with particular psychological traits or cultural beliefs that correlate strongly with the decision to start a business. It may be that more adventurous or self-confident individuals are over-represented in immigrant groups. Of course, cultural traits encouraging business participation may also be formed after migration. Immigrants may take a decision to exploit entrepreneurial opportunities as a response to the external hostility (Bonacich, 1973). The clash of values between the groups drives potential entrepreneurs into self-employment. Alternatively, immigrants embedded in ethnic subcultures may be encouraged to start a business following the expectations of their co-ethnics. The decision to exploit an entrepreneurial opportunity is easier to take when co-ethnic peers, neighbors and relatives show respect and moral support for business people.

Resource Acquisition

Exploitation of entrepreneurial opportunities demands the acquisition and mobilization of key resources, including monetary capital, labor, real estate, equipment and so on. Shane (2004) points to the importance of asymmetric information for adequate financing of ventures. In order to overcome the problems associated with asymmetric information, Shane (2004) argued, entrepreneurs and investors may rely on self-financing, contractual constraints, pre- and post-investment tools, social ties and quality signaling.

Financial resources are, of course, a critical resource in the start-up of any business, largely because money can be converted relatively easily into the other required resources (Elam, 2008). We further adopt the view that other resources, like social ties, credibility and human capital, can also be converted into financial and other material resources. For immigrants, pre-migration experiences can provide some advantages where resource acquisition is concerned. Specific accomplishments, reputations and social ties from the home country can help establish immigrant entrepreneurs within host country ethnic networks. Because immigrants often experience difficulties when applying for bank loans (Bruder et al., 2007), these ethnic network ties often provide critical access to financial and other resources for immigrant entrepreneurs. Pakistani and Indian Sikh groups in the UK have been found to rely on some form of introduction or recommendation to local banks by co-ethnic business associations (Fadahunsi et al., 2000). Additionally, Chinese (Wong, 1998) and Korean (Park, 1997; Raijman and Tienda, 2003) immigrants in the USA have been found to use ethnic rotating credit associations more broadly compared to others.

Whether formal sources of finance are available for immigrant entrepreneurs or not, many prefer informal borrowing for its expeditiousness and absence of paperwork (Portes and Zhou, 1992). It is also observed that Korean retailers are likely to obtain credits from Korean wholesalers despite a relatively high credit risk involved (Kim and Hurh, 1985). Co-ethnic loans may be mediated through less or more formalized rotating credit associations called, for example, 'sangue' or 'min' among Haitian immigrants in New York (Laguerre, 1998). Immigrants sometimes also qualify for special funds for minorities, or microcredits provided exclusively for immigrants.

In addition to providing access to credit, ethnic networks of immigrants are an important source of the experience relevant for entrepreneurial ventures. Employment in a co-ethnic firm may serve as preparation for becoming a business owner (Portes and Bach, 1985; Raijman and Tienda, 2000) and can provide additional human capital or compensate for low human capital (Potocky-Tripodi, 2004).

SUMMARY AND CONCLUSION

The purpose of this chapter is to develop a process model of immigrant venture creation integrating existing findings. We argue that the recent intellectual advancements developed within the field of general entrepreneurship provide a firm theoretical foundation for such a model. We draw on Shane's (2004) entrepreneurial process theory for the basis of our model and link previously known immigrant specific factors to certain stages in the entrepreneurial process.

The proposed process model of immigrant entrepreneurship provides a guideline for answering the following research question: What factors differentiate immigrant entrepreneurs from others at different levels of analysis and at different stages in the entrepreneurial process? At the societal level immigrant entrepreneurs are different if or when the special rules and consumer preferences create or ban certain entrepreneurial opportunities compared to the opportunities available to native entrepreneurs. At the group level ethnic culture, discrimination, blocked mobility and extensive use of ethnic resources and networks make immigrants different from the mainstream population. Finally, at the individual level immigrant entrepreneurs are different if the relevant stages of the entrepreneurial process are affected by insufficient language abilities and unfamiliarity with the host country context. Most importantly, we propose that immigrant entrepreneurs may be different given the influence of pre-migration experiences and selective migration processes on individual characteristics relevant to entrepreneurial process.

Insofar as we were able to establish the link between key factors that make immigrant entrepreneurs different from their native counterparts at different points in the entrepreneurship process, we expect this theoretical model will serve as the basis for future theory development and research on the ways in which pre-migration, selective migration and host country conditions are likely to affect immigrant entrepreneurship. More work is needed on how macro level factors shape the existence of opportunities for immigrants. Research on the extent to which immigrants draw on ethnic resources to discover, acquire resources and exploit opportunities will help complete the picture. Additional theorizing is needed as well on the parts of the process not addressed in this development effort – namely, how pre-migration, selective migration and host country requirements influence the strategies and organizational approaches that immigrants take towards the launch of the ventures and the resulting performance. Finally, research is needed on how immigrants approach and experience the start-up process. It is our hope that this work will occur and that an understanding of immigrant entrepreneurship which highlights the great advantages (in addition to the disadvantages) of transnational and/or migration experiences will emerge.

REFERENCES

Aldrich, H. and R. Waldinger (1990), 'Ethnicity and entrepreneurship', *Annual Review of Sociology*, **16**, 111–35.

Baker, T. and R.E. Nelson (2005), 'Creating something from nothing: resource construction through entrepreneurial bricolage', *Administrative Science Quarterly*, **50**(3), 329–66.

Baker, T., E. Gedajlovic and M. Lubatkin (2005), 'A framework for comparing entrepreneurship processes across nations', *Journal of International Business Studies* **36**(5), 492–504.

Barrett, G., T. Jones, D. McEvoy and C. McGoldrick (2002), 'The economic embeddedness of immigrant enterprise in Britain', *International Journal of Entrepreneurial Behaviour and Research*, **8**(1/2), 11–31.

Basu, A. and E. Altinay (2002), 'The interaction between culture and entrepreneurship in London's immigrant businesses', *International Small Business Journal*, **20**(4), 371–93.

Bonacich, E. (1973), 'A theory of middleman minorities', *American Sociological Review*, **38**(5), 583–94.

Bruder, J., D. Neuberger and S. Rathke-Doepner (2007), 'Financial constraints of ethnic entrepreneurship: evidence from Germany', working paper no. 84, University of Rostock, Rostock, Germany.

Chaganti, R. and P.G. Greene (2002), 'Who are ethnic entrepreneurs? A study of entrepreneurs' ethnic involvement and business characteristics', *Journal of Small Business Management*, **40**(2), 126–43.

Chotigeat, T., P.W. Balsmeier and T.O. Stanley (1991), 'Fueling Asian immigrants' entrepreneurship: a source of capital', *Journal of Small Business Management*, **29**(3), 50–61.

Clark, K. and S. Drinkwater (1998), 'Ethnicity and self employment in Britain', *Oxford Bulletin of Economics and Statistics*, **60**(3), 383–407.

Cobas, J.A. (1986), 'Paths to self employment among immigrants: an analysis of four interpretations', *Sociological Perspectives*, **29**(1), 101–20.

Cormack, J. and J. Niessen (2002), 'Immigrant and minority businesses: making the policy case', *European Journal of Migration and Law*, **4**(3), 329–37.

Davidsson, P. and J. Wiklund (1997), 'Values, beliefs and regional variations in new firm formation rates', *Journal of Economic Psychology*, **18**(2–3), 179–99.

De Carolis, D.M. and P. Saparito (2006), 'Social capital, cognition, and entrepreneurial opportunities: a theoretical framework', *Entrepreneurship Theory and Practice*, **30**(1), 41–56.

Ekberg, J. and M. Hammarstedt (1999), 'Egenföretagare bland invandrare', *Arbetsmarknad och Arbetsliv*, **5**(3), 207–17.

Elam, A.B. (2008), *Gender and Entrepreneurship: A Multilevel Theory and Analysis*, Cheltenham, UK and Northampton, MA, USA: Edward Elgar.

Enger, A., E. Langset, A. Skeidsvoll and M. Solaas (1992), *Innvandrere: dynamiske etablerere?: en intervjuundersøkelse blant innvandrere i Bydel 4, 5 og 6 i Oslo*, Oslo, Norway: Prosjektforum for Arbeidslivsstudier.

Fadahunsi, A., D. Smallbone and S. Supri (2000), 'Networking and ethnic minority enterprise development: insights from a North London study', *Journal of Small Business and Enterprise Development*, **7**(3), 228–40.

Gartner, W.B. (1985), 'A conceptual-framework for describing the phenomenon of new venture creation', *Academy of Management Review*, **10**(4), 696–706.

Greene, P.G. (1997), 'A call for conceptual clarity. Comments on Bates: why are firms owned by Asian immigrants lagging behind black-owned businesses?', *National Journal of Sociology*, **10**(2), 49–55.

Hammarstedt, M. (2001), 'Immigrant self employment in Sweden – its variation and some possible determinants', *Entrepreneurship and Regional Development*, **13**(2), 147–61.

Harper, D.A. (2003), *Foundations of Entrepreneurship and Economic Development*, London: Routledge.

Hayton, J.C., G. George and S.A. Zahra (2002), 'National culture and entrepreneurship: a review of behavioral research', *Entrepreneurship Theory and Practice*, **26**(4), 33–52.

Johnson, P.J. (2000), 'Ethnic differences in self employment among southeast Asian refugees in Canada', *Journal of Small Business Management*, **38**(4), 78–85.

Kim, K.C. and W.M. Hurh (1985), 'Ethnic resources utilization of Korean immigrant entrepreneurs in the Chicago Minority Area', *International Migration Review*, **19**(1), 82–111.

Kirzner, I.M. (1985), *Discovery and the Capitalist Process*, Chicago, IL: University of Chicago Press.

Kloosterman, R. and J. Rath (2001), 'Immigrant entrepreneurs in advanced economies: mixed embeddedness further explored', *Journal of Ethnic and Migration Studies*, **27**(2), 1–10.

Kloosterman, R. and J.P. Van Der Leun (1999), 'Just for starters: commercial gentrification by immigrant entrepreneurs in Amsterdam and Rotterdam neighbourhoods', *Housing Studies*, **14**(5), 659–77.

Laguerre, M.S. (1998), 'Rotating credit associations and the diasporic economy', *Journal of Developmental Entrepreneurship*, **3**(1), 23–34.

Levie, J. (2007), 'Immigration, in-migration, ethnicity and entrepreneurship in the United Kingdom', *Small Business Economics*, **28**(2–3), 143–69.

Light, I. (1980), 'Asian enterprise in America', in S. Cummings (ed.), *Self-help in Urban America: Patterns of Minority Business Enterprise*, Port Washington, NY: Kennikat Press, pp. 33–57.

Light, I. (1984), 'Immigrant and ethnic enterprise in North America', *Ethnic and Racial Studies*, **7**, 195–216.

Light, I., P. Bhachu and S. Karageorgis (1993), 'Migration networks and immigrant entrepreneurship', in I. Light and P. Bhachu (eds), *Immigration and Entrepreneurship: Culture, Capital, and Ethnic Networks*, New Brunswick, NJ: Transaction Publishers, pp. 25–49.

Magatti, M. and F. Quassoli (2003), 'Italy: between legal barriers and informal arrangements', in J. Rath and R. Kloosterman (eds), *Immigrant Entrepreneurs: Venturing Abroad in the Age of Globalization*, Oxford: Berg, pp. 147–71.

Marlow, S. (1992), 'The take-up of business growth training schemes by ethnic minority-owned small firms in Britain', *International Small Business Journal*, **10**(4), 34–46.

Park, K. (1997). *The Korean American Dream: Immigrants and Small Business in New York City*, Ithaca, NY: Cornell University Press.

Peberdy, S. and C.M. Rogerson (2003), 'South Africa: creating new spaces?', in J. Rath and R. Kloosterman (eds), *Immigrant Entrepreneurs: Venturing Abroad in the Age of Globalization*, Oxford: Berg, pp. 79–99.

Portes, A. and R.L. Bach (1985), *Latin Journey: Cuban and Mexican Immigrants in the United States*, Berkeley, CA: University of California Press.

Portes, A. and M. Zhou (1992), 'Gaining the upper hand: economic mobility among immigrant and domestic minorities', *Ethnic and Racial Studies*, **14**(4), 491–522.

Potocky-Tripodi, M. (2004), 'The role of social capital in immigrant and refugee economic adaptation', *Journal of Social Service Research*, **31**(1), 59–91.

Raijman, R. and M. Tienda (2000), 'Immigrants' pathways to business ownership: a comparative ethnic perspective', *International Migration Review*, **34**(3), 682–706.

Raijman, R. and M. Tienda (2003), 'Ethnic foundations of economic transactions: Mexican and Korean immigrant entrepreneurs in Chicago', *Ethnic and Racial Studies*, **26**(5), 783–801.

Rath, J. and R. Kloosterman (2003), *Immigrant Entrepreneurs: Venturing Abroad in the Age of Globalization*, Oxford: Berg.

Razin, E. and D. Scheinberg (2001), 'Immigrant entrepreneurs from the former USSR in Israel: not the traditional enclave economy', *Journal of Ethnic and Migration Studies*, **27**(2), 259–76.

Reynolds, P.D. (1991), 'Sociology and entrepreneurship: concepts and contributions', *Entrepreneurship Theory and Practice*, **16**(2), 47–70.

Reynolds, P.D. and S.B. White (1997), *The Entrepreneurial Process: Economic Growth, Men, Women, and Minorities*, Westport, CT: Quorum Books.

Reynolds, P., N. Bosma, E. Auito et al. (2005), 'Global Entrepreneurship Monitor: data collection design and implementation 1998–2003', *Small Business Economics*, **24**(3), 205–31.

Sarasvathy, S.D. (2001), 'Causation and effectuation: toward a theoretical shift from economic inevitability to entrepreneurial contingency', *Academy of Management Review*, **26**(2), 243–63.

Schumpeter, J.A. (1934), *The Theory of Economic Development: An Inquiry into Profits, Capital, Credit, Interest, and the Business Cycle*, Cambridge, MA: Harvard University Press.

Shane, S. (2004), *A General Theory of Entrepreneurship: The Individual-opportunity Nexus*, Cheltenham, UK and Northampton, MA, USA: Edward Elgar.

Shane, S. and S. Venkataraman (2000), 'The promise of entrepreneurship as a field of research', *Academy of Management Review*, **25**(1), 217–26.

Terjesen, S.A. and A.B. Elam (2009), 'Transnational entrepreneurs' venture internationalization strategies: a practice theory approach', *Entrepreneurship Theory and Practice*, **33**(5), 1093–120.

Tong, C.K., B.S.A. Yeoh and M.W. Charney (2003), *Approaching Transnationalisms: Studies on Transnational Societies, Multicultural Contacts, and Imaginings of Home*, Boston, MA: Kluwer Academic.

Venkataraman, S. (1997), 'The distinctive domain of entrepreneurship research: an editor's perspective', in J. Katz and R. Brockhaus (eds), *Advances in Entrepreneurship, Firm Emergence, and Growth*, Greenwich, CT: JAI Press, pp. 119–58.

Wadhwa, V., A.L. Saxenian, B. Rissing and G. Gereffi (2008), 'Skilled immigration and economic growth', *Applied Research in Economic Development*, **5**(1), 6–14.

Waldinger, R., R. Ward and H. Aldrich (1990), *Ethnic Entrepreneurs: Immigrant Business in Industrial Societies*, Newbury Park, CA: Sage Publications.

Weber, M. (1958), *The Protestant Ethic and the Spirit of Capitalism*, New York: Charles Scribner's Sons.

Wilpert, C. (2003), 'Germany: from workers to entrepreneurs', in J. Rath and R. Kloosterman (eds), *Immigrant Entrepreneurs: Venturing Abroad in the Age of Globalization*, Oxford: Berg, pp. 233–59.

Wilson, F., D. Marlino and J. Kickul (2004), 'Our entrepreneurial future: examining the diverse attitudes and motivations of teens across gender and ethnic identity', *Journal of Developmental Entrepreneurship*, **9**(3), 177–97.

Wong, B. (1998), *Ethnicity and Entrepreneurship: The New Chinese Immigrants in the San Francisco Bay Area*, Boston, MA: Allyn and Bacon.

Yoon, I.J. (1991), 'The changing significance of ethnic and class resources in immigrant businesses: the case of Korean immigrant businesses in Chicago', *International Migration Review*, **25**(2), 303–31.

Yuengert, A.M. (1995), 'Communication: testing hypotheses of immigrant self employment', *Journal of Human Resources*, **30**(1), 194–204.

8. Decision-making disagreements and performance in venture capital backed firms*

Truls Erikson and Bradley A. George

INTRODUCTION

The creation and growth of new ventures is often cited as a key component of wealth creation (Birch, 1987; Kirchhoff, 1991; Robinson and McDougall, 2001). Because of their economic and social value, improved understanding of the determinants of new venture performance has become increasingly important (Chrisman et al., 1998). Early models proposed that new venture performance was a function of characteristics of the entrepreneur, the organization's strategy and the industry structure (Sandberg and Hofer, 1987). While this model has received empirical support in previous studies, Chrisman and colleagues noted that these models should be expanded to include business strategy, resources and organizational structure, processes and systems (Chrisman et al., 1998). While there are a number of organizational processes that may be theoretically linked to new venture performance, a critical process which has received limited treatment in the entrepreneurship research is the decision-making process (Forbes, 2000).

New ventures have a number of important differences that need to be considered when examining the relationship between decision processes and performance. Traditional models of the rational actor have been challenged by theorists from the Carnegie school (for example, Simon, 1957; March and Simon, 1958; Cyert and March, 1963), who noted that decision makers have cognitive limitations that inhibit their ability to be perfectly rational. Decision makers often draw upon past experience to form heuristics and decision routines which aid in future decision making. New ventures, by their very nature, lack this experience (Gartner et al., 1992). They are dealing with additional uncertainties such as the relative competence of competitors, customer preferences (Bhide, 1994) and, to some extent, unknown internal capabilities as well. This is particularly true of high potential, high risk ventures such as those typically backed by venture capitalists.

Decision-making processes are typically affiliated with disagreements over ends and means. Differences of opinions regarding ends and means to achieve these ends are not only imperative to operational decision making, but also to decisions regarding business strategy. The lack of accepted decision-making norms or organizational history in new ventures, coupled with an uncertain environment, invites differing perceptions of the correct course of action among the decision-making team. Undoubtedly, creative debates and conflicts can lead to more thorough decisions. However, disagreements can also hinder decision-making processes, and there is a need to address what type of disagreements may benefit or hamper the performance of potential high growth, venture capital backed new ventures.

Jehn and Mannix (2001) address three types of conflicts: affective, task and procedural. In short, affective conflict refers to the tension and relationship friction between decision-making parties. Task conflict within the manage-ment team refers to the awareness in differences of viewpoints and opinions regarding a task. Process conflict within the management team refers to perceptions of how task accomplishments will proceed (Jehn and Mannix, 2001). While each of these types of conflict have often been examined in isolation, researchers have called for new directions for understanding how managerial decision makers can capture the benefits of certain types of conflict without incurring the costs associated with other types (Eisenhardt and Zbaracki, 1992). To accomplish this requires examining the relationship between the various types of conflict, which led Jehn and Chatman (2000) to propose that it is the proportion of total conflict attributable to each type of conflict that is important rather than the degree of each type of conflict alone.

We contribute to the literature and practice in three important ways. First, the study contributes to the entrepreneurship literature by extending the model of firm performance by examining how a key characteristic of the decision-making process, that of management team conflict, may affect new venture performance. Second, we build on the work of Jehn and Chatman (2000) by examining the effects of proportional conflict in multiple firms and industries, providing a more general examination of the effects of proportional conflict when compared to their work utilizing teams within a single firm. Finally, given the uncertain environment in which high potential new ventures operate, there is a high probability that conflict in the decision-making process will occur. By extending the work of Jehn and Chatman (2000) on proportional conflict, we hope to provide a better understanding of how the combination of various types of conflict influences new venture performance. This will give managers better guidance as to how to manage the various types of conflict in the decision-making process in order to maximize firm performance. The chapter will begin with a discussion of the different types of conflict and their relationship to performance using an information processing theory lens. This theoretical framework will then be used to develop hypotheses regarding the relationship between proportional conflict and new venture performance. Next we describe the sample and methodology used to test these hypotheses. This is followed by a discussion of our results, the limitations of the current research and suggestions for future research.

THEORETICAL BACKGROUND AND HYPOTHESES

Research on group processes has illustrated the impact of decision processes on group outcomes as well as organizational outcomes (Olson et al., 2007). As noted by Steiner (1979), the manager's decision quality will be dependent on the process that the group uses to make their decision, a key aspect of which is how the individuals in the group and the group as a whole collect and analyse information relevant to the decision at hand. Information processing theory suggests that decisions are based on what information a particular individual pays attention to and how that information is interpreted (Barr et al., 1992). While the theoretical origins were initially related to how organizations process information (Galbraith, 1973), the theory has been expanded to the consideration of groups as information processors in our efforts to understand the decision processes of teams (Hinsz et al., 1997).

At the individual level the mind can be considered a human information processing system (Lord and Maher, 1990). Consistent with the behavioral theory of the firm (Cyert and March, 1963), managers are considered to be boundedly rational as well as having multiple and conflicting goals and aspiration levels. In addition, they often have unique backgrounds and experiences which will influence not only the parts of the environment that a manager pays attention to, but how they interpret those inputs as well (Hambrick and Mason, 1984). The end result is that managers will often interpret environmental inputs differently, leading to differing opinions on an appropriate course of action, paving the way for conflict in decision making (Sapienza and Gupta, 1994).

This can be particularly true for management teams in high risk, high potential firms such as those that attract venture capital financing. The environment in which these entrepreneurs find themselves is often one of rapid change and uncertainty. They are often focusing on new products or processes, often in emerging markets with little or no history to rely on when making key decisions. As such, it is likely that individuals faced with these conditions will often have differing interpretations of the environment based on their own unique backgrounds. Given the lack of existing heuristics or organizational experience, differences of opinion regarding what action should be taken and how it should be executed could be expected to be more common for entrepreneurial teams dealing with the unknown.

As a result, one aspect of the process that has garnered much attention is that of conflict in decision making resulting from real or perceived differences among team members (Wall and Callister, 1995; De Dreu and Weingart, 2003). Unfortunately, while group conflict is recognized by theorists as being an important characteristic of the decision process (Mintzberg et al., 1976; Janis, 1982; Hickson et al., 1986; Schweiger et al., 1986; Cosier and Schwenk, 1990; Amason, 1996), its effects on decision and organizational outcomes are not well understood (Eisenhardt and Zbaracki, 1992). Early theorists focused on the negative effects of conflict (Pondy, 1969; Brown, 1983; Wall and Callister, 1995). However, later researchers proposed that there were three different types of conflict that must be considered and which may have different effects on organizational and group outcomes (Amason, 1996; Amason and Sapienza, 1997; Jehn and Chatman, 2000; Jehn and Mannix, 2001). These are affective conflict (involving personal issues such as dislike among group members), task conflict (conflict about ideas and differences of opinion about the task itself) and procedural conflict (disagreement about how to accomplish the task). Information processing theory suggests that we consider how conflict affects the way in which members process, interpret and act on information if we are to understand how team conflict can affect decision and organizational outcomes.

Due to the fact that managers will have different backgrounds that will influence the information they pay attention to as well as how they interpret that information, task conflict has been considered to be inevitable in decision making (Amason, 1996). However, it has long been argued that task conflict can be beneficial in that it forces people to consider different perspectives and confront issues (Coser, 1956; Deutsch, 1973). Task conflict essentially expands the information available and provides a variety of information filters that lead to a wider view of the issue in question, resulting in higher quality decisions and organizational performance. Researchers have reasoned that exposure to opposing views provides additional information for the team members to process, allowing them to develop a more complete understanding of the problem and potential solutions (Pelled et al., 1999). A lack of task conflict may result in 'groupthink' (Janis, 1982), with managers overlooking important details or considering different alternatives, resulting in sub-optimal solutions.

This line of reasoning has received some empirical support. For example, Olson et al. (2007) found that task conflict positively influenced decision understanding, decision quality and decision commitment in a study of 85 senior management teams in hospitals. Similarly, Amason (1996) found that task conflict was positively related to decision quality, decision understanding and affective acceptance. Simons and Peterson (2000) summarized the literature by concluding that groups which experience task conflict tend to make better decisions. In spite of these examples, a meta-analysis of 30 empirical studies on team conflict conducted by De Dreu and Weingart (2003) found that the corrected mean correlation between task conflict and team performance was significant and negative with $\rho = -0.23$.

Affective conflict, also referred to as emotional conflict (Pelled et al., 1999) and relationship conflict (Jehn and Mannix, 2001; De Dreu and Weingart, 2003), involves disagreements based on personal and social issues that are not work related (Jehn and Chatman, 2000). It is theorized that this type of conflict impairs the processing of information in the decision process (Pelled et al., 1999), adversely affecting the decision process. Increasing levels of affective conflict can create a hostile environment in which members become reluctant to share differing perspectives (Pelled et al., 1999), decreasing the amount of information available to the group. Similarly, the animosity associated with affective conflict can lead team members to disregard information and viewpoints that are shared within the group.

Support for the negative effects of affective conflict have been found for decision quality (Amason, 1996), group performance (Jehn and Mannix, 2001) and firm performance (Eisenhardt et al., 1997). In addition, De Dreu and Weingart's (2003) meta-analysis reported a mean corrected correlation of $\rho = -0.22$; support for a negative relationship. However, support has not been universal, with some studies finding a small positive relationship between affective conflict and team performance (for example, Barsade et al., 2000; De Dreu and Van Vianen, 2001).

While previous studies have focused primarily on task conflict and affective conflict, researchers have more recently identified a third type of conflict, labeled process conflict (Amason, 1996; Jehn, 1997; Jehn and Mannix, 2001). As opposed to task conflict, which focuses on differences with regards to what needs to be done, process conflict is defined as an awareness of controversies about aspects of how the task will proceed (Jehn and Mannix, 2001). As noted by Amason (1996), if managers cannot agree on how a decision will be implemented, the quality of the decision itself will mean little. As such, researchers have argued that process conflict interferes with the implementation of a decision, resulting in a negative relationship with team performance. Furthermore, since process conflict focuses on task strategy and delegation of duties and resources, conflict in this area may be interpreted as questioning one's abilities or making a political move to control resources and power within the organization. Jehn and Mannix (2001), on the other hand, argued that process conflict early in a group's life would have a positive effect by allowing the team to establish work norms and make decisions about task responsibilities, milestones and deadlines. This would then allow the team to focus on the content of the tasks.

The lack of agreement between the theoretical relationships and empirical results has prompted scholars to propose that the three types of conflict cannot be viewed in isolation from each other. This is further supported by the fact that De Dreu and Weingart's (2003) meta-analysis found that the mean corrected correlation between task conflict and affective conflict was $\rho = 0.54$, suggesting that treating the three types of conflict separately may inhibit our ability to test proposed causal relationships. Following along these lines, Jehn and Chatman (2000) suggest that the more important issue is the proportion of conflict that is either task related, affective or procedural. They refer to this as proportional conflict composition. Proportional conflict composition describes the relationship among the three types of conflict (task, affective and process), as the level of each type of conflict proportional to the total amount of conflict in the group rather than the absolute level of any one type of conflict.

As noted earlier, task conflict is often argued to be positively related to team performance and decision quality. By presenting differing views on the task, decision makers are presented with additional information with which to make their decision. A structured form of this, devil's advocacy, has been shown to improve decision quality (Schwenk, 1990). However, as affective conflict increases, team members may view opposing viewpoints as more personal attacks on their own opinions, lessening their willingness to objectively debate and process the new information, reducing the effectiveness of the process and the subsequent quality of the decisions. When examining the effects of the decision-making process at the management team level in new ventures, a reduction in decision quality or process effectiveness would be expected to result in a decrease in firm performance as these teams are directly responsible for setting the strategic direction of the firm.

As venture capital backed firms are often operating in dynamic, uncertain environments, poor decision making can result in mistakes from which the firm may be unable to recover. Process conflict, on the other hand, will lead to disagreements as to how to implement the solution. For entrepreneurial firms in high growth areas, such as those financed by venture capitalists, decision speed and implementation speed can be critical in enabling the firm to act quickly and take advantage of opportunities in the marketplace. Therefore, we would expect increasing process conflict to detract from the positive effects of task conflict on firm performance.

Proportional task conflict (*PTC*) is calculated as follows:

$$PTC = TC/(TC + AC + PC)$$

where TC = task conflict, AC = affective conflict and PC = process conflict.

From the equation above it can be seen that for a given amount of task conflict, increases in affective conflict, process conflict or both will decrease the proportional task conflict. Increases in proportional task conflict result from either increases in task conflict or decreases in affective and process conflict. For a given amount of process and affective conflict, we propose that increases in task conflict will result in an increase in the information available to be processed, improved decision making and higher firm performance. As affective and/or process conflict increase for a given amount of task conflict, the quality of the decisions will suffer and their implementation will be delayed, resulting in a decrease in firm performance. Therefore, we hypothesize that:

Hypothesis 1: Proportional task conflict is positively related to new venture performance in venture capital backed firms.

Process conflict relates to disagreements with regards to how to proceed with the solution rather than disagreements about the solution, or decision, itself. Jehn and Chatman (2000) found a negative, but not significant relationship between proportional process conflict and group performance in their study of managers in a large, established firm. While it may be argued that disagreement about task allocation may improve the fit between skills and duties within the team (Jehn, 1997), we argue that in a dynamic, uncertain market such as that faced by venture capital backed firms, the ability to act quickly once a decision is made is critical in order to capture opportunities that arise. A failure to act can result in lost opportunities that may be difficult to capture from competitors at a later date, resulting in fewer growth opportunities and lower firm performance. As such, it is expected that increasing amounts of process conflict will lead to delays in the implementation of the decision and negatively affect new venture performance. Increases in task conflict will further adversely affect the decision process speed and firm performance. Increases in affective conflict will lead to a negative decision-making environment and a decrease in trust among the team members. As a result, team members may begin to doubt the rationale behind the process conflict, attributing it to an attempt to gain resources or power within the organization. This will decrease the commitment of the team members to the eventual implementation plan and adversely affect its success.

Hypothesis 2: Proportional process conflict is negatively related to new venture performance in venture capital backed firms.

Affective conflict has generally been found to be negatively related to team performance and decision quality. Therefore, we would expect the highest levels of performance to be related to a low level of affective conflict in relation to the other two types of conflict. This would be reflective of a group which welcomes differing views on both task and process and is willing to objectively process and analyse that information. As the proportion of total conflict in the team attributable to affective conflict increases, the team environment is likely to become increasingly hostile, leading team members to view dissenting views as personal attacks and detracting from the ability and willingness of the participants to process additional information. This will result in a decrease in both the amount of information shared and the willingness of the decision makers to consider this information in their cognitive processing with the end result being a decrease in the number of opportunities considered and the quality of the evaluation process, which will subsequently have a negative effect on the firm's performance.

Hypothesis 3: Proportional affective conflict is negatively related to new venture performance in venture capital backed firms.

RESEARCH METHODOLOGY

Data Collection

This study is based on 45 venture capital backed firms from Norway. The data are derived from a survey mailed to the CEOs of 240 companies funded by Norwegian venture capital funds. The sample reflects the portfolios of the primary members of the Norwegian Venture Capital Association as of March 2004. Seventy companies returned their questionnaires. Twenty-five firms failed to provide complete information and were removed from the sample.

Dependent Variables

In this study we use revenue growth as a measure of new venture performance. Delmar et al. (2003) argue for sales as the most appropriate measure of new venture growth since it is more or less insensitive to capital intensity. Similar measures are employed by Shelton (2006), Ardishvili et al. (1998) and Hoy et al. (1992). Sales are appropriate because they tend to be a precursor of other growth indicators such as increase in assets, employees and profits (Delmar, 1997; Shelton, 2006). And it is the growth measure preferred by the entrepreneurs (Barkham et al., 1996; Shelton, 2006). Additionally, venture capitalists are generally interested in investing in firms with the potential for high levels of revenue growth, making this an appropriate measure of performance for our particular study. We employ the difference between the 2004 and 2000 sales data and calculate the growth in percentage. Since the survey was administered in March 2004, respondents are expected to have based their response on the past few years' management experience.

Independent Variables

In measuring the three types of conflicts, the Intragroup Conflict Scale of Jehn (1995) was used. The procedural conflict measures originate from Shah and Jehn (1993). Jehn and Chatman (2000) tested out the same measures on 545 employees within one organization, whereas we use the same pre-tested measures on the management team in 45 smaller organizations. A 5-point Likert scale was employed. Each of the items was translated into Norwegian and back-translated to check for accuracy. A factor analysis was run on all of the items to ensure that they retain their factor structure following translation. The factor analysis indicated problems with one item on each of the scales in that they failed to load sufficiently on the appropriate factor. Because these items have been shown in numerous previous studies to be reliable, it is quite possible that the interpretation of the translated version of the items resulted in their not reflecting the intended construct. Due to concerns regarding the item validity of the translated items, a decision was made to drop each of the items and use two item scales for each construct. Chronbach's alpha for the three constructs are 0.834 for affective conflict, 0.724 for task conflict and 0.919 for process conflict, which is beyond the recommended 0.70 by Nunnally (1967).

Correlation Analysis

Correlation analysis is employed in analysing the hypothesized relationships. The results of the correlation analysis are shown in Table 8.1. The first three rows of the table show the correlations between various conflict types and proportional conflicts, while the last row addresses the three hypotheses. In this study we are primarily concerned with if, and to what extent, the various types of conflicts covariate with performance. Since we assume directionality in testing the hypotheses, we use one-tailed Pearson's product-moment correlations for these relationships.

Table 8.1   Correlation matrix

	Proportional affective conflict	Proportional task conflict	Proportional process conflict
Affective conflict	0.541**	−0.298*	−0.229†
Task conflict	−0.147	0.455**	−0.386**
Process conflict	−0.058	−0.322*	0.449**
Revenue growth	−0.266*	0.484**	−0.335*

Note: Significance levels are for one-tail tests for revenue growth; † $p < 0.1$ level, * $p < 0.05$ level, ** $p < 0.01$ level.

As can be seen from Table 8.1, proportional conflicts differ from their original conflict types, indicating that they indeed capture other facets not accounted for in the original measures. With regards to the hypothesis tests, we find support ($p < 0.05$) for Hypothesis 1 regarding the affective component's negative effect on new venture performance. We find strong support ($p < 0.01$) for Hypothesis 2 that proportional task conflict is positively associated with new venture performance. We also find support ($p < 0.05$) for Hypothesis 3 regarding the negative effect of proportional process conflict on performance.

DISCUSSION

Addressing the Effects of Conflicts on New Venture Performance

This study supports the contention that compositional task conflict has a positive effect, and that compositional procedural conflict has a negative effect on new venture performance. Thus, it appears that compositional task conflict is beneficial for the performance of a new venture, whereas compositional procedural conflict is not. This finding makes sense, as when the parties have debated over the main task and purposes of the company, disagreements over who should be responsible do not necessarily contribute to enhance performance. As expected, we also found support for the contention that compositional affective conflict has a negative effect on firm performance.

Compositional task conflict is apparently an important measure, and owners or board directors should seek to stimulate an open atmosphere and environment that facilitates creative debates over purposes and tasks. This could be accomplished, for instance, by establishing a wider advisory board, or the like. For instance, increasing the number of owners could also prove useful.

Compositional procedural conflict was found to have a significant negative effect on new venture performance. Apparently, debate over responsibilities and resource allocation appears to be less beneficial to the development process. In other words, it appears that debates over how tasks should proceed or debates over responsibilities signals either a lack of personal capacity or dislike for the assigned responsibility. It may also reflect that the right persons are not assigned appropriate responsibility. Could it be that debates over tasks and goals are beneficial to the performance, whereas debates over responsibilities are expressions of not having accomplished the tasks, or not having the ability to accomplish the assigned tasks? Since this is a cross-sectional correlation study, it could also be that this correlate only reflects dislike over the situation, and that these dislikes are associated with poor performance – not necessarily the cause of it. However, addressing this issue calls for another methodology than employed here.

Limitations and Weaknesses

As mentioned above, the study is correlational. We still do not know the long-term effect of managerial disagreements on new venture performance. Moreover, whereas the present data can be claimed to be homogeneous, as the data are limited to venture capital backed firms, the strength of this sample is that we are dealing with the most promising high growth firms in the industry. All the companies have passed a rigorous selection hurdle. Additionally, the conflict measures used in this study were developed by previous researchers for use at the employee level, whereas we have used them at the management level. They turned out to work rather well with the exception of a few items. Indeed, it may have been due to weak wording of these items, but we made every attempt to capture the meaning through back-translation of the items (an iterative process).

Future Research

Future studies should seek to employ a larger sample size. Researchers could also survey firms across cultures and simultaneously test the cross-cultural validity of these findings, as we experienced difficulties with regard to item loadings on a few items. That is, future studies could also attempt to develop and test other conflict measures, as we found that some of the items applied in this study did not receive support in the Norwegian context. For instance, items measuring policy to a larger extent than employed in this study could prove valuable. Presently, the procedural conflict measure captures primarily disagreements over responsibilities rather than disagreements over policy or means.

Future studies should also be expanded to include additional industries and non-venture capital backed firms if we hope to be able to generalize results outside of this context. While venture capital backed firms are important in that they typically represent high potential firms, they represent only a very small fraction of the total number of new ventures that are started. Therefore, it is important to understand whether these relationships hold not only across industries, but also outside the small world of venture capital backed firms. Future studies could also seek to address the relationship of decision making and capabilities within management teams. These future studies could also attempt to measure these conflict types in a longitudinal manner. For instance, it would be viable to measure the effect of conflicts over time, and assess why they occur and how they emerge. Future research could also seek to address the long-term effect of managerial disagreements.

CONCLUSION

The findings of this study are significant from both a theoretical and practical point of view. From a theoretical standpoint this study illustrates how key process characteristics can affect new venture performance in venture capital backed firms. This highlights the need for researchers to consider aspects of the decision process, such as management team conflict, when developing models for understanding the influences on new venture performance. Also it further illustrates the point made by Jehn and Chatman (2000) that we must consider context when studying managerial decision-making disagreements in venturing firms. That is, we should consider other types of conflicts at work and not look at them in isolation.

From a practical standpoint the results of this study suggest that managerial decision-making disagreements have both negative and positive effects on the performance of venturing firms. Managers are interested in gaining the benefits of conflict, but simultaneously want to avoid the negative costs associated with it. While conflict may be inherent in any team functioning, this study shows that the managers should focus on how best to manage the portfolio of team conflict, rather than on controlling a single type in order to maximize firm performance.

NOTE

* An earlier version of this chapter was presented at the 2009 BCERC conference.

REFERENCES

Amason, A.C. (1996), 'Distinguishing the effects of functional and dysfunctional conflict on strategic decision making: resolving a paradox for top management teams', *Academy of Management Journal*, **39**(1), 123–48.

Amason, A.C. and H.J. Sapienza (1997), 'The effects of top management team size and interaction norms on cognitive and affective conflict', *Journal of Management*, **23**, 496–516.

Ardishvili, A.S., S. Cardoza, S. Hammon and S. Vadakath (1998), 'Towards a theory of new venture growth', paper presented at the 1998 Babson Entrepreneurship Research Conference, Ghent, Belgium.

Barkham, R. G. Gudgin, M. Hart and E. Hanvey (1996), *The Determinants of Small Firm Growth*, vol. 12, Gateshead, Tyne and Wear, UK: Athenaeum Press.

Barr, P., J. Stimpert and A.S. Huff (1992), 'Cognitive change, strategic action, and organizational renewal', *Strategic Management Journal*, **13**, 15–36.

Barsade, S.G., A.J. Ward, J.D.F. Turner and J.A. Sonnenfeld (2000), 'To your heart's content: a model of affective diversity in top management teams', *Administrative Science Quarterly*, **45**, 802–36.

Bhide, A. (1994), 'How entrepreneurs craft strategies that work', *Harvard Business Review*, **72**(2), 150–61.

Birch, D.L. (1987), *Job Creation in America*, New York: Free Press.

Brown, L.D. (1983), *Managing Conflict at Organizational Interfaces*, Reading, MA: Addison-Wesley.

Chrisman, J.J., A. Bauerschmidt and C.W. Hofer (1998), 'The determinants of new venture performance: an extended model', *Entrepreneurship Theory and Practice*, **23**(1), 5–29.

Coser, L.A. (1956), *The Functions of Social Conflict*, New York: Free Press.

Cosier, R.A. and C.R. Schwenk (1990), 'Agreement and thinking alike: ingredients for poor decisions', *Executive*, **4**(1), 69–74.

Cyert, R.M. and J.G. March (1963), *A Behavioral Theory of the Firm*, Englewood Cliffs, NJ: Prentice-Hall.

De Dreu, C.K.W. and A.E.M. Van Vianen (2001), 'Responses to relationship conflict and team performance', *Journal of Organizational Behavior*, **22**, 309–28.

De Dreu, C.K.W. and L.R. Weingart (2003), 'Task versus relationship conflict, team performance, and team member satisfaction: a meta-analysis', *Journal of Applied Psychology*, **88**(4), 741–9.

Delmar, F. (1997), 'Measuring growth: methodological considerations and empirical results', in R. Donkels and A. Miettinen (eds), *Entrepreneurship and SME Research: On its Way to the Next Millennium*, Aldershot, UK: Ashgate, pp. 199–216.

Delmar, F., P. Davidsson and W.B. Gartner (2003), 'Arriving at the high-growth firm', *Journal of Business Venturing*, **18**, 189–216.

Deutsch, M. (1973), *Conflict Resolution: Constructive and Destructive Processes*, New Haven, CT: Yale University Press.

Eisenhardt, K.M. and M.J. Zbaracki (1992), 'Strategic decision making', *Strategic Management Journal (1986–1998)*, **13** (special issue), 17–37.

Eisenhardt, K.M., J.L. Kahwajy and L.J. Bourgeois III (1997), 'Conflict and strategic choice: how top management teams disagree', *California Management Review*, **39**(2), 42–62.

Forbes, D.P. (2000), 'The strategic implications of managerial cognition and firm decision processes: evidence from a new venture context', unpublished dissertation, Leonard N. Stern School of Business, New York University, New York.

Galbraith, J. (1973), *Designing Complex Organizations*, Reading, MA: Addison-Wesley Publishing.

Gartner, W.B., B.J. Bird and J.A. Starr (1992), 'Acting as if: differentiating entrepreneurial from organizational behavior', *Entrepreneurship Theory and Practice*, **16**(3), 13–31.

Hambrick, D.C. and P.A. Mason (1984), 'Upper echelons: the organization as a reflection of its top managers', *Academy of Management Review*, **9**(2), 193–206.

Hickson, D.J., R.J. Butler, D. Cray, G.R. Mallory and D.C. Wilson (1986), *Top Decisions: Strategic Decision-making in Organizations*, San Francisco, CA: Jossey-Bass.

Hinsz, V.B., R.S. Tindale and D.A. Vollrath (1997), 'The emerging conceptualization of groups as information processors', *Psychological Bulletin*, **121**, 43–64.

Hoy, F., P. McDougall and D. D'souza (1992), 'Strategies and environments of high growth firms', in D. Sexton and J. Kasarda (eds), *The State of the Art of Entrepreneurship*, Boston, MA: PWS-Kent Publishing, pp. 341–57.

Janis, I.L. (1982), *Victims of Groupthink*, Boston, MA: Houghton Mifflin.

Jehn, K.A. (1995), 'A multimethod examination of the benefits and detriments of intragroup conflict', *Administrative Science Quarterly*, **40**, 256–82.

Jehn, K.A. (1997), 'A qualitative analysis of conflict types and dimensions in organizational groups', *Administrative Science Quarterly*, **42**, 530–57.

Jehn, K.A. and J.A. Chatman (2000), 'The influence of proportional and perceptual conflict composition on team performance', *International Journal of Conflict Management*, **11**(1), 56–73.

Jehn, K.A. and E.A. Mannix (2001), 'The dynamic nature of conflict: a longitudinal study of intragroup conflict and group performance', *Academy of Management Journal*, **44**(2), 238–51.

Kirchhoff, B.A. (1991), 'Entrepreneurship's contribution to economics', *Entrepreneurship Theory and Practice*, **15**(1), 93–112.

Lord, R.G. and K.J. Maher (1990), 'Alternative information-processing models and their implications for theory, research, and practice', *Academy of Management Review*, **15**(1), 9–28.

March, J.G. and H.A. Simon (1958), *Organizations*, New York: Wiley.

Mintzberg, H., D. Raisinghani and A. Theoret (1976), 'The structure of "unstructured" decision processes', *Administrative Science Quarterly*, **21**, 246–75.

Nunnally, J.C. (1967), *Psychometric Theory*, New York: McGraw-Hill.

Olson, B.J., S. Parayitam and Y. Bao (2007), 'Strategic decision making: the effects of cognitive diversity, conflict, and trust on decision outcomes', *Journal of Management*, **33**(2), 196–222.

Pelled, L.H., K.M. Eisenhardt and K.R. Xin (1999), 'Exploring the black box: an analysis of work group diversity, conflict, and performance', *Administrative Science Quarterly*, **44**, 1–28.

Pondy, L.R. (1969), 'Varieties of organizational conflict', *Administrative Science Quarterly*, **14**, 499–506.

Robinson, K.C., and P.P. McDougall (2001), 'Entry barriers and new venture performance: a comparison of universal and contingency approaches', *Strategic Management Journal*, **22**, 659–85.

Sandberg, W.R. and C.W. Hofer (1987), 'Improving new venture performance: the role of strategy, industry structure, and the entrepreneur', *Journal of Business Venturing*, **2**(1), 5–28.

Sapienza, H.J. and A.K. Gupta (1994), 'Impact of agency risks and task uncertainty on venture capitalists-CEO interaction', *Academy of Management Journal*, **39**, 544–74.

Schweiger, D.M., W.R. Sandberg and J.W. Ragan (1986), 'Group approaches for improving strategic decision making: a comparative analysis of dialectical inquiry, devil's advocacy, and consensus', *Academy of Management Journal*, **29**(1), 51–71.

Schwenk, C.R. (1990), 'Conflict in organizational decision making: an exploratory study of its effects in for-profit and not-for-profit organizations', *Management Science*, **36**(4), 436–48.

Shah, P. and K.A. Jehn (1993), 'Do friends perform better than acquaintances? The interaction of friendship, conflict and task', *Group Decision and Negotiation*, **2**, 149–66.

Shelton, L.M. (2006), 'Female entrepreneurs, work-family conflict, and venture performance: new insights into the work-family interface', *Journal of Small Business Management*, **44**(2), 285–97.

Simon, H.A. (1957), *Models of Man: Social and Rational*, New York: Wiley.

Simons, T. and R.A. Peterson (2000), 'Task conflict and relationship conflict in top management teams: the pivotal role of intragroup trust', *Journal of Applied Psychology*, **85**, 102–11.

Steiner, G.A. (1979), *Strategic Planning: What Every Manager Must Know*, New York: Free Press.

Wall, V. and R. Callister (1995), 'Conflict and its management', *Journal of Management*, **21**, 515–58.

9. Board features associated with new team member addition in academic spin-offs

Ekaterina S. Bjørnåli and Truls Erikson

INTRODUCTION

The strategic management and organizational behaviour literature contains an extensive body of work that has examined the relationship between management change characteristics and the need for organizational change. Managerial turnover as a form of organizational adaptation has been widely studied in the context of large, established organizations (Wiersema and Bantel, 1993), in which the replacement of top executives provides an important mechanism for the organization to overcome inertia (Tushman and Romanelli, 1985) and adapt strategically to changing contexts (Pfeffer and Salancik, 1978). However, studies focusing on top management teams (TMT) in large, established firms have failed to distinguish between the factors associated with team member entry and those associated with team member exit (Ucbasaran et al., 2003).

In sharp contrast to large, established firms, management turnover in the context of new ventures has almost been neglected. Few studies have attempted to address this gap (for example, Forbes et al., 2006; Erikson and Berg-Utby, 2009). However, entrepreneurship scholars and theorists have begun to acknowledge that the teams that lead entrepreneurial firms change over time, and that 'new team members need to be brought in and founders, whose skills may become outdated, need to be replaced' (Beckman et al., 2007, p. 149). Overall, the studies of team dynamics demonstrate that the managerial transitions in new ventures may not always go smoothly and even be detrimental to the firm (for example, Chandler et al., 2005; Beckman et al., 2007). Still, these managerial transitions have not been studied extensively, and more research is required to examine the reasons for and skills of those entering and leaving the firm (Beckman et al., 2007). The range of issues associated with managerial transitions is wide, including the dismissal and replacement of team members (for example, Fiet et al., 1997; Boeker and Karichalil,

2002) and team member entry (Forbes et al., 2006). Some studies have attempted to address both additions and departures (for example, Ucbasaran et al., 2003; Chandler et al., 2005). In this chapter we focus on team member addition, which allows us to examine issues more thoroughly.

In evolving team-based ventures the addition of the new member is a critical and common development (Forbes et al., 2006). The decision about choosing and adding a new member is important because it may considerably change the existing human capital. In terms of achieved attributes such as experience, this is linked to increased levels of productivity (Becker, 1975). Academic spin-off firm (ASO) founders need to fill skill gaps to facilitate the development of resources and capabilities which enable the firm's transition from a non-commercial environment to the market (Vohora et al., 2004). Entrepreneurship scholars have demonstrated the positive linkages between the quality of the team's past experience and firm performance (Burton et al., 2002). Therefore, adding a new member to the team may potentially affect ASO firm growth and survival.

Although the idea of increasing team diversity by adding a new member is not new, we have little knowledge of the factors associated with team member addition (Ucbasaran et al., 2003; Vanaelst, 2006). Vanaelst et al. (2006) have studied the entrepreneurial team development in ten Belgian spin-off cases. They examined the heterogeneity of the team members which evolved through the firm's life cycle, suggesting that people enter the team due to the firm's resource needs. Forbes et al. (2006) have explored team formation and elaborated on strategic choice perspective, for example, resource seeking and interpersonal attraction/social motives of team member addition. Drawing on resource dependence theory, Huse (2007b) identified the importance of the board's role of using a network when recruiting new TMT members in privately held threshold firms.

The purpose of this chapter is to increase our understanding of the factors associated with team member entry. We address this research gap by exploring the factors associated with the new member addition to the team in ASO companies which are usually based on technology formally transferred from the university or research institute. Since many ASOs, as high tech firms, operate in industry niches characterized by high levels of growth and require highly skilled board members, the boards in these firms may play a greater role and have stronger influence on firm activities compared to other types of companies (Hambrick and Abrahamson, 1995; Forbes and Milliken, 1999). Several entrepreneurial firm studies have demonstrated an active involvement of board members in the firm's strategic decisions, playing roles such as providing a sounding board and a source of advice in decision making rather than merely performing monitoring and control (Deakins et al., 2000; Johannisson and Huse, 2000). Furthermore, ASOs usually have a significant demand for finance and human capital, for example, industry-specific knowledge and commercial expertise (Clarysse et al., 2007; Wright et al., 2007). ASOs may attract experienced and well-connected directors to their boards who can aid in accessing critical external resources (Lynall et al., 2003). Consequently, in this chapter we attempt to examine the role of the board as a pool of helpers, and as an important predictor of new team member addition. We consider board size, number of outsiders, board members who are not part of the TMT and the university community, and board contribution of networking.

Our chapter extends previous research and makes a number of contributions. It studies managerial transitions in high tech new ventures rarely addressed by TMT studies which mainly focused on mature firms (Ensley et al., 2002). It responds to suggestions in the entrepreneurial team literature to use a broader definition of team turnover considering team member entry and exit (Ucbasaran et al., 2003). We gather additional insights into team member additions in ASOs by considering board features associated with team member addition. We contribute to the governance research on privately held firms, which emphasizes the need to go beyond agency theory (Uhlaner et al., 2007). We draw on the resource dependence perspective on the board's role in TMT dynamics and then we focus explicitly on the board in ASOs. Thus, we add to academic entrepreneurship where the number of studies on team and board level is still limited (Rothaermel et al., 2007).

HYPOTHESES DEVELOPMENT

Board Resources and Size

The resource role of board members in start-ups is particularly important for increasing strategic flexibility and enabling firm growth and survival (Filatochev et al., 2006). Resource theories have been used to argue for a positive relationship between board size and corporate financial performance (Huse, 2007b). Resource dependency view holds that boards help firms to establish links with an external environment in order to secure resources, and a large board will fulfil this task better than a small board. The argument is that the greater the need for external linkages, the larger the board should be (Pfeffer and Salancik, 1978).

Larger boards have more contacts in or connections with stakeholder groups, other boards and other organizations, which increase their chance of receiving new information and gaining new insights to help to solve non-routine challenges (George et al., 2001). Thus, each director may bring different linkages and resources to a board. Larger boards may therefore be better at identifying the appropriate member which the TMT might need. This leads to the following hypothesis:

Hypothesis 1: Board size is positively associated with subsequent team member addition in academic spin-offs.

Board Resources and Outsiders

Research also suggests that the proportion of inside versus outside members will affect the board's involvement and influence (Sapienza et al., 2000). The proportion of outside board members has been found to be positively related to board involvement in strategic decisions (Johnson et al., 1993). Outside directors are classified as non-management members of the board (Rosenstein et al., 1993). Outside directors bring in new resources and diversity of perspectives (Pfeffer and Salancik, 1978). They also bring their networks into the company. It is generally noted that firms with a higher proportion of outside board members who have greater number of interlocks (that is, sit on two or more boards) will experience superior performance (Johnson et al., 1996). Also, the service role of directors – that is, providing advice and counsel to the Chief Executive Officer (CEO) – may impact new venture performance (George et al., 2001).

Vanaelst et al. (2006) illustrate how the entrepreneurial team evolves from the pre-founding team, consisting mainly of the researchers, to the founding team, which may include a surrogate (external) entrepreneur and is ready to legally incorporate the ASO venture. Once the new venture is legally established, the founding team divides into two major teams: the management team and the board of directors (Vanaelst et al., 2006). The management team and the board of directors may represent separate entities or they may overlap. For instance, the scientist entrepreneur may be a member of both the management team and the board, while a university technology transfer office (TTO) may place its representative on the board of the ASO. In this study we define management, such as scientist entrepreneurs, as board insiders. We also consider TTO members involved in ASOs as insiders since they are a part of the university environment, and in the academic entrepreneurship literature they are shown to still need to develop networking and commercial skills if spin-offs are to be successful (Lockett et al., 2005). Other external board members who are not part of the TMT and do not belong to the university community are conceived of as outsiders. Outside board members may be, for instance, venture capital investors and industrial partners (Clarysse et al., 2007; Wright et al., 2004). The larger the number of outsiders on the board, the more external and diverse connections and interlocks the board will have. This increases the probability of finding an appropriate team member candidate from outside the academic environment. Thus, we propose the existence of a relationship as follows:

Hypothesis 2: The number of outsiders on the board is positively associated with subsequent team member addition in academic spin-offs.

Board Networking Role

In threshold firms, as ASO ventures, the outside directors develop the contributions of the boards by using their networks (Huse, 2007b). An active networking strategy requires increased board involvement and a greater number of interlocks (George et al., 2001). Informal strategic networks are of great importance to small firms, and directorates play a central role in creating, maintaining and influencing important external contacts of the firm (Borch and Huse, 1993). The board's networking involvement is connected to the creation of personal contacts with representatives of its exchange partners or other people involved, and the board members' involvement in environment influencing activities such as legitimizing, door opening and lobbying (Borch and Huse, 1993).

In this respect, the outside directors are found to be mainly active in using their networks to find and recruit key personnel and in receiving additional financial resources during the stages of external capitalization (Rosenstein, 1988; Deakins et al., 2000). Finding appropriate team members can be challenging for scientist entrepreneurs with networks limited to peers within academia (Ensley and Hmieleski, 2005; Mosey and Wright, 2007). The board members can aid them in finding and recruiting appropriate top management candidates using their connections. Previous studies also show that outside directors aid entrepreneurs in the decision-making process within the firm through contacts, experience and other expertise they bring to the firm (Deakins et al., 2000). Board members with well-developed networks have information that may improve their skills and competence to fulfil their strategic function (George et al., 2001), enabling them to give better advice to entrepreneurs. ASOs may benefit from boards that actively use their networks. Thus, we propose the existence of a relationship as follows:

Hypothesis 3: Board contribution of networking is positively associated with subsequent team member addition.

Data and Methods

The dataset originates from a survey given to the CEOs of 353 companies derived from Norwegian universities and public research institutes in the autumn of 2008. This sample constitutes the 318 companies that are registered as having used the university TTO or technology licensing-like organization in the FORNY database. FORNY is a government programme (under the Research Council of Norway) designed to increase the creation of wealth in Norway by supporting the commercialization of R&D results. The rest of the companies were found from other sources. Anonymity for all companies and informants was assured. Fifty-three firms reported that they are not academic spin-offs or they are no longer active. One hundred and thirty-five academic spin-off companies returned their questionnaires resulting in a response rate of 45 per cent. Due to missing values, 95 cases were included in the analysis. We registered 64 firms with new team member addition.

Our dependent variable is new team member addition. We asked the respondents to consider the most important/critical membership change. Then we asked them whether it was the person who entered – not left – the TMT. The firm was allocated a value of 1 if the new team member addition occurred, and a value of 0 otherwise.

Board size was measured with the question: how many persons are on the board? The number of outsiders was measured as the number of external board members who are neither TMT members nor TTO representatives. With regard to board contribution of networking, we asked a respondent to indicate to what extent they agree with the following statements on the board networking role (Huse, 2007a), that is, to which degree on the Likert 7-point scale ranging from 1 (to a very small degree) to 7 (to a very large degree): (a) the board contributes to networking (that is, network building) and (b) the firm and board use the board member's network to get advice. The networking variable was constructed by summating scales (Cronbach's alpha = 0.855).

We controlled for firm stage since ASO companies that are in later development stages may have more resources, experience, information and relationships (Finkle, 1998), and the skills required by a team may vary between early-stage and late-stage firms (Hambrick and Mason, 1984).

We also controlled for firm performance since firms with very poor and very high performance are shown to experience TMT change more often (Boeker and Wiltbank, 2005). Firm performance is often measured by sales revenues. As many of our firms have no sales, traditional measures are not appropriate. As suggested by Fredriksen and Klofsten (1999), a way to deal with this issue is by using an all subjective measure of how the companies are developing according to a business plan. Hence, we used multiple measures that captured performance pertaining to growth (Cronbach's alpha = 0.859) and product (Cronbach's alpha = 0.711). The growth measure captures how the firm's growth in sales, growth in market share, profitability and financing as measured since the firm's foundation. The product measure includes the quality of the firm's product/service, the innovation in the form of new products/services and customer satisfaction since the firm's foundation. We also measured the firm's overall satisfaction with performance, that is, to what degree the firm is satisfied with its market share, profit, sales and return on assets (ROA) (Cronbach's alpha = 0.937).

Finally, we controlled for team size, tenure and team heterogeneity in functional and industry backgrounds as they, in previous studies, have been hypothesized and tested to moderate team member addition (for example, Ucbasaran et al. 2003; Chandler et al., 2005). Team size is the number of persons who are in the management team – not included in the board. Heterogeneity in functional (sales, finance and so on) and industry backgrounds was measured on the Likert 7-point scale ranging from 1 (to a very small degree) to 7 (to a very large degree), adapted from the survey carried out by Huse (2007a). This measure was composed by summated scales (Cronbach's alpha = 0.660). Team tenure indicates the total sum of years the members have been on the TMT.

RESULTS

Measures of correlation and descriptive statistics are reported in Table 9.1.

To test the significance in predicting the new team member addition of the independent variables over the control variables, we used a two-step logistic regression. All control variables were entered in the first step (Model 1) whereas all the focal variables were entered in the second step (Model 2).

Table 9.2 presents the results of our two-step regression. Model 1 representing only the control variables (that is, firm growth, product, satisfaction with performance, development stage, team size, team tenure, team functional and industrial heterogeneity) is significant at the 0.01 level. One control variable, team functional and industrial heterogeneity, is positively and significantly related to subsequent team member addition at the 0.01 level.

The focal variables (that is, board size, outsiders, board networking) were entered as a block in Model 2. The addition of the board variables to Model 1 with the control variables resulted in an improved model. This block is significant at the 0.001 level and the overall model is significant at the 0.000 level. Two control variables, firm growth and team functional and industrial diversity, are significantly related to the subsequent team member entry at the 0.1 and 0.05 levels, respectively. Board size is positively and marginally significantly related to the subsequent new team member addition ($p < 0.1$). Hence, Hypothesis 1 is marginally supported. The number of outsiders is positively, but not significantly related to the new member addition. Thus, Hypothesis 2 is not supported. Hypothesis 3, regarding the positive relation-

Table 9.1 Pearson correlation matrix with all the variables and descriptive statistics

	Mean	SD	1	2	3	4	5	6	7	8	9	10	11
Addition (1)	0.57	0.50	1.000										
Firm growth (2)	4.27	1.36	-0.100	1.000									
Firm product (3)	5.00	0.97	-0.114	0.451**	1.000								
Satisfaction with firm performance (4)	3.38	1.63	-0.061	0.568**	0.168	1.000							
Development stage (5)	2.14	0.99	-0.044	0.267**	0.041	0.260**	1.000						
Team size (6)	2.62	1.70	0.241**	0.280**	0.157	0.248**	0.076	1.000					
Team tenure (7)	12.13	10.71	0.051	0.249**	0.125	0.282**	0.267**	0.513**	1.000				
Team functional and industrial heterogeneity (8)	4.65	1.79	0.222*	-0.036	0.139	-0.093	-0.198*	0.063	-0.057	1.000			
Board size (9)	3.80	1.16	0.272**	0.073	0.214*	0.005	-0.156	0.384*	0.124	0.379**	1.000		
Board outsiders (10)	2.05	1.66	0.262**	-0.017	0.094	-0.118	-0.195*	0.125	-0.096	0.378**	0.535**	1.000	
Board networking (11)	4.76	1.61	0.209*	0.020	-0.012	0.006	-0.329**	-0.063	-0.129	0.173	0.003	0.167	1.000

Note: $N = 95$; * $p < 0.05$; ** $p < 0.01$; SD Standard Deviation.

Table 9.2 Results of the logistic regression on team member addition

Levels	Variables	Model 1	Model 2
Firm controls	Firm growth	0.70	0.60†
		(−0.37)	(−0.53)
	Firm product	0.92*	0.86
		(−0.08)	(−0.15)
	Satisfaction with firm performance	1.10	1.12
		(0.09)	(0.11)
	Life cycle stage	0.98	1.32
		(−0.02)	(0.28)
Team controls	Team size	1.40	1.40
		(0.34)	(0.34)
	Team tenure	1.01	1.03
		(0.01)	(0.03)
	Functional and industrial heterogeneity	1.67**	1.58*
		(0.52)	(0.46)
Board	Board size (H1)		1.81†
			(0.60)
	Board outsiders (H2)		1.06
			(0.06)
	Board networking (H3)		1.67**
			(0.51)
	Constant	0.45	0.01*
	Block χ^2 significance	0.01**	0.001***
	Model χ^2	18 580	31 498
	Model χ^2 significance	0.01**	0.000***
	−2 log likelihood	101 412	88 494
	Overall predictive accuracy	70.5 %	81.1%
	Cox and Snell R^2	0.178	0.282
	Nagelkerke R^2	0.248	0.393
	Number of firms	95	95

Note: *** $p < 0.001$, ** $p < 0.01$, * $p < 0.05$, † $p < 0.10$.

ship between board contribution of networking and subsequent new member addition, is supported. The level of board network building activity is positively and significantly associated with adding new members to the TMT ($p < 0.01$).

In summary, ASO companies that have heterogeneous teams with regard to functional and industry backgrounds as well as larger and more active networking boards are more likely to add new members to their TMTs. As to firm growth, our findings seem to indicate that the better the firm's growth is, the less need there is for adding new members to the team.

DISCUSSION

In this chapter we sought to explore board factors associated with new team member addition in ASOs. Drawing on the resource dependence perspective of active boards in small companies (Huse, 2007b), we examined the role of the board, including composition and networking contribution, as the driver of new team member entry. Our findings suggest that the board plays an important role in the team member addition process. In particular, we find that board size and networking activity level facilitate the team member addition process in ASOs, while the number of outsiders – people who do not belong to either the TMT or university community – was not significant with regard to adding a new member to the TMT.

Our investigation represents a useful addition to team literature and governance literature, since little is known about the role of the board in TMT dynamics in academic spin-offs as high tech new ventures (Ensley et al., 2002; Clarysse et al., 2007). We contribute by drawing on the resource dependence perspective of the board's role as an important predictor of team member entry in ASO companies (Uhlaner et al., 2007). An empirical contribution of our study to academic entrepreneurship is identifying factors associated with team member addition in ASOs (Rothaermel et al., 2007). ASO companies which have larger active networking boards are more likely to add new members to the team. However, a firm's growth, which includes growth in sales, market share, profitability and financing, seems to lessen the likelihood of adding a new member. In other words, lack of growth increases the likelihood of new team member additions. This is consistent with open answers from the survey, in which the respondents mentioned 'improved growth' and 'increase in sales' as consequences of team member entry.

A positive relationship between the functional and industry background diversity among TMT members and additions is similar to the findings demonstrated by previous studies (Chandler et al., 2005). In contrast to the Ucbasaran et al. (2003) study of family firms, and the Chandler et al. (2005) study of five-year-old emerging ventures, we do not find that team size is associated with subsequent team member addition. This may be due to the origin of ASOs from a non-commercial academic environment and that the firms we studied represented all development stages.

For academic entrepreneurship and research on governance in privately held firms, our study adds board composition and networking measures as variables that should be considered. The exploration of the factors at the board level shows that board size and board networking contribution are positively related to new team member entry. This is in line with previous studies on boards that demonstrate the active role of the board recruiting key personnel and engaging in network building activities in venture capital backed small and medium-sized enterprises (Deakins et al., 2000; Huse, 2007b). Also, we accounted for the firm's development stage, which is important since various studies show that ASOs are threshold companies that go through several stages of activity and thus influence TMT development (for example, Vohora et al., 2004; Vanaelst et al., 2006). The number of outsiders – board members who are neither TMT members nor TTO representatives – was not found to be significantly associated with the additions of new team members in ASOs. This may suggest that what matters is the joint engagement in networking activities by both internal and external board members and those whom these board members know when it comes to finding new members for the TMT.

This study has several implications. First, the study indicates that the diversity in functional and industrial backgrounds of the team members is positively related to new member addition. Early-stage technology based firms were shown to overcome various thresholds (for example, receiving venture capital funding, going public) when they had teams that were heterogeneous in functional backgrounds (Beckman et al., 2007; Zimmerman, 2008) and industry experience (Chandler et al., 2005). For managers seeking further ASO development, this implies that they should adjust the team's functional and industrial diversity as early as possible by adding members with relevant expertise in order to enable growth and overcome the thresholds that an ASO faces.

Second, additional analyses do not uncover any significant interactions between the studied variables and the firm's development stage. Neither could we find significant interactions between the studied variables and firm performance except for the interaction between the board size and firm growth, which was marginally significant ($p < 0.1$) and positively related to subsequent team member entry. This suggests that the larger the board and the better the growth, the more likely it is a new team member will be added. The additional analyses also support our suggestion about the importance of the joint networking effort of both internal and external board members in the new team member addition process. Although it is not significant, our third performance variable, which measures the satisfaction with firm performance regarding market share, profit, sales and ROA, is positively related to subsequent team member addition. Most of the survey respondents are CEOs and original founders in CEO, board chair and other positions. Thus, this positive relationship may indicate that when the CEO/founder is satisfied with firm performance they will most probably have a positive attitude towards the addition of new TMT members. Our results are only indicative. Hence, future research is needed to explore in depth the role of team and board in various stages of firm development and under which conditions these factors become more pronounced. For instance, previous high tech start-up studies have demonstrated the U-shaped relationship between TMT change – including founder departure and general additions and departures – and firm growth (Boeker and Karichalil, 2002; Boeker and Wiltbank, 2005). Both fast growth and a lack of start-up growth create the need for different top managers, but in the latter case 'to help turn the new venture around' (Boeker and Wiltbank, 2005, p. 125).

Finally, our study suggests that ASOs with larger boards and greater levels of networking activity are more likely to add new members to their management teams. For academic founders, this means that when forming a board or negotiating board seats with, for example, powerful investors, they should pay attention to the records of potential board members with respect to previous networking and recruiting activities in other companies.

Our study has a number of limitations which will hopefully be addressed by future research. First, we considered only the strategic choice perspective, which implies the addition of the member according to the wishes of the existing team members. An institutional perspective, according to which the addition may be imposed by external institutional forces, such as influential owners, is outside the scope of this study. Second, our study is cross-sectional, which means that we could not capture the underlying processes behind the relationships assessed. Third, this is a study of Norwegian ASOs, and there is obviously a need for more studies in other comparable countries and contexts. Fourth, we have only focused on team member addition, while the other side of team turnover – team member exit – could also be investigated as these events are apparently related, although they may have different drivers. Future research should investigate what drives team member exits. Consequences of TMT member addition are important as well. For instance, Beckman et al. (2007) show that high tech venture teams that add members obtain initial public offering (IPO) faster. The results of our survey seem to indicate that most important additions to the team were usually positive with a stronger competence brought by the new member to the team as a result. This adds new growth opportunities and the chance of increased sales. However, future research should address the question of the consequences of team member entry for the new venture.

REFERENCES

Becker, G.S. (1975), *Human Capital*, New York: National Bureau of Economic Research.
Beckman, C.M., M.D. Burton and C. O'Reilly (2007), 'Early teams: the impact of team demography on VC financing and going public', *Journal of Business Venturing*, **22** (2), 147–73.
Boeker, W. and R. Karichalil (2002), 'Entrepreneurial transitions: factors influencing founder departure', *Academy of Management Journal*, **45**(4), 818–26.
Boeker, W. and R. Wiltbank (2005), 'New venture evolution and managerial capabilities', *Organization Science*, **16**(2), 123–33.

Borch, O.J. and M. Huse (1993), 'Informal strategic networks and the board of directors', *Entrepreneurship Theory and Practice*, **18**(1), 23–6.

Burton, M.D., J.B. Sorensen and C.M. Beckman (2002), 'Coming from good stock: career histories and new venture formation', in M. Lounsbury and M. Ventresca (eds), *Research in the Sociology of Organizations*, Greenwich, CT: JAI Press, pp. 229–62.

Chandler, G.N., B. Honig and J. Wiklund (2005), 'Antecedents, moderators, and performance consequences of membership change in new venture teams', *Journal of Business Venturing*, **20**(5), 705–25.

Clarysse, B., M. Knockaert and A. Lockett (2007), 'Outside board composition in high tech start-ups', *Small Business Economics*, **29**(3), 243–60.

Deakins, D., E. O'Neill and P. Mileham (2000), 'The role and influence of external directors in small, entrepreneurial companies: some evidence on VC and non-VC appointed external directors', *Venture Capital*, **2**(2), 111–27.

Ensley, M.D. and K.M. Hmieleski (2005), 'A comparative study of new venture top management team composition, dynamics and performance between university-based and independent start-ups', *Research Policy*, **34**(7), 1091–105.

Ensley, M.D., A.W. Pearson and A.C. Amason (2002), 'Understanding the dynamics of new venture top management teams: cohesion, conflict, and new venture performance', *Journal of Business Venturing*, **17**(4), 365–86.

Erikson, T. and T. Berg-Utby (2009), 'Preinvestment negotiation characteristics and dismissal in venture capital-backed firms', *Negotiation Journal*, **25**(1), 41–57.

Fiet, J.O., L.W. Busenitz, D.D. Moesel and J.B. Barney (1997), 'Complementary theoretical perspectives on the dismissal of new venture team members', *Journal of Business Venturing*, **12**(5), 347–66.

Filatotchev, I., S. Toms and M. Wright (2006), 'The firm's strategic dynamics and corporate governance life-cycle', *International Journal of Managerial Finance*, **2**(4), 256–79.

Finkle, T.A. (1998), 'The relationship between boards of directors and initial public offerings in the biotechnology industry', *Entrepreneurship Theory and Practice*, **22**(3), 5–29.

Forbes, D.P. and F.J. Milliken (1999), 'Cognition and corporate governance: understanding boards of directors as strategic decision-making groups', *Academy of Management Review*, **24**(3), 489–505.

Forbes, D.P., P.S. Borchert, M.E. Zellmer-Bruhn and H.J. Sapienza (2006), 'Entrepreneurial team formation: an exploration of member addition', *Entrepreneurship Theory and Practice*, **30**(2), 225–48.

Fredriksen, Ø. and M. Klofsten (1999), 'CEO vs board typologies in venture-capital-entrepreneur relationships', in P.D. Reynolds, W.D. Bygrave, K.G. Shaver, C.M. Mason and S. Manigart (eds), *Frontiers of Entrepreneurship Research*, Wellesley, MA: Babson College, pp. 335–48.

George, G., D. Robley Wood Jr and R. Khan (2001), 'Networking strategy of boards: implications for small and medium-sized enterprises', *Entrepreneurship and Regional Development*, **13**(3), 269–85.

Hambrick, D.C. and E. Abrahamson (1995), 'Assessing managerial discretion across industries – a multimethod approach', *Academy of Management Journal*, **38**(5), 1427–41.

Hambrick, D. and P. Mason (1984), 'Upper echelons: the organization as a reflection of its top managers', *Academy of Management Review*, **9**(2), 193–206.

Huse, M. (2007a), *Styret: Tante, barbar eller klan?*, Bergen, Norway: Fagbokforlaget.

Huse, M. (2007b), *Boards, Governance and Value Creation: The Human Side of Corporate Governance*, Cambridge: Cambridge University Press.

Johannisson, B. and M. Huse (2000), 'Recruiting outside board members in the small family business: an ideological challenge', *Entrepreneurship and Regional Development*, **12**(4), 353–78.

Johnson, R.A., R.E. Hoskisson and M.A. Hitt (1993), 'Board of director involvement in restructuring: the effects of board versus managerial controls and characteristics', *Strategic Management Journal*, **14**(1), 33–50.

Johnson, J.L., C.M. Daily and A.E. Ellstrand (1996), 'Board of directors: a review and research agenda', *Journal of Management*, **22**(3), 409–38.

Lockett, A., D. Siegel, M. Wright and M.D. Ensley (2005), 'The creation of spin-off firms at public research institutions: managerial and policy implications', *Research Policy*, **34**(7), 981–93.

Lynall, M.D., B.R. Golden and A.J. Hillman (2003), 'Board composition from adolescence to maturity: a multitheoretic view', *Academy of Management Review*, **28**(3), 416–31.

Mosey, S. and M. Wright (2007), 'From human capital to social capital: a longitudinal study of technology-based academic entrepreneurs', *Entrepreneurship Theory and Practice*, **31**(6), 909–35.

Pfeffer, J. and G. Salancik (1978), *The External Control of Organizations: A Resource Dependence Perspective*, New York: Harper & Row.

Rosenstein, J. (1988), 'The board and strategy: venture capital and high technology', *Journal of Business Venturing*, **3**(2), 159–70.

Rosenstein, J., A.V. Bruno, W.D. Bygrave and N.T. Taylor (1993), 'The CEO, venture capitalists and the board', *Journal of Business Venturing*, **8**(2), 99–113.

Rothaermel, F.T., S.D. Agung and L. Jiang (2007), 'University entrepreneurship: a taxonomy of the literature', *Industrial and Corporate Change*, **16**(4), 691–791.

Sapienza, H.J., M.A. Korsgaard, P.K. Goulet and J.P. Hoogendam (2000), 'Effects of agency risks and procedural justice on board processes in venture capital-backed firms', *Entrepreneurship and Regional Development*, **12**(4), 331–51.

Tushman, M. and E. Romanelli (1985), 'Organizational evolution: a metamorphosis model of convergence and reorientation', in L. Cummings and B. Staw (eds), *Research in Organizational Behavior*, Vol. 7, Greenwich, CT: JAI Press, pp. 171–222.

Ucbasaran, D., A. Lockett, M. Wright and P. Westhead (2003), 'Entrepreneurial founder teams: factors associated with member entry and exit', *Entrepreneurship Theory and Practice*, **28**(2), 107–27.

Uhlaner, L., M. Wright and M. Huse (2007), 'Private firms and corporate governance: an integrated economic and management perspective', *Small Business Economics*, **29**(3), 225–41.

Vanaelst, I. (2006), 'Essays on entrepreneurial teams in innovative high-tech start-ups', PhD dissertation, Vrije Universiteit Brussel–Universiteit Gent.

Vanaelst, I., B. Clarysse, M. Wright, A. Lockett, N. Moray and R. S'Jegers (2006), 'Entrepreneurial team development in academic spinouts: an examination of team heterogeneity', *Entrepreneurship Theory and Practice*, **30**(2), 249–71.

Vohora, A., M. Wright and A. Lockett (2004), 'Critical junctures in the development of university high-tech spinout companies', *Research Policy*, **33**(1), 147–75.

Wiersema, M.F. and K.A. Bantel (1993), 'Top management team turnover as an adaptation mechanism: the role of the environment', *Strategic Management Journal*, **14**(7), 485–504.

Wright, M., A. Vohora and A. Lockett (2004), 'The formation of high-tech university spinouts: the role of joint ventures and venture capital investors', *Journal of Technology Transfer*, **29**(3–4), 287–310.

Wright, M., B. Clarysse, P. Mustar and A. Lockett (2007), *Academic Entrepreneurship in Europe*, Cheltenham, UK and Northampton, MA, USA: Edward Elgar.

Zimmerman, M.A. (2008), 'The influence of top management team heterogeneity on the capital raised through an initial public offering', *Entrepreneurship Theory and Practice*, **32**(3), 391–414.

10. Design characteristics associated with venture capital acquisitions in academic spin-offs

Ekaterina S. Bjørnåli, Roger Sørheim and Truls Erikson

INTRODUCTION

The formation of high growth academic spin-off companies is one of the main policy goals of governments and universities (Rothaermel et al., 2007; Wright et al., 2007b). Academic spin-offs are usually based on technology formally transferred from the parent organization, which is a university or research institute. Equity finance is conducive to the creation of wealth through spin-off formation; however access to finance and, more particularly finance from venture capitalists, is a major barrier that academic spin-offs face (Wright et al., 2006). The concerns of venture capitalists are related to the quality of the management team and that scientist entrepreneurs may not have the credibility to recruit management with commercial expertise or to attract customers (Wright et al., 2006).

The importance of the topic of firm creation is also reflected by the increasing literature related to academic spin-offs (Rothaermel et al., 2007; Djokovic and Souitaris, 2008). Spin-off researchers have primarily tried to explain the variation in spin-off activity and identify factors that would increase this activity in the universities. Previous studies have mainly focused on the university related factors, for example, universities' and technology transfer offices' (TTO) policies, practices and faculty characteristics, rather than on the development of spin-off companies after their legal establishment and the success factors outside the research environment.

The success behind spin-off firm creation is attributed to the quality of human resources (that is, faculty, TTO personnel, founding team) and funding from university, industry and venture capitalists (Shane and Stuart, 2002; O'Shea et al., 2005). Few studies have investigated the link between human resources embodied in the top management team (TMT) and firm performance. For instance, Ensley and Hmieleski (2005) show that academic spin-offs have less diverse TMTs and perform significantly lower in terms of net cash flow and revenue growth than independent new ventures. Even fewer studies have addressed the role of boards in academic spin-offs (Clarysse et al., 2007). This is surprising because the resources and knowledge of board members may be particularly important for increasing a firm's strategic flexibility and ensuring long-term growth and survival (Filatotchev et al., 2006).

A venture capital (VC) firm's supply of risk capital has been considered a primary source of funds for academic spin-offs (Zucker et al., 1998). However, there is a mismatch between the expectations of spin-offs and VC providers, which results in the so-called equity gap (Wright et al., 2006). While spin-offs consider VC as more important in the early seed stage, the venture capitalists prefer to invest after the seed stage. Spin-off studies demonstrate that a number of public and private financing initiatives have been developed aiming to support early-stage spin-offs and to fill the financing gap (Leleux and Surlemont, 2003; Wright et al., 2006). However, there has been little research regarding the extent to which these public and private financing initiatives have actually improved the development of academic spin-offs and helped them in obtaining VC financing.

The purpose of this chapter is to examine the role of prior finance and a firm's internal human resources in VC acquisition in academic spin-offs. We draw on resource-based theory. A resource-based theory views the managerial team and the firm's board as internal resources that can give a competitive advantage to a firm and thus be associated with organizational success (Barney, 1991, 2001; Barney and Wright, 1998). A firm's human resources include the knowledge, experience, skills and competencies of people involved in the organization (Barney and Wright, 1998). Including people on the management team and board whose resources are valuable, rare, inimitable, non-substitutable and non-transferable may be a way of providing the firm with sustainable competitive advantage. In other words, the unique configuration of the human resources provided by team and board members will enhance the firm's prospects for success.

In this study academic spin-offs are viewed as facing VC financing constraint (Westhead and Storey, 1997; Wright et al., 2006). Because VC investors are concerned with managerial talent and credibility, a firm that has the unique configuration of managerial resources may be more likely to overcome this constraint and thus outperform its competitors. Size of and diversity in both the management team and board are, as we contend, the most important structural design features generally considered as advantageous to entrepreneurial firms (Beckman et al., 2007; Zimmerman, 2008). In line with Cohen and Bailey (1997, p. 243), the design features are defined as characteristics of 'the task, group, and organization that can be directly manipulated by managers to create the conditions for effective performance' (Stewart, 2006).

Furthermore, on the analogy of the pecking order hypothesis applied in the spin-off literature (Wright et al., 2006), we expect that academic spin-offs look for internal (seed fund) and alternative forms of external financing (from informal and industrial investors) before they seek VC. For potential VC investors the way a spin-off was previously financed may serve as an indication of the firm's uniqueness in terms of managerial resources and credibility which can provide a firm with a competitive advantage. Applying resource-based theory, the unique configuration of the prior financial resources may increase the firm's chances of receiving VC financing.

This chapter extends previous research and makes a number of contributions. First, we contribute to academic entrepreneurship and VC literature by linking several types of early-stage finance (from the seed funds to the informal investors and industry) to the spin-off ability to acquire VC capital. We find that portfolio seed funding and capital from industrial partners, but not the support from informal investors, are design features associated with successful VC acquisitions. Second, the chapter extends our understanding of the role of the TMT (Ensley and Hmieleski, 2005) and boards (Clarysse et al., 2007) in academic spin-offs by linking their design characteristics to VC financing. We find that only team size and cognitive diversity among management team members are design features associated with VC acquisitions. Thus, the chapter contributes to new venture team research (Wright et al., 2007a) and adds to research on boards in privately held firms (Uhlaner et al., 2007), which calls for going beyond agency theory.

Below we start by outlining the development of our hypotheses. Next, we discuss the research design and data collection methods. Then we provide definitions of the selected dependent, independent and control variables, followed by a discussion of the findings. Finally, we conclude and discuss implications, future research directions and limitations of the study.

HYPOTHESES DEVELOPMENT

Prior Finance Characteristics and Venture Capital Acquisition

Drawing an analogy with the pecking order hypothesis previously applied in the spin-off studies (Wright et al., 2006), we expect that spin-offs first attract internal start-up financial support, for example, from a university and/or government seed funds, then the capital from informal investors (so-called business angels) and in some cases from industry until the VC investors become interested in the venture. The gap between the demand for finance from scientist entrepreneurs and the willingness of financiers to supply this funding is recognized by policy makers in many countries (Feldman et al.,

2002; Wright et al., 2006). This recognition has led governments around the world to increasingly channel public financing to research and early-stage ventures (Lerner, 2002; Wright et al., 2006). In Europe seed capital funds are usually set up as an intermediary in order to reduce uncertainty related to technical and commercial issues (Murray, 2007). Thus, one should expect that some of the spin-offs financed with governmental and seed capital funds will be capable of securing VC funding as they become more mature and uncertainty related to technical and commercial issues is reduced.

Informal investors, as is often claimed, do seed stage deals that they hope will develop into ventures that attract start-up financing from venture capitalists (De Clercq et al., 2006). The assumption whether there is a relay race between informal and VC investors has been previously questioned (Sørheim, 2005) since the informal and VC investors have different investment strategies and the informal investors are more concerned about avoiding bad investments rather than 'hitting a home run' (Mason and Harrison, 2002).

Finally, academic spin-offs face the challenge of making the venture 'investor ready' (Douglas and Shepherd, 2002) to acquire VC by, for example, developing successful prototypes, assembling an experienced TMT, customer testing and early sales, and thorough intellectual property (IP) due diligence. The support of the industrial partner may make it easier to access necessary resources. The decision to invest and the level of investment committed to a venture is contingent upon VC investors' perception of the credibility of the venture in terms of whether the risks involved are acceptable. Collaboration with an industrial partner generates the credibility of a venture early on and may facilitate greater commitment by VC investors (Wright et al., 2004).

This means that financial choices made in the very early stages of an academic spin-off are expected to heavily influence the capital acquisition process in later stages. Thus, we propose the following hypothesis:

Hypothesis 1: Prior finance design characteristics will make an independent contribution to the venture capital acquisition function in academic spin-offs.

Management Team Design Characteristics and Venture Capital Acquisition

Team size and diversity among TMT members are generally considered as advantageous to entrepreneurial firms and conducive to achieving important milestones, for example, attracting VC financing and going public (Beckman et al., 2007; Zimmerman, 2008). Larger teams have been found to be linked to better performance and growth in high tech ventures (Eisenhardt and Schoonhoven, 1990). Chandler et al. (2005) demonstrate that larger initial team size provides an advantage for organizations that are not more than five years old. The diversity dimensions that have systematically been studied are different demographic diversity characteristics like gender and age, personality diversity and more directly task-related cognitive (or background) diversity characteristics (Stewart, 2006; Kearney et al., 2009). Following this distinction we focus on demographic, personality and cognitive diversity, respectively.

For spin-off teams having personality diversity may be advantageous because it can be helpful in creating innovative and new insights with respect to technology development, product improvement and marketing tasks. Similar to Kearney et al. (2009), we argue that age diversity is a more appropriate indicator of demographic diversity than gender, ethnicity or nationality in an entrepreneurial setting. Age diversity in management teams reflects a varied set of experiences, views and social ties that may ultimately appear attractive to external financiers.

When tasks are complex and non-routine – as with spin-off development – cognitive diversity should also have a beneficial effect on firm performance (Stewart, 2006; Beckman et al., 2007). Prior research demonstrates that new ventures benefit from having teams that are heterogeneous in educational, functional and industrial backgrounds and include members with diverse start-up, management and international experiences. For instance, Zimmerman (2008) found that diversity in the TMT's educational background is associated with greater capital raised through an initial public offering (IPO). The positive relationship between functional heterogeneity and firm performance has been widely supported in previous new venture studies (Ensley and Hmieleski, 2005; Beckman et al., 2007; Zimmerman, 2008). Diversity in industry backgrounds reflects a varied set of different points of view on technology, competitive tactics and knowledge of how industry operates, all of which may produce innovative solutions, enhanced understanding of customer demands and consequently give competitive advantage to the new venture (Eisenhardt and Schoonhoven, 1990). The positive consequences of diversity in start-up experience are that they may enhance a team member's human capital (Ucbasaran et al., 2003) since many tasks in new ventures are unique and tacit in nature and can only be learned by doing (Shepherd et al., 2000). Diversity in management experience may indicate quality of the management team in a venture, which is one of the major concerns of the VC investors (Wright et al., 2006).

Finally, since academic spin-offs are often based on completely new technologies and enter or even create new markets and industries for their technologies and products, for example, the biotechnology industry (Zucker et al., 1998; Shane, 2004), they are forced to interact with strategic partners and customers across borders. Team members with international experience are better equipped to deal with the uncertainties and ambiguities associated with international operations and are more confident and effective in foreign envi-ronments (Sambharya, 1996). International background diversity may, thus, be a positive signal to potential investors. Hence, variation along all these back-ground characteristics makes a new venture more attractive to external stake-holders and to investors. In summary, we therefore hypothesize:

Hypothesis 2: Management team design characteristics will make an inde-pendent contribution to the venture capital acquisition function in academic spin-offs.

Board Design Characteristics and Venture Capital Acquisition

We contend that board size and diversity among board members are the most important design characteristics that give an advantage to spin-offs when attracting VC financing (Milliken and Martins, 1996). Larger boards may provide a broader set of needed resources, including finance, knowledge and competence, than smaller boards. Gabrielsson and Huse (2002) found that the board size was larger in Swedish VC backed industrial firms compared to non-VC backed firms. Hence, we expect a positive relationship between a large board and company's ability to attract VC.

As with the TMT, we distinguish between demographic (age), personal-ity and cognitive diversity characteristics. The most relevant knowledge and skills of the board are the functional area knowledge and skills that include accounting, finance, marketing and law, and firm-specific knowledge and skills, including the knowledge of how the firm operates, how technology works, how to develop the product and set it into production (Forbes and Milliken, 1999). The board members who represent a broader range of work experience in related industries may make better use of the firm-specific knowledge and skills than the members with almost no or single industry experience. Hence, among cognitive diversity characteristics we emphasize diversity in industry and functional backgrounds as more appropriate design features. We also consider diversity in educational and international back-grounds as important components of board cognitive diversity. Board members with varied industry, education, functional and international back-grounds may have alternative networks with several representatives of the firm's exchange partners and other informants, for example, potential VC investors (Huse, 2007b). Hence, having diverse and well-experienced board members may make a new venture more attractive to VC investors. Therefore, we hypothesize that:

Hypothesis 3: Board design characteristics will make an independent contri-bution to the venture capital acquisition function in academic spin-offs.

DATA AND METHODS

In autumn 2008 a questionnaire was sent to the chief executive officers of 353 companies considered as originating from Norwegian universities and public research institutes. The sample constitutes the 318 companies which are registered as having used the university TTO in the FORNY database. FORNY is a government program designed to increase creation of wealth in Norway by supporting the commercialization of R&D results. The rest of the companies were found in other sources. Anonymity for all informants was assured. Fifty-three firms reported that they are not academic spin-offs or they are no longer active. We received 135 questionnaires. The response rate was 45 percent. Due to missing values, 106 cases were included in the analysis.

We registered 28 firms with VC financing. The firms represent a broad range of industries such as information technology, health, oil and gas, energy and environment, medical and biotechnology, maritime and offshore, and others. As for the innovation degree and scope, 93 firms were highly innovative and the product/service or technology they develop or the markets they aim at are completely new. Ninety-eight firms had a new product/service, technology or market internationally.

Our dependent variable is whether or not the spin-off received funding from a venture capitalist coded as a dummy variable, that is, the firm was allocated a value of 1 if a respondent reported that the firm had received external capital from VC investors, and the firm was allocated a value of 0 if the firm had never received external capital from venture capitalists. We have two separate markers for VC finance: the first is a direct question, the second question addresses how many rounds of VC finance the company has received. When the latter is dichotomously coded, they exhibit a perfect correlation with the employed measure (1.000, $p < 0.001$).

As to independent variables on the financial level, we asked the firms to check a set of alternatives with regard to prior finance. These measures were coded dichotomously into seed capital, industrial capital and private (informal) capital. To measure team member diversity, we asked a respondent to which degree the TMT members represented a variety in the functional background, education, age and so on, on the Likert 7-point scale ranging from 1 (to a very small degree) to 7 (to a very large degree). The index was inspired by Huse's (2007a) comprehensive study of value creating boards. Similar questions were posed with regard to personality, age, education and industry backgrounds, start-up, management and international experience. Team size was measured as the number of persons in the management team. To measure board member heterogeneity, we asked a respondent to which degree the board members represented a variety in the functional background, education, age and so on on the Likert 7-point scale. Board size is the number of members on the board.

We control for firm stage, age and size as larger and older firms may have more resources, experience, more information and relationships (Huse, 2007b). The skills required by a team/board may vary between younger and older firms (Hambrick and Mason, 1984). We used five categories of cycle stages from product development to maturity and declining stages (Kazanjian, 1988). Firm age is the number of years since the business was formally incorporated. Firm size is measured as full-time employment equivalents.

FINDINGS

Hierarchical logistic regression analysis is an appropriate technique when assessing multiple themes against a binary dependent variable. Since we hypothesized on the overall theme level, we present and assess four blocks: the first block includes the control variables, the second block adds the prior financing measures, the third, management team variables and the fourth, the board measures. Thus, three models beyond the control variables are presented in order to assess design characteristics associated with VC acquisitions in academic spin-offs.

Our four step model is shown in Table 10.1.

Model 1 contains the control variables. Model 2 demonstrates support for Hypothesis 1. This model is significant at the 0.001 level. Prior seed and industry funding are both found to be significant at the 0.05 level. Financing by informal investors has apparently no effect on subsequent VC acquisition. In fact, the data indicate that the presence of informal investors may have a negative effect on subsequent VC financing.

Model 3 demonstrates support for Hypothesis 2. This model includes management team member heterogeneity and team size variables. It appears that team size and functional and industry backgrounds are positively associated with attracting VC financing ($p < 0.05$ and $p < 0.1$). Personality diversity is negatively associated with receiving VC financing ($p < 0.1$). Model 4 does not exhibit support for Hypothesis 3, although educational diversity in boards, which is negatively related to VC acquisition, is found to be significant at the 0.05 level.

In summary, prior portfolio seed and industry financing appear to be the predominant predictors of subsequent VC funding. However, cognitive diversity in terms of variation in functional and industry backgrounds and management team size are both associated with VC financing, although team personality diversity and board educational diversity are negatively associated. The presence of the positive relationship for functional background and team size in our findings seems to be in line with the literature on diversity and performance. Meta-analytical studies of teams and performance provide

Table 10.1   Hierarchical logistic regression model results

Variables	Block 1	Block 2	Block 3	Block 4
Firm size	1.00	1.00	0.99	0.99
Firm age	0.98	0.94	0.88	0.84
Cycle stage	0.97	0.86	1.53	1.64
Seed financing		4.63**	3.89*	5.30*
Informal investors		0.84	0.79	0.75
Industrial investors		3.33*	3.40†	5.14*
Team size			1.51*	1.54*
Team diversity in:				
Functional background			1.78*	2.29**
Industry background			1.40	1.59†
Education			0.90	0.94
Start-up experience			1.45	1.44
Management experience			0.82	1.01
International experience			0.86	0.73
Personality			0.68†	0.73
Age			0.80	0.79
Board size				0.89
Board diversity in:				
Functional background				0.86
Industry background				0.89
Education				0.56*
International experience				1.31
Personality				1.00
Age				0.96
Constant				0.02
Model χ^2	0.248	16 296	34 810	42 762
Model χ^2 significance	n.s.	0.012	0.003	0.005
Δ Model χ^2	0.248	16 048	18 514	7 952
Δ Model χ^2 significance	n.s.	0.001	0 030	n.s.
-2 log likelihood	122 151	106 103	87 589	79 640
Overall predictive accuracy	73.6%	75.5%	79.2%	82.1%
Cox & Snell R^2	0.002	0.143	0.280	0.332
Nagelkerke R^2	0.003	0.208	0.409	0.485
Number of firms	106	106	106	106

Notes: † $p < 0.1$, * $p < 0.05$, ** $p < 0.01$.

support for cognitive diversity (for example, functional heterogeneity and so on) being desirable in creative settings, as in an academic spin-off context, which requires the teams' engagement in applying knowledge and expertise in non-routine tasks (Stewart, 2006). Similar support is provided for team size, and is consistent with the notion that additional members are desirable when the team (as in an academic spin-off context) is required to interact with and obtain resources such as supplies and expertise from a complex environment. A negative relationship of personality diversity may be rooted in the conflict. When negative sides of the conflict prevail upon positive (task) conflict on the team it may result in poor performance (Ensley et al., 2002).

While knowledge and skills of the board members are about doing, other characteristics including age and education or school attended are about being (Huse 2007a). Board members may have a good reputation providing firms with prestige and helping with networking and resource tasks, but they do not necessarily need to have relevant education or competence with respect to key issues that spin-offs face (for example, technology development). This may be reflected in the negative relationship of educational diversity. Alternatively, the negative relationship may be due to educational diversity among board members in our context resembling an ascribed (demographic) rather than a more directly task-related (cognitive) characteristic. As shown in meta-analytical group studies, demographic diversity typically has a slightly negative effect (Stewart, 2006).

CONCLUSIONS

This chapter has sought to explore the role of prior finance and a firm's internal human resources embodied in the management team and the board in VC acquisition in academic spin-offs. Our study brings a novel contribution to academic entrepreneurship research by relating early-stage finance and team and board design characteristics to academic spin-off performance. Our investigation also represents a useful addition to the team and governance literature, since little is known about the TMT and the board's role in VC acquisition in high tech new ventures (Ensley and Hmieleski, 2005; Clarysse et al., 2007; Uhlaner et al., 2007; Wright et al., 2007a). Overall, we find that prior portfolio seed and industry financing are the predominant predictors of subsequent VC funding. We find that academic spin-offs with larger teams and higher cognitive diversity previously financed by seed funds and industry are more likely to attract VC funding than academic spin-offs with board educational diversity and with support from informal investors.

The chapter's contribution is manifold. First, we consider early types of financing from the seed funds, informal investors and industry as important predictors of VC acquisition by academic spin-offs. Second, we find that management teams with higher cognitive diversity in terms of functional and industry background are more likely to receive VC funding. These findings extend and refine previous research, confirming that the unique configuration of managerial team resources may usefully predict entrepreneurial success (Beckman et al., 2007; Zimmerman, 2008). Third, as boards in high tech ventures exhibit greater levels of influence on firm development compared to other types of firms (Forbes and Milliken, 1999; Huse, 2007b), we tried to integrate board design features associated with receiving VC financing into our model.

Our findings indicate that previous funding by informal investors does not assure obtaining VC financing. The question is whether it is due to, as it is often assumed, informal investors investing in ventures whose growth prospects are too small to be of interest to venture capitalists (De Clercq et al., 2006). Additional analysis shows that there are no significant differences in perceptually measured growth variables (for example, the firm's satisfaction with performance in terms of market share and firm sales) between the groups of spin-offs financed by informal and VC investors. Hence, this could rather be explained by the nature of the informal investors. They are often interlinked with other informal investors (Sørheim and Landström, 2001; Sørheim, 2003). This means that informal investors probably will be the main source of finance in future financing rounds. Another explanation for this could be that informal investors and entrepreneurs respond negatively to VC terms (which could be considered as negative treatment of current owners). The reader should also bear in mind that in total venture capitalists make very few investments compared to the total of investments from informal investors and only a small fraction of investments from informal investors would be of interest to venture capitalists.

This study has several implications and offers several future research avenues. First, this study suggests that prior seed funding and alliances with industrial partners are positively associated with VC acquisitions. For policy makers, this means that seed funds could be extended and different types of public support schemes could be designed in order to facilitate involvement from strategic industrial partners. Future research could investigate whether there is a 'lock in' effect, meaning that funding from informal investors in early stages is a negative signal to potential VC investors and, thus, an obstacle for obtaining future financing from VC investors. Second, when forming a team, TTOs and entrepreneurs should pay attention to the cognitive diversity. As in other high tech ventures the diversity in functional and industry backgrounds is positively associated with the academic spin-off's ability to attract VC funding. Yet, our results demonstrate that prior portfolio seed and industry financing appear to be the more important predictors of receiving VC financing than a management team's cognitive diversity. This may imply that the management team's ability to accumulate seed and industrial financing prior to seeking VC support plays a greater role than the team's cognitive diversity per se. Future investigations may test this hypothesis. Third, board design characteristics do not appear to be as important as prior finance and TMT design features, yet the overall model remains strong. For future research on boards in high tech firms, this means that the board's role and, particularly, the extent to which the human aspects of the board (not mere control function) contribute to entrepreneurial success is an attractive research path, which needs more systematical investigation.

Our study has a number of limitations. First, our study is cross-sectional, and some of the team and board characteristics found may be attributed to the teams and boards after they have received VC funding. We could partially control for this issue. We performed an additional analysis with the variable that accounts for whether there were changes in the management team after the investment was made and we received similar results as in our main analysis. Yet, future researchers need to attempt to conduct a longitudinal study to ensure the proper sequence of events and characteristics measured. Second, even if this study indicates that cooperation between informal investors and venture capitalists is limited when it comes to investments in academic spin-offs, we still have limited knowledge about this phenomenon. Future studies could address the issues of finance, the TMT and the board in academic spin-offs in more detail. Third, this is a study of Norwegian spin-offs, and more studies could be done in other comparable countries and contexts. For example, risk capital markets in the USA are far more developed compared to Norway. A marketplace with more professional actors might influence the interplay between investors focusing on different stages of the life cycle of a firm.

REFERENCES

Barney, J. (1991), 'Firm resources and sustained competitive advantage', *Journal of Management*, **17**(1), 99–120.
Barney, J. (2001), 'Is the resource-based "view" a useful perspective for strategic management research? Yes', *Academy of Management Review*, **26**(1), 41–56.
Barney, J. and P.M. Wright (1998), 'On becoming a strategic partner: the role of human resources in gaining competitive advantage', *Human Resource Management*, **37**(1), 31–46.
Beckman, C.M., M.D. Burton and C. O'Reilly (2007), 'Early teams: the impact of team demography on VC financing and going public', *Journal of Business Venturing*, **22**(2), 147–73.
Chandler, G.N., B. Honig and J. Wiklund (2005), 'Antecedents, moderators, and performance consequences of membership change in new venture teams', *Journal of Business Venturing*, **20**(5), 705–25.

Clarysse, B., M. Knockaert and A. Lockett (2007), 'Outside board composition in high tech start-ups', *Small Business Economics*, **29**(3), 243–60.

Cohen, S.G. and D.E. Bailey (1997), 'What makes teams work: group effectiveness research from the shop floor to the executive suite', *Journal of Management*, **23**(3), 239–90.

De Clercq, D., V. Fried, O. Lehtonen and H.J. Sapienza (2006), 'An entrepreneur's guide to the venture capital galaxy', *Academy of Management Perspectives*, **20**(3), 90–112.

Djokovic, D. and V. Souitaris (2008), 'Spinouts from academic institutions. A literature review with suggestions for further research', *Journal of Technology Transfer*, **33**(3), 225–47.

Douglas, E.J. and D. Shepherd (2002), 'Exploring investor readiness: assessments by entrepreneurs and investors in Australia', *Venture Capital*, **4**(3), 219–36.

Eisenhardt, K.M. and C.B. Schoonhoven (1990), 'Organizational growth: linking founding team, strategy, environment, and growth among U.S. semiconductor ventures 1978–1988', *Administrative Science Quarterly*, **35**(3), 504–29.

Ensley, M.D. and K.M. Hmieleski (2005), 'A comparative study of new venture top management team composition, dynamics and performance between university-based and independent start-ups', *Research Policy*, **34**(7), 1091–105.

Ensley, M.D., A.W. Pearson and A.C. Amason (2002), 'Understanding the dynamics of new venture top management teams: cohesion, conflict, and new venture performance', *Journal of Business Venturing*, **17**(4), 365–86.

Feldman, M.P., A.N. Link and D.S. Siegel (2002), *The Economics of Science and Technology: An Overview of Initiatives to Foster Innovation, Entrepreneurship, and Economic Growth*, Boston, MA: Kluwer Academic Publishers.

Filatotchev, I., S. Toms and M. Wright (2006), 'The firm's strategic dynamics and corporate governance life-cycle', *International Journal of Managerial Finance*, **2**(4), 256–79.

Forbes, D.P. and F.J. Milliken (1999), 'Cognition and corporate governance: understanding boards of directors as strategic decision-making groups', *Academy of Management Review*, **24**(3), 489–505.

Gabrielsson, J. and M. Huse (2002), 'The venture capitalist and the board of directors in SMEs: roles and processes', *Venture Capital*, **4**(2), 125–46.

Hambrick, D. and P. Mason (1984), 'Upper echelons: the organization as a reflection of its top managers', *Academy of Management Review*, **9**(2), 193–206.

Huse, M. (2007a), *Styret: Tante, barbar eller klan?*, Bergen, Norway: Fagbokforlaget.

Huse, M. (2007b), *Boards, Governance and Value Creation: The Human Side of Corporate Governance*, Cambridge: Cambridge University Press.

Kazanjian, R.K. (1988), 'Relation of dominant problems to stages of growth in technology-based new ventures', *Academy of Management Journal*, **31**(2), 257–79.

Kearney, E., D. Gebert and S.C. Voelpel (2009), 'When and how diversity benefits team – the importance of team members' need for cognition', *Academy of Management Journal*, **52**(3), 581–98.

Leleux, B. and B. Surlemont (2003), 'Public versus private venture capital: seeding or crowding out? A pan-European analysis', *Journal of Business Venturing*, **18**(1). 81–104.

Lerner, J. (2002), 'When bureaucrats meet entrepreneurs: the design of effective "public venture capital" programmes', *Economic Journal*, **112**(477), 73–84.

Mason, C. and R. Harrison (2002), 'Is it worth it? The rates of return from informal venture capital investments', *Journal of Business Venturing*, **17**(3), 211–36.

Milliken, F.J. and L.L. Martins (1996), 'Searching for common threads: understanding the multiple effects of diversity in organizational groups', *Academy of Management Review*, **21**(2), 402–33.

Murray, G. (2007), 'Venture capital and government policy', in H. Landström (ed.), *Handbook of Research on Venture Capital*, Cheltenham, UK and Northampton, MA, USA: Edward Elgar, pp. 98–123.

O'Shea, R.P., T.J. Allen, A. Chevalier and F. Roche (2005), 'Entrepreneurial orientation, technology transfer and spinoff performance of U.S. universities', *Research Policy*, **34**(7), 994–1009.

Rothaermel, F.T., S.D. Agung and L. Jiang (2007), 'University entrepreneurship: a taxonomy of the literature', *Industrial and Corporate Change*, **16**(4), 691–791.

Sambharya, R.B. (1996), 'Foreign experience of top management teams and international diversification strategies of U.S. multinational corporations', *Strategic Management Journal*, **17**(9), 739–46.

Shane, S. (2004), *Academic Entrepreneurship: University Spinoffs and Wealth Creation*, Cheltenham, UK and Northampton, MA, USA: Edward Elgar.

Shane, S. and T. Stuart (2002), 'Organizational endowments and the performance of university start-ups', *Management Science*, **48**(1), 157–70.

Shepherd, D.A., E.J. Douglas and M. Shanley (2000), 'New venture survival: ignorance, external shocks, and risk reduction strategies', *Journal of Business Venturing*, **15**(5–6), 393–410.

Sørheim, R. (2003), 'The pre-investment behaviour of business angels: a social capital approach', *Venture Capital*, **5**(4), 337–64.

Sørheim, R. (2005), 'Business angels as facilitators for further finance – an exploratory study', *Journal of Small Business and Enterprise Development*, **12**(2), 178–90.

Sørheim, R. and H. Landström (2001), 'Informal investors – a categorization, with policy implications', *Entrepreneurship and Regional Development*, **13**(4), 351–70.

Stewart, G.L. (2006), 'A meta-analytic review of relationships between team design features and team performance', *Journal of Management*, **32**(1), 29–55.

Ucbasaran, D., A. Lockett, M. Wright and P. Westhead (2003), 'Entrepreneurial founder teams: factors associated with member entry and exit', *Entrepreneurship Theory and Practice*, **28**(2), 107–27.

Uhlaner, L., M. Wright and M. Huse (2007), 'Private firms and corporate governance: an integrated economic and management perspective', *Small Business Economics*, **29**(3), 225–41.

Westhead, P. and D. Storey (1997), 'Financial constraints on the growth of high technology small firms in the UK', *Applied Financial Economics*, **7**, 197–201.

Wright, M., A. Vohora and A. Lockett (2004), 'The formation of high-tech university spinouts: the role of joint ventures and venture capital investors', *Journal of Technology Transfer*, **29** (3–4), 287–310.

Wright, M., A. Lockett, B. Clarysse and M. Binks (2006), 'University spin-out companies and venture capital', *Research Policy*, **35**(4), 481–501.

Wright, M., K.M. Hmieleski, D.S. Siegel and M.D. Ensley (2007a), 'The role of human capital in technological entrepreneurship', *Entrepreneurship Theory and Practice*, **31**(6), 791–806.

Wright, M., B. Clarysse, P. Mustar and A. Lockett (2007b), *Academic Entrepreneurship in Europe*, Cheltenham, UK and Northampton, MA, USA: Edward Elgar.

Zimmerman, M.A. (2008), 'The influence of top management team heterogeneity on the capital raised through an initial public offering', *Entrepreneurship Theory and Practice*, **32**(3), 391–414.

Zucker, L.G., M.R. Darby and M.B. Brewer (1998), 'Intellectual human capital and the birth of U.S. biotechnology enterprises', *American Economic Review*, **88**(1), 290–306.

PART IV

Growth and early stage financing

11. Exploring the venture capitalist/ entrepreneur relationship: the effect of conflict upon confidence in partner cooperation

Truls Erikson and Andrew Zacharakis

INTRODUCTION

The entrepreneurship literature has long explored how venture capitalists (VCs) add value after they have made an investment in an entrepreneur's company (for example, Sapienza, 1992; Cable and Shane, 1997). Timmons and Bygrave (1986) propose that the cooperative relationship between a VC and entrepreneur is more important to the success of the business than the capital itself. Yet much can interfere in the relationship and impede its effectiveness, such as the threat of opportunism (Williamson, 1985) that both parties to the deal face (Cable and Shane, 1997). From a strong agency perspective, the underlying assumption is that the entrepreneur (agent) is motivated to act opportunistically to the detriment of the VC (principal) (Sahlman, 1990). The threat of opportunistic behavior lowers confidence in partner cooperation which refers to the perceived level of certainty that one's partner will pursue mutually compatible interests in the relationship (Das and Teng, 1998). While self-interested behavior to the detriment of the other party is a problem, cooperation can also be hampered when both parties are acting in good faith. Conflict can also impede efficiency in the relationship. Whenever two parties cooperate, there is potential for conflict in both the means (strategy) and ends (goals) that they hope to accomplish (Jehn, 1997; Jehn and Mannix, 2001). In highly uncertain environments, such as those categorized around new venture funding, the possibility of conflict increases, especially as ventures face unexpected difficulties and bumps in the road (Sapienza and Gupta, 1994). As such, conflict within the VC/entrepreneur dyad is to be expected (Higashide and Birley, 2002; Parhankangas and Landström, 2004). Conflict is not necessarily negative. Amason (1996) points out that conflict can improve decision quality as people challenge each other and better alternatives are developed. However, conflict can potentially damage consensus and create a negative affective environment. Such affective conflict diminishes confidence in partner cooperation and hinders the ability of VCs to add value to the entrepreneur and venture.

The current chapter follows the lead of Higashide and Birley (2002) and Parhankangas and Landström (2004) and investigates conflict within the VC/entrepreneur dyad. From a survey of VCs, Higashide and Birley (2002) find that conflict does exist and can have both a positive and a negative impact on venture performance depending on the type of conflict that occurs. Parhankangas and Landström (2004) use a broader definition of conflict, terming it as contract violations, ranging from disagreement on goals and means all the way to opportunism. In their survey of 78 Nordic VCs they find that the VC's reaction to the contract violation is a function of the severity of that violation. Disagreements, which are similar to the good faith conflicts explored by Higashide and Birley (2002) and in the current chapter, tend to lead to more constructive VC responses such as voicing the VC's opinion and working towards a resolution, or silence, which is hoping that the situation will turn out well.

The current chapter contributes to this previous work in several ways. First, we capture conflict from the perspective of the entrepreneur rather than the VC. As such, we examine whether entrepreneurs view conflict similarly or differently from VCs which helps complete the picture that Higashide and Birley (2002) and Parhankangas and Landström (2004) started to develop. Our second contribution is adding process conflict into the equation (Jehn, 1997). While Higashide and Birley (2002) examine the interplay of cognitive conflict (how best to achieve common goals) and affective conflict (dysfunctional and emotional conflict which arises from incompatibilities), this chapter also looks at process conflict (who is responsible for what tasks). For example, it is easy to envision that the entrepreneur would believe that the VC should lead the effort to seek new financing, whereas the VC might feel that this is the entrepreneur's responsibility. In such a situation process conflict would arise. Our final contribution goes beyond conflict between the entrepreneur and VC (intergroup conflict) and examines how intragroup conflict within the entrepreneurial team impacts the team's relationship with the VC. Specifically, we expect that higher levels of conflict within the entrepreneurial team will carry over and increase conflict between the entrepreneur and VC. Ensley et al. (2002) find that negative affective conflict is more likely the lower the cohesion of the founding team. This is problematic according to Amason (1996) because teams with weak consensus have difficulty implementing decisions effectively. Therefore, a conflicted entrepreneurial team may have greater conflict with its value added partner, the VC. To the best of our knowledge, this is the first research that looks at how intragroup conflict interacts with intergroup conflict when looking beyond the organization's boundaries.

THEORETICAL DEVELOPMENT

Information processing theory (Carnvale and Probst, 1998) looks at how people make decisions (Anderson, 1990). A simplified model of information processing (Barr et al., 1992) describes decisions as a function of what information attracts a person's attention, how that information is interpreted and what actions follow from that interpretation. Many decisions within an organization involve several people who gather and share information. Conflict may encourage or impede the full and systematic evaluation of all the pertinent information surrounding a decision, depending on the type of conflict, the intensity and the context surrounding the decision (De Dreu, 2007).

Intergroup Conflict

Extensive research speculates that cognitive conflict (how to best achieve common goals) improves decision quality because it encourages people to challenge each other's assumptions and collectively find innovative solutions (for example, Tjosvold, 1997; Schulz-Hardt et al., 2002). In the case of the VC/entrepreneur dyad, the common goal is to fuel the growth of the venture. Higashide and Birley (2002) found that cognitive conflict is indeed beneficial in the VC/entrepreneur dyad during the post-investment period. Specifically, cognitive conflict on the goals of the venture was found to positively impact performance. However, De Dreu and Weingart (2003) conducted a meta-analysis on previous research and found that cognitive conflict has a negative impact on performance and team satisfaction except at very low levels of conflict. They suggested this finding holds for both routine and non-routine tasks. The question becomes why the Higashide and Birley (2002) results differ from De Dreu and Weingart's (2003) meta-analysis.

De Dreu (2007) suggests that cognitive conflict is more effective the more complex the task. In complex tasks where the parties perceive outcome interdependence they are more likely to share information and learn from each other, which should lead to greater cooperation. Growing an entrepreneurial venture fits the complexity criterion (Zahra et al., 2006). The venture needs to build and grow an organization, develop and refine a product or service and solicit new customers, all while suffering from the liability of newness (Stinchcombe, 1965). Olson et al. (2007) offer another critique of the De Dreu and Weingart (2003) meta-analysis saying that most of the included studies look at lower level employees. When looking at top management teams, Olson et al. (2007, p. 202) argue that these managers have more experience dealing with conflict and have learned to 'separate the meaning from the message'. Thus, more experienced business people dealing with a complex task are seeking more information so as to develop innovative strategies to succeed. That means they are inclined to solicit input, both positive and negative, and consider that information in the decision. So while cognitive conflict is expected to impact how people perceive and interpret information often result-ing in certain information being ignored or discarded (Carnvale and Probst, 1998), more recent research suggests that skilled business people operating in a complex environment perceive more information when moderate levels of cognitive conflict are present (De Dreu, 2007; Olsen et al., 2007).

VCs are experienced business people, experts in funding and growing new ventures (Shepherd and Zacharakis, 2001). Likewise, entrepreneurs who secure VC financing are likely more sophisticated and experienced, or often bring on a more experienced CEO as a condition for receiving the financing (Rosenstein et al., 1993). So theory would suggest that moderate levels of cognitive conflict should improve confidence in cooperation. However, there are some reasons to expect that cognitive conflict could be negative in the new venture context. First, entrepreneurs are emotionally attached to their ventures (Baron, 1998) so they might misinterpret or feel threatened by the VC's input. Second, there is relatively lower cohesion between the VC and the entrepre-neur than is true for top management teams. Ensley et al. (2002) find that high levels of cohesion minimize the negative effect of cognitive conflict, but VCs and entrepreneurs have less time to form a cohesive bond than is the case for the venture founders.

Theory around the direction of cognitive conflict is mixed. There is evidence to expect cognitive conflict to have a positive impact on confidence in coopera-tion, namely the nature of the task and the skilled, experienced parties involved. There is also evidence to suggest a negative impact such as the strong emotional attachment that entrepreneurs have to their venture and the lower cohesion between the VC and the entrepreneur relative to cohesion within top manage-ment teams. Based upon this mixed evidence, we hypothesize the relationship both ways. This discussion leads to the following hypotheses:

Hypothesis 1a: Cognitive conflict is positively associated with confidence in partner cooperation.
Hypothesis 1b: Cognitive conflict is negatively associated with confidence in partner cooperation.

Process conflict, which refers to differences in preference in how the parties will achieve the task (Jehn and Mannix, 2001), can also impede confidence in cooperation. When growing a venture, there are many tasks that need to be accomplished. Entrepreneurs have certain expectations on how and where VCs should help. Timmons and Sapienza (1994) surveyed entrepreneurs asking them about the roles that VCs should play in the partnership. They found three categories around strategy, social support and networking.

Entrepreneurs felt that the greatest value added that a VC could offer was around strategic decisions. Entrepreneurs seem to feel that the biggest gap between expectations and VC effectiveness involves the VC's help in recruiting new team members and networking to important industry contacts (Timmons and Sapienza, 1994). From an information processing perspective, process conflict can lead to distorted information flows as entrepreneurs perceive that VCs should take certain actions (and vice versa) and each party adjusts their own conduct accordingly. In situations where process conflict exists it will have a negative impact on confidence in partner cooperation. This leads to the next hypothesis:

Hypothesis 2: The presence of process conflict is negatively associated with confidence in partner cooperation.

Affective conflict (dysfunctional and emotional conflict which arises from incompatibilities) can also impede cooperation. This threat is particularly heightened in the VC/entrepreneur dyad because unlike conflict within the founding team, cohesion is likely lower due to the shorter tenure of the relationship (Ensley et al., 2002). Affective conflict is individual oriented disagreements arising from personal disaffection. Amason and Schweiger (1994) say affective conflict is emotional and dysfunctional and can lead to distrust and hostility within the team. Entrepreneurs are emotionally attached to their venture (Baron, 1998) and the very negotiation that brings the entrepreneur and VC together can lead to affective feelings (Shepherd and Zacharakis, 2001). In the VC/entrepreneur dyad affective conflict might lead to confrontation and the firing of key members of the entrepreneurial team (Bruton et al., 2000) or avoidance. In either case both parties will likely have lower confidence in the other's actions leading to poor performance.

Affective conflicts are detrimental to individual and group performance and the likelihood that a group will work together in the future (Shah and Jehn, 1993; Jehn and Mannix, 2001). Applied to the VC/entrepreneur context, there is empirical support that affective conflict will result in a detrimental effect in the relationship between the VC and the entrepreneur (Higashide and Birley, 2002). Affective conflict is also expected to interfere with task-related efforts as the parties will focus on reducing threats, increasing power and attempting to build cohesion rather than working on the task (Jehn, 1997). Thus, from an information processing perspective, affective conflict encourages parties to withhold information from each other and to interpret exchanged information in a biased manner. Accordingly, the following hypothesis:

Hypothesis 3: The presence of affective conflict is negatively associated with confidence in partner cooperation.

De Dreu and Weingart (2003) conducted a meta-analysis on the relationship between affective and cognitive conflict with performance measured as team performance and member satisfaction. They found strong and negative relationships between the affective components and team performance and member satisfaction. Thus, there is a very real danger that cognitive and process conflict could lead to affective conflict. Accordingly, the following two hypotheses:

Hypothesis 4a: Task conflict is highly associated with affective conflict.
Hypothesis 4b: Process conflict is highly associated with affective conflict.

Intragroup Conflict

To this point we have focused solely on the conflict between the entrepreneur and the VC. This assumes that the VC/entrepreneur relationship is in a vacuum, but there is another relationship central to the success of the venture and that is within the entrepreneurial team. How does conflict between the VC and the entrepreneur interact with conflict on the entrepreneurial team? Carnvale and Probst (1998) conducted an experiment where groups of individuals needed to act cooperatively in order to win prizes over competing groups. They found that intergroup competition led to greater intragroup cooperation. Without that intergroup competition the level of conflict within teams tends to be higher and more negatively related to performance (Carnvale and Probst, 1998). In a sense, entrepreneurs are in competition with VCs to get the best valuation possible. We expect that this pre-investment mentality carries through to the post-investment period, diminishing over time as the entrepreneur and VC build trust in each other (Shepherd and Zacharakis, 2001). This competition with the VC could lead to greater cohesion within the entrepreneurial team and lower intragroup conflict.

On the other hand, if there is already intragroup conflict, it can lead to stress within the entrepreneurial team and suboptimal decision processes (Ellis, 2006). From an information process perspective, teams under stress have difficulty communicating effectively and generally communicate less (Driskell and Johnston, 1998). Considering the interdependent nature of teams, the lower the level of communication may lead to conflict as different team members perceive that information is being purposely withheld (Shepherd and Zacharakis, 2001). Das and Teng (1998) assert that frequent and open communication strengthens commitment between parties. Open communication also aids research and discovery (Sheppard and Sherman, 1998). Thus, stress hinders communication which lowers trust and commitment to each other within the team.

The tension within the entrepreneurial team (intragroup) leads to tension between the entrepreneur and VC (intergroup). Labianca et al. (1998) find that low intragroup cohesiveness is significantly related to higher perceptions of intergroup conflict. This intragroup tension may lead to cognitive conflict in the VC/entrepreneur dyad as the entrepreneur may be preoccupied with how to manage the intragroup stress. Ellis (2006) finds that transactive memory, defined as the distributed memory and expertise across team members, is hindered by stress and may impede the sharing of cognitive processes. In other words, the entrepreneur may not fully engage the VC, leading to cognitive conflict. Intragroup stress can also lead to process conflict in that the entrepreneur may have unrealistic expectations of what role the VC should take in advising and assisting the entrepreneurial team. Finally, it may enhance affective conflict as the stress heightens the entrepreneur's emotional state.

As such, we expect that intragroup conflict leads to intergroup conflict. We also assert that conflict within the entrepreneurial team will lead to lower confidence in cooperation in the VC/entrepreneur dyad as the VC becomes aware and concerned about how that stress will influence the entrepreneur's ability to execute the plan. This leads to our last series of hypotheses.

Hypotheses 5abc: Intragroup conflict is positively associated with various intergroup conflicts.
Hypothesis 5d: Intragroup conflict is negatively associated with confidence in intergroup cooperation.

METHODOLOGY

The dataset originates from a survey mailed to the CEOs of 240 portfolio companies of Norwegian venture capital funds. Seventy companies returned their questionnaire. Due to some missing data, we have intact data from 58 companies (an effective response rate of 24 percent). We use multiple regressions in the assessment of the hypothesized relationships.

Main Dependent Variable

Directly measuring partner cooperation represents a challenge because it is difficult to quantify it. In this study we capture the entrepreneur's perception or confidence in partner cooperation. It is measured with the 'reliance on relational norm' construct advocated by Zhang et al. (2003). The Chronbach alpha is 0.800. Principal component analysis (PCA) was employed to reduce the items into an overall measure.

Independent Variables

When measuring intragroup conflict within the new venture management team (ENT), we used pre-tested measurement items from Jehn and Mannix (2001) that originate from the Intragroup Conflict Scale (Jehn, 1995). PCA was employed to reduce the nine items into a general conflict measure which is labeled general intrateam conflict. Chronbach's alpha is 0.916.

When measuring the various types of intergroup conflict between the entrepreneur and the VC, we used interpersonal conflict measurement items from Jehn and Mannix (2001) as measures for affective conflict. When measuring cognitive conflict, we used Sapienza's (1992) divergence of perspective measures and we used process conflict measures from Shah and Jehn (1993). Chronbach's alphas are well beyond the recommended 0.70 (Nunnally, 1967).

RESULTS

Table 11.1 shows correlations, means and the standard deviations for the computed variables (multiple items were aggregated and averaged). It can be seen that the cognitive and affective conflict types co-vary significantly and negatively with confidence in partner cooperation. It can also be seen that general intragroup conflict co-varies significantly and positively with all the VC/entrepreneur conflict types. Table 11.1 also shows that those management teams which perceive an affective conflict with the VC also have an internal conflict within the management team.

The results of the regression analysis are shown in Table 11.2. We do not find support for Hypothesis 1a which suggests that cognitive conflict has a direct positive effect on confidence in partner cooperation. On the contrary, we find strong support for Hypothesis 2b which asserts that cognitive conflict has a direct negative effect on confidence in partner cooperation.

Table 11.1   Descriptive statistics and Pearson's product moment correlations

N = 57	Mean	SD	1	2	3	4
1. CPC	0.00	1.00				
2. ENT intrateam conflict	2.52	1.16	−0.178			
3. ENT/VC affective conflict	2.16	1.07	−0.384	0.579		
4. ENT/VC cognitive conflict	3.05	1.43	−0.489	0.324	0.561	
5. ENT/VC process conflict	1.75	0.73	−0.066	0.398	0.491	0.297

Note: Except for confidence in partner cooperation (CPC), these variables are based on manually aggregated and averaged items. Correlations larger than +/− 0.258 are significant at the 0.05 level. Correlations larger than +/− 0.324 are significant at the 0.01 level (two-tailed).

Table 11.2   Results from regression analyses on the two dependent variables

Dependent variables:	Affective conflict	CPC
Independent variables		
ENT intrateam conflict		0.044
ENT/VC affective conflict		−0.454***
ENT/VC process conflict	0.355**	0.040
ENT/VC cognitive conflict	0.456***	−0.305*
R^2	0.430	0.283
Adj. R^2	0.409	0.228
F	20.390***	5.134***

Note: * $p < 0.05$, ** $p < 0.01$, *** $p < 0.001$ (VIF measures ranging from 1.038 to 1.599). The regression analysis with affective conflict as the dependent variable uses manually aggregated and averaged items as independent variables. The regression analysis with confidence in partner cooperation (CPC) as dependent variable has factorized variables (principal components) as input variables.

We do not find support for Hypothesis 2 which addresses the relationship between process conflict and confidence in partner cooperation. However, we do find support for Hypothesis 3 which examines the negative relationship between affective conflict and confidence in partner cooperation. Moreover, we find strong support for Hypotheses 4a and 4b which look at the relationship between cognitive and process conflict's effect on affective conflict, and thus their indirect effect on confidence in partner cooperation.

With regard to Hypotheses 5a–d, we find that general intragroup conflict in the management team influences confidence in partner cooperation indirectly through their effect on various conflict types in the VC/entrepreneur relationship. Thus we have support for Hypotheses 5a, 5b and 5c. However, we do not find support for Hypothesis 5d regarding the direct effect of general intragroup conflict on confidence in partner cooperation.

DISCUSSION

This study supports the idea that strong debates within the VC/entrepreneur dyad are highly associated with affective conflict which leads to negative relationship (Hypotheses 4a and 4b), supporting the contention that cognitive and process conflict affects the relationship indirectly. Our study is also in line with De Dreu and Weingart's (2003) meta-analysis that implies that cognitive conflict often results in affective conflict. Conflict has a stronger negative relationship with team performance in highly complex tasks (De Dreu and Weingart, 2003) which typifies the new venture environment (Sapienza and Gupta, 1994). While team cohesion can reduce the probability that cognitive conflict will result in affective conflict (Ensley et al., 2002), cohesion within the VC/entrepreneur dyad is likely low. First, VCs and entrepreneurs often have limited prior experience with each other, so relationship tenure is low. Second, entrepreneurs are conflicted in accepting VC investment because of the equity and control they must relinquish, which may lead entrepreneurs to keep information from the VCs (Shepherd and Zacharakis, 2001). This information asymmetry inhibits strengthening cohesion within the dyad.

The current study goes beyond the work of Higashide and Birley (2002) and Parhankangas and Landström (2004) by looking at how general intragroup conflict is related to intergroup conflict (Hypotheses 5a–c). General intragroup conflict is highly correlated with intergroup conflict across all dimensions, on cognitive, affective and process conflict. Similar to Ellis (2006), we suspect that intragroup conflict creates stress within the entrepreneurial team that is transferred and creates intergroup conflict. Part of the explanation may be that Carnvale and Probst (1998) examined intra/intergroup conflict within the confines of a large existing corporation. Small work groups within that organization are competing for favor higher up the hierarchy. Thus, individuals within that group recognize that cooperation will better allow them to gain that recognition. Within the domain of the current study the VC/entrepreneurial team investment process is adversarial. Members of the entrepreneurial team may have felt differently about how well the company made out in the negotiations and these different perspectives can create emotional stress that continues during the post-investment period. This is the first work to our knowledge that looks at intra/intergroup conflict between two separate entities (the entrepreneur and the VC) that are partnering for mutual benefit.

The current research suggests that general intragroup conflict is highly correlated with intergroup conflict which may lead to affective conflict. As suggested in the discussion section, the adversarial nature of the pre-investment process can continue into the post-investment phase. Thus, structuring the relationship in purely contractual terms can lead to problems. Both VCs and entrepreneurs need to work with each other to build trust (Shepherd and Zacharakis, 2001) which should increase cohesion (Ensley et al., 2002). That process begins in the pre-investment phase. Considering the likelihood for some difficulties in the new venture creation process, it is particularly important for VCs and entrepreneurs to manage their conflicts.

Like all research, this study has limitations. First, in the validity assessment a few conflict items did not load as expected, which is always a challenge. This may be due to weak wording, or simply minor cultural differences due to differences in language. Another issue is that it may have been difficult for respondents to separate the meaning in all items posed. Second, the employed cross-sectional research design only demonstrates correlations, and directionality is thus argued from a theoretical point of view. As such, the current cross-sectional study matches other studies (Ensley et al., 2002; Higashide and Birley, 2002). Although longitudinal studies are preferred, the very nature of the addressed relationships does not facilitate a longitudinal inquiry because longitudinal data with this level of sensitivity/confidentiality are extremely difficult to collect as one basically excavates into what may be perceived as personally and potentially conflicting issues. Moreover, future studies should look into the combined effect of the various types of conflicts. For instance, cognitive conflict may be perceived as positive for confidence in partner cooperation, but together with affective conflict, the very same level of cognitive conflict may then be perceived differently. Hence, future research should also seek to address the interactional effects of various types of conflicts.

The current study does not extend into performance. As demonstrated in this study, the likely beneficial effects of good faith disagreements regarding means and ends remain largely unresolved, although we have generated some valuable insights.

CONCLUSION

In this chapter we have demonstrated that conflict is detrimental to the relationship between the VC and the entrepreneur and make three contributions. First, whereas Higashide and Birley (2002) and Parhankangas and Landström (2004) looked at conflict from the VC's point of view, we find that the entrepreneur perspective views cognitive conflict as detrimental. Implications for investors and entrepreneurs are to be cautious in how they handle (good faith) disagreements, as they may turn into often irreparable, affective conflicts. Second, we look at process conflict within the VC/entrepreneur dyad. Although we do not find a direct correlation with confidence in partner cooperation, it has an indirect negative effect through the affective conflict component. Finally, this study looks at how general intragroup conflict can transfer and lead to intergroup conflict. Considering that the volatile environment surrounding new ventures is conducive to conflict, more research needs to be conducted on how conflict can be effectively managed in the VC/entrepreneur dyad.

REFERENCES

Amason, A.C. (1996), 'Distinguishing the effects of functional and dysfunctional conflict on strategic decision making: resolving a paradox for top management teams', *Academy of Management Journal*, **391**, 123–48.

Amason, A.C. and D. Schweiger (1994), 'Resolving the paradox of conflict, strategic decision making, and organizational performance', *International Journal of Conflict Management*, **53**, 239–53.

Anderson, J. (1990), *Cognitive Psychology and its Implications*, New York: W.H. Freeman.

Baron, R. (1998), 'Cognitive mechanisms in entrepreneurship: why and when entrepreneurs think differently than other people', *Journal of Business Venturing*, **134**, 275–94.

Barr, P., J. Stimpert and A. Huff (1992), 'Cognitive change, strategic action, and organizational renewal', *Strategic Management Journal*, **13**, 15–36.

Bruton, G., V. Fried and R. Hisrich (2000), 'CEO dismissal in venture capital-backed firms: further evidence from an agency perspective', *Entrepreneurship Theory and Practice*, **244**, 69–78.

Cable, D. and S. Shane (1997), 'A prisoner's dilemma approach to the entrepreneur-venture capitalist relationship', *Academy of Management Review*, **22**, 142–76.

Carnvale, P. and T. Probst (1998), 'Social values and social conflict in creative problem solving and categorization', *Journal of Personality and Social Psychology*, **745**, 1300–309.

Das, T. K. and B. Teng (1998), 'Between trust and control: developing confidence in partner cooperation in alliances', *Academy of Management Review*, **233**, 491–512.

De Dreu, C. (2007), 'Cooperative outcome interdependence, task reflexivity, and team effectiveness: a motivated information processing perspective', *Journal of Applied Psychology*, **923**, 628–38.

De Dreu, C. and L. Weingart (2003), 'Task versus relationship conflict, team performance, and team member satisfaction: a meta-analysis', *Journal of Applied Psychology*, **884**, 741–9.

Driskell, J. and J. Johnston (1998), 'Stress exposure in training', in J. Cannon-Bowers and E. Sales (eds), *Making Decisions Under Stress: Implications for Individual and Team Training*, Washington, DC: American Psychological Association, pp. 191–218.

Ellis, A. (2006), 'System breakdown: the role of mental models and transactive memory in the relationship between acute stress and team performance', *Academy of Management Journal*, **493**, 376–89.

Ensley, M., A. Pearson and A. Amason (2002), 'Understanding the dynamics of new venture top management teams: cohesion, conflict, and new venture performance', *Journal of Business Venturing*, **174**, 365–86.

Higashide, H. and S. Birley (2002), 'The consequences of conflict between the venture capitalist and the entrepreneurial team in the United Kingdom from the perspective of the venture capitalist', *Journal of Business Venturing*, **17**, 59–81.

Jehn, K. (1995), 'A multimethod examination of the benefits and detriments of intragroup conflict', *Administrative Science Quarterly*, **40**, 256–82.

Jehn, K. (1997), 'A qualitative analysis of conflict types and dimensions in organizational groups', *Administrative Science Quarterly*, **42**, 530–57.

Jehn, K. and E. Mannix (2001), 'The dynamic nature of conflict. A longitudinal study of intragroup conflict and group performance', *Academy of Management Journal*, **442**, 238–51.

Labianca, G., D. Brass and B. Gray (1998), 'Social networks and perceptions of intergroup conflict: the role of negative relationships and third parties', *Academy of Management Journal*, **411**, 55–67.

Nunnally, J.C. (1967), *Psychometric Theory*, New York: McGraw-Hill.

Olson, B., S. Parayitam and Y. Bao (2007), 'Strategic decision making: the effects of cognitive diversity, conflict, and trust on decision outcomes', *Journal of Management*, **332**, 196–222.

Parhankangas, A. and H. Landström (2004), 'Responses to psychological contract violations in the entrepreneur-venture capitalist relationship: an exploratory study', *Venture Capital: An International Journal of Entrepreneurial Finance*, **64**, 217–42.

Rosenstein, J., A. Bruno and W. Bygrave (1993), 'The CEO, venture capitalists and the board', *Journal of Business Venturing*, **82**, 99–113.

Sahlman, W. (1990), 'The structure and governance of venture capital organizations', *Journal of Financial Economics*, **27**, 473–521.

Sapienza, H. (1992), 'When do venture capitalists add value', *Journal of Business Venturing*, **71**, 9–27.

Sapienza, H. and A. Gupta (1994), 'Impact of agency risks and task uncertainty on venture capitalists-CEO interaction', *Academy of Management Journal*, **376**, 1618–32.

Schulz-Hardt, S., M. Jochims and D. Frey (2002), 'Productive conflict in group decision making: germaine and contrived dissent as strategies to counteract biased information seeking', *Organizational Behavior and Human Decision Processes*, **88**, 563–86.

Shah, P. and K. Jehn (1993), 'Do friends perform better than acquaintances? The interaction of friendship, conflict and task', *Group Decision and Negotiation*, **2**, 149–66.

Shepherd, D.A. and A. Zacharakis (2001), 'The venture capitalist-entrepreneur relationship; control, trust and confidence in co-operative behavior', *Venture Capital*, **32**, 129–49.

Sheppard, B. and D. Sherman (1998), 'The grammars of trust: a model and general implications', *Academy of Management Review*, **233**, 422–37.

Stinchcombe, A. (1965), 'Social structure and organizations', in J. March (ed.), *Handbook of Organizations*, Chicago, IL: Rand McNally, pp. 142–93.

Timmons, J. and W. Bygrave (1986), 'Venture capital's role in financing innovation for growth', *Journal of Business Venturing*, **12**, 161–76.

Timmons, J. and H. Sapienza (1994), 'Venture capital: more than money', in S.E. Pratt and J.K. Morris (eds), *Pratt's Guide to Venture Capital Resources*, Oryx Press, 49–55.

Tjosvold, D. (1997), 'Conflict within interdependence: its value for productivity and individuality', in C. De Dreu and E. Van de Vllert (eds), *Using Conflict in Organizations*, London: Sage, pp. 23–37.

Williamson, O. (1985), *The Economic Institutions of Capitalism: Firms, Markets, Relational Contracting*, New York: Free Press.

Zahra, S., H. Sapienza and P. Davidsson (2006), 'Entrepreneurship and dynamic capabilities: a review, model and research agenda', *Journal of Management Studies*, **434**, 917–55.

Zhang, C., S.T. Cavusgil and A.S. Roath (2003), 'Manufacturer governance of foreign distributor relationships: do relational norms enhance competitiveness in the export market?', *Journal of International Business Studies*, **34**, 550–66.

12. New business founders: perceptions about and the use of external funding

Roger Sørheim and Espen J. Isaksen

INTRODUCTION

Throughout the last three decades there have been a number of studies indicating that small and medium-sized enterprises (SMEs) are the most important contributors of new jobs in the private sector (Birch, 1979, 1987; Davidsson et al., 1994; Storey, 1994; Cassar, 2004). This means that SMEs play a key role as a vehicle for economic growth and wealth creation. However, not all SMEs are creators of jobs; the vast majority of them (more than 90 percent) remain in the lifestyle category (Lumme et al., 1998; Van Osnabrugge and Robinson, 2000). Moreover, how business start-ups are financed is one the fundamental issues of enterprise research as financial capital is a necessity for new firms who want to compete in the marketplace (Cassar, 2004). Moreover, financial constraints are often claimed to be the reason why only a small part of new small businesses actually grow (Greene and Brown, 1997; Cassar, 2004). The rationale for this reasoning is that external financiers (that is, banks, informal investors and venture capital firms) are reluctant to finance new small firms because of the risk involved (related to information asymmetries and lack of track record) (Binks, 1996; Winborg, 2000; Sørheim, 2003). This implies a supply side view of small business finance, focusing on how external financiers evaluate new firms. This rationale has been questioned over the last decade: (1) by focusing on the heterogeneity among small firms, that many firms prefer to remain 'lifestyle' firms and (2) that many business founders have a strong propensity to retain total control over their businesses (Cressy and Olofsson, 1996; Berggren et al., 2000). This indicates that it is important to look at different categories of small firms in terms of their perception of and actual use of external funding.

In a Norwegian context hiring a person permanently is considered a big step for the newly established firm (due to legislation that protects the employee). Based on unique data from newly established firms in this chapter we will examine if prospective employers differ from other non-prospective employers when it comes to perceptions of financial prerequisites and actual financial behavior.

THEORETICAL BACKING AND HYPOTHESES DEVELOPMENT

A number of studies focusing on small business managers' preferences towards financial means have introduced the 'pecking order approach' as a point of departure (Holmes and Kent, 1991; Reed, 1996; Winborg, 2000; Cassar, 2004). This 'pecking order approach' was originally designed in order to study financial preferences in large listed firms (Myers and and Majluf, 1984). The approach implies that managers' attitudes towards financial sources are ranked in the following way: (1) internally generated equity, (2) debt financing and (3) external equity from new owners (Myers, 1984; Myers and Majluf, 1984). This ranking is presumed to occur because of the information asymmetries between business managers and financiers. That is, uneven distribution of information between the business manager and financiers results in different evaluations of the firm. So, it is supposed that the firm, compared with the external financier, has better knowledge about the real value. The majority of studies undertaken of financial preferences among small businesses seems to support the underlying notion that small businesses are reluctant to make use of external funding, thus supporting the 'pecking order approach' (Reed, 1996; Paul et al., 2007). However, the application of the pecking order framework in SMEs could be questioned. The framework was introduced for large firms who actually could choose between different types of financial sources. This will not usually be the case for newly established firms (Paul et al., 2007). This means that even if newly established firms act in line with the pecking order hypothesis, they will not necessarily use a pecking order reasoning when they deal with financial issues. A more fruitful approach for newly established firms seems to be a 'muddling through approach' introduced by Winborg (2000). He claims that small business managers are pragmatic and quite flexible when it comes to the handling of financial needs, where business managers with the need for external finance are more positive towards external finance than managers not facing such a need. A 'muddling through approach' takes into account that business founders may change goals and means and that this is reflected in their perception and actual use of external means in order to develop their business.

There are a number of aspects that seem to be unique for new small firms. The lack of track record makes it difficult to achieve any kind of external funding without sufficient collateral (Binks, 1996; Cassar, 2004). Another important element seems to be growth and size. The attitudes towards growth may affect the perceived view of potential external resources (Cressy, 1995). Hall (1989) has provided indications that ambition to grow is related to financial search activity. An ambition to grow leads to a larger capital need and these growth aspiring firms seem to be more active in their search for external funding

(Cressy, 1995). Moreover, several studies emphasize that small business managers' preferences towards risk and desire for control influence attitudes and use of external funding (Cressy, 1995; Cassar, 2004). The role of individual attributes is not taken into account when examining large public firms (Cassar, 2004). Finally, Winborg (2000) demonstrated that most small business managers, in general, are not interested in obtaining external funding. Berggren et al. (2000) related this attitude towards external funding to small business managers' propensity to retain absolute control over the business (control aversion) and they claim that the reason for this is asymmetric relationships. We believe that they are stretching their empirical results when claiming information asymmetry is manifested in small business managers' control aversion (Berggren et al., 2000). From our point of view this picture is somewhat more complex and we find it difficult to accept that business managers' wish to maintain control of their business is mainly related to potential information asymmetry between the founder and the financier. In order to explore this further we have examined prospective and non-prospective employers' perceptions about and actual use of financial sources. We employ four different concepts reflecting the new business founder's perception of different dimensions concerning possible prerequisites for external funding. These are perceived environmental munificence, perceived self-efficacy for investor relationships, control aversion and perceived financial risk associated with the business start-up. Since prospective employers view the hiring of others as a likely event to occur, it is probable that these prerequisites match their aspirations.

Perceived environmental munificence refers to perceptions of availability of critical resources in the external environment (Brown and Kirchhoff, 1997). Thus, business founders that perceive the environment to be munificent regard the environment to be rich concerning important resources. Brown and Kirchhoff (1997) found empirical evidence that small business owner's perception of environmental munificence was positively related to the owner's entrepreneurial orientation. Entrepreneurial orientation was found to be positively associated with a firm's growth rate in terms of employment growth and sales growth. In this study it is expected that there is a positive relationship between reporting to be a prospective employer and perceived environmental munificence regarding financing. The following hypothesis is therefore derived:

Hypothesis 1: Prospective employers, compared with other new business founders, perceive the environment to be more munificent.

Perceived self-efficacy (Bandura, 1997) refers to people's beliefs in their own capability or competence in performing tasks leading to a specific behavior. In the context of new business start-ups, founders who express higher levels of self-efficacy regarding important tasks in the start-up process can be expected to be more likely to reach their goals. One of the most important tasks in the business start-up process may concern the ability to get connected to financial capital sources. De Noble et al. (1999) developed several measures of entrepreneurial self-efficacy, among them a measure they named 'initiating investor relationships'. This study applies an adjusted measure based on De Noble et al.'s (1999) investor relationship measure. The following hypothesis is suggested:

Hypothesis 2: Prospective employers, compared with other new business founders, report higher levels of perceived self-efficacy with regard to developing viable investor relationships.

Berggren et al. (2000) found, in their study of 281 Swedish SMEs, a significant negative relationship between growth pressure (perceived importance of growth to survive) and control aversion. We expect a similar relationship in our study. Thus the following hypothesis is suggested:

Hypothesis 3: Prospective employers, compared with other new business founders, have lower levels of control aversion reflected by more positive perceptions of new external owners.

Growth oriented business founders may to a larger degree than other business founders perceive that there are financial risks associated with the start-up process. It is likely that entrepreneurs intending to hire employees already in an initial phase have used and plan to use more of their own and other financial resources than non-prospective employers; thus, prospective employers may experience that they have more to lose than the other group. The following hypothesis is suggested:

Hypothesis 4: Prospective employers perceive the financial risk associated with the business founding as higher than non-prospective employers.

With regard to financial behavior it is expected that prospective employers express a greater demand for financial capital than the other group of new business founders. This is manifested through a more active financing behavior. Hence, since this group of business founders plan to hire, it is likely that these founders match their actions according to their aspirations. More specifically, the following hypotheses are suggested:

Hypothesis 5a: Prospective employers, compared with other new business founders, are more active in their search for external funding (debt and equity).

Hypothesis 5b: Prospective employers, compared with other new business founders, are more likely to have received offers concerning external funding (debt and equity).

Hypothesis 5c: Prospective employers, compared with other new business founders, are more likely to have accepted offers concerning external funding (debt and equity).

Hypothesis 5d: Prospective employers have, to a larger extent than other new business founders, received external funding (debt and equity).

DATA AND METHOD

The sample used in this study consists of new entries in a Norwegian business register (the Norwegian Central Coordinating Register for Legal Entities). This is a comprehensive business register that coordinates information that exists in other government registers such as the register of employers, the register of business enterprises and the Value Added Tax register (see Brønnsundregisterene, 2004). Consequently, businesses that are obliged to enter one of these registers will be included in the coordinating register. In addition, businesses can voluntarily choose to register in order to get a unique organization number.

A structured questionnaire was constructed to include issues concerning the financing of new businesses. In order to get the questionnaire pre-tested, academics and practitioners (six persons following a training course for entrepreneurs) commented upon the content and the structure of an early version of the form.

In order to approach the businesses as early as possible after they entered the register, the business register was contacted. The register supplied lists containing the name, address and additional information about the firms within one week after the businesses entered the register. We received these lists in four rounds. The lists contained all limited liability companies, sole proprietorships, general partnerships and limited partnerships that entered the register in the period from 20 May to 15 June 2002. Within one week after we received the lists the questionnaires were mailed out to the businesses. A reminder with a copy of the questionnaire was sent out in four rounds, three weeks after the initial mailings. Of the total 3121 business founders approached, 126 of the mailings were returned as unreachable. Of the remaining 2995 questionnaires, 1048 were received. This represents a 35 percent response rate.

In order to ensure that we were studying new entries, we removed 17 respondents that did not return the questionnaires within 90 days after the registration date. Further, we also removed 204 respondents that reported one of the following: (1) the business was not started from scratch; (2) they were not alone or with partners responsible for the business start-up and (3) the business was a subsidiary of another business. Of the remaining 827 businesses, 64 responses had missing data on one or more of the variables of interest. These respondents were also excluded from the sample. After eliminations the sample consisted of 763 respondents.

In order to check for the possibility of response bias we first compared the respondents (1048 businesses) with the non-respondents (1947 businesses) with regard to legal form and localization (county). Cross-tabulation with Chi-square tests did not reveal any significant differences (at the 0.1 level of significance) between the two groups, suggesting that the respondents are representative of the population. Subsequently, we compared the final sample (763 businesses) to the non-respondents and excluded businesses (in total 2232 businesses) regarding the same two variables. The analysis did not reveal any significant differences (at the 0.1 level of significance) with regard to localization; however, a significant effect concerning legal form was detected ($p < 0.01$). Limited liability companies were under-represented and sole proprietorships were over-represented in the final sample. The main issue is whether the sample is representative of new entries that are *de novo* independent start-ups. As limited liability companies were over-represented among subsidiaries and acquisitive entries, legal form may not be an appropriate variable for checking response bias. Hence, despite the difference with regard to legal form identified, there is no reason to expect that the final sample is biased in any systematic way.

Measures

Prospective and non-prospective employers were classified based on a single question: 'how likely is it that the business in one year has employed anyone other than you?' Responses were reported along a 7-point scale where 1 = very unlikely, 4 = neither likely or unlikely and 7 = very likely. The variable was recoded into a categorical variable in which responses stating that employment of others was likely (5 to 7) were coded 1 (yes), otherwise 0 (no). Only 190 (24.9 percent) of the 763 businesses were classified as prospective employers, indicating modest employment growth objectives among Norwegian independent start-ups. In order to investigate differences concerning characteristics of prospective versus non-prospective employers, financial characteristics and future ideal size in terms of employees and sales turnover were compared. The ideal business size measures are based on a similar type of measures appearing in Wiklund (1998). Results of the non-parametric tests (Mann-Whitney U) are shown in Table 12.1. Compared to the non-prospective employers, prospective employers reported: significantly more invested total financial capital, significantly higher financial requirement within one year as well as three years and significantly larger ideal business size in terms of sales turnover and employment in one year and three years. These results indicate that the two categories are different along dimensions referring to initial size, future financial needs and growth aspiration.

RESULTS AND ANALYSIS

In order to test the hypotheses with regard to perceptions of financial pre-requisites, t-tests were carried out. The four perception variables are detailed and the results are displayed in Table 12.2.

Environmental munificence is in this context related to perceived growth in business industry and the perceived interest from external financiers. Table 12.2 shows that prospective employers, compared with other new business founders, see their business environment as more favourable. There is therefore support for Hypothesis 1.

The results presented in Table 12.2 indicate that all new business founders in Norway have perceived a rather strong self-efficacy for developing viable relationships with external financiers. Nevertheless, according to Hypothesis 2 prospective employers should have higher perceived capability to build the needed investor relationships; thus this hypothesis is also supported.

Empirical results regarding new business founders' perception about new external owners indicate prospective employers are more open-minded towards new external owners, that they to a larger extent are willing to abandon a control averse position. Thus, there is support for Hypothesis 3.

A striking point when addressing the question about risk is that both prospective and non-prospective employers consider the financial risk associated with the business to be quite low. However, compared with other new business founders, prospective employers perceive their financial risk to be higher. This means that Hypothesis 4 is supported. Furthermore, the perceived risk is consistent with the business characteristics reported in Table 12.1.

Hypotheses relating to initial financing behavior were tested using cross-tabulation with Chi-square tests and empirical findings are displayed in Table 12.3. The results show that prospective employers are far more active than non-prospective employers in their search for loans/credits. The reader must also bear in mind that this is a search for finance from the period when the business was officially founded. Moreover, it is interesting to notice that more than one in five of the prospective employers have searched for external equity for their business (the corresponding number for non-prospective businesses is

Table 12.1 Business characteristics of prospective and non-prospective employers

Variable	Prospective employers		Mann-Whitney U statistics	Significance level (two-tailed)
	Yes	No		
Total financial capital (loans and equity) invested in the business				
n = 717	177 (24.7%)	540 (75.3%)		
Mean	407	210		
Median	100	13	26 639.0	0.0000
Financial requirement within one year				
n = 740	182 (24.6%)	558 (75.4%)		
Mean	219	90		
Median	0	0	44 036.5	0.0007
Financial requirement within three years				
n = 625	152 (24.3%)	473 (75.7%)		
Mean	977	310		
Median	0	0	29 081.0	0.0000
Ideal business size: no. of employees including the founder in one year				
n = 723	181 (25.0%)	542 (75.0%)		
Mean	3.23	1.19		
Median	2.00	1.00	12 274.5	0.0000
Ideal business size: no. of employees including the founder in three years				
n = 712	179 (25.1%)	533 (74.9%)		
Mean	5.7	1.74		
Median	4.0	1.00	16 463.0	0.0000
Ideal business size: sales turnover in one year				
n = 699	176 (25.2%)	523 (74.8%)		
Mean	3070	763		
Median	2000	400	12 729.0	0.0000
Ideal business size: sales turnover in three years				
n = 683	173 (25.3%)	510 (74.7%)		
Mean	7441	2052		
Median	4000	650	16 433.0	0.0000

Notes: Figures with regard to total financial capital, financial requirement and ideal size and sales turnover are reported in 1000 NOK (1 NOK = approx. 0.14 USD).

Table 12.2   Perceptions of financial prerequisites

Variable	Prospective employers		t-value	Significance level (two-tailed)
	Yes ($n = 190$)	No ($n = 573$)		
Perceived environmental munificence			−3.586	0.0004
Mean	3.87	3.51		
Median	4.00	3.75		
Perceived self-efficacy for investor relationships			−3.225	0.0013
Mean	7.22	6.62		
Median	7.50	7.00		
Control aversion			4.824	0.0000
Mean	3.99	4.73		
Median	4.00	4.00		
Perceived financial risk associated with the business founding			−6.721	0.0000
Mean	2.76	2.01		
Median	3.00	2.00		

Notes:
1. Environmental munificence was measured using similar dimensions as those developed by Brown and Kirchhoff (1997). The measure used in this study consisted of four items: 'The business's industry may in general be characterized as high growth,' 'Banks and other suppliers of loan capital are generally very interested in financing businesses like mine', 'Investors are generally very interested in financing businesses like mine' and 'Investors would generally quite easily understand the technology used in my business'. The items were measured using a 7-point Likert scale: 1 = strongly disagree, 4 = neither agree nor disagree and 7 = strongly agree. Responses on the four statements were averaged. Chronbach's alpha = 0.77.
2. Three items of perceived self-efficacy for investor relationships were taken from De Noble et al. (1999): 'Develop and maintain favorable relationships with potential investors', 'Develop relationships with key people who are connected to capital sources' and 'Identify potential sources of funding for investments'. In addition, one item was added: 'Be able to obtain sufficient funds for the founding'. The items were measured according to Bandura (2001) and Betz and Hackett (1998) recommendations. The respondents were asked to indicate their degree of confidence in performing the tasks successfully. The scale ranged from 0 = 'no confidence at all', 5 = 'some confidence' and 10 = 'complete confidence'. Responses on the four statements were averaged. Chronbach's alpha = 0.90.
3. Two items referring to control aversion were used. These items were developed based on Berggren et al.'s (2001) study. The actual items used in this study were the following: 'New owners are favorable for the business' and 'New owners renew and develop the business'. The items were measured using a 7-point Likert scale: 1 = strongly disagree, 4 = neither agree nor disagree and 7 = strongly agree. The scores on the two variables were reversed and averaged. Chronbach's alpha = 0.92.
4. Perceived financial risk was measured using a single item and a 7-point scale: 1 = very low risk and 7 = very high risk.

Table 12.3 *Financing behavior among prospective and non-prospective employers*

| Variable | Prospective employers | | | | Chi-square statistic | Significance level (two-tailed) |
| | Yes ($n = 190$) | | No ($n = 573$) | | | |
	Count	%	Count	%		
Has the founder(s) applied for loans/credits to the business?					42.99	0.0000
No	93	48.9	427	74.5		
Yes	97	51.1	146	25.5		
Has the founder(s) received offers concerning loans/ credits to the business?					35.83	0.0000
No	104	54.7	443	77.3		
Yes	86	45.3	130	22.7		
Has the founder(s) accepted offers concerning loans/ credits to the business?					34.82	0.0000
No	111	58.4	458	79.9		
Yes	79	41.6	115	20.1		
Has the founder(s) applied for external equity to the business?					15.33	0.0001
No	149	78.4	513	89.5		
Yes	41	21.6	60	10.5		
Has the founder(s) received offers concerning external equity to the business?					27.39	0.0000
No	144	75.8	519	90.6		
Yes	46	24.2	54	9.4		
Has the founder(s) accepted offers concerning external equity to the business?					14.77	0.0001
No	157	82.6	529	92.3		
Yes	33	17.4	44	7.7		
Has the business received external financing (external loans, external credits or external equity)?					42.16	0.0000
No	107	56.3	459	80.1		
Yes	83	43.7	114	19.9		

Note: The actual questions with regard to applied, received and accepted loans/credits and external equity were 'how many sources have you applied/received/accepted loans/credits and external equity from?'. The variables were recoded to '0' (no) if the respondents reported 0 sources and '1' (yes) if the respondents reported sources ≥ 1.

one in ten). According to Hypothesis 5a, prospective employers are more active in their search for external funding, the hypothesis is supported.

Moreover, it is interesting to notice that some prospective employers receive offers of external equity without applying for such funds. This can be explained by the fact that some investors are very proactive in their search for potential investment opportunities (Sørheim, 2003). Furthermore, a striking point seems to be the high acceptance rate: most of the new business founders that apply for external funding will actually receive some kind of external funding. Nevertheless, a significant larger share of prospective employers had received offers concerning loans/credits as well as external equity. With regard to accepted offers concerning loans/credits and external equity, prospective employers are significantly more likely to have accepted offers than non-prospective employers. Thus, Hypotheses 5b and 5c are supported.

Addressing the final hypothesis, Table 12.3 suggests that prospective employers receive external funding to a larger extent than other new businesses, so Hypothesis 5d is supported. These empirical findings are consistent with the business characteristics, which indicate that prospective employers in general have a higher capital need (see Table 12.1).

DISCUSSION AND IMPLICATIONS

The empirical findings in this study suggest that a separation between prospective and non-prospective employers is a viable approach in order to examine financial perceptions and actual financial behavior of new business founders. The results show that non-prospective employers by and large are without growth aspirations. Prospective employers, on the other hand, have growth aspirations in terms of number of employees, financial requirements and sales. Another intriguing finding from this study is related to the acceptance rate when prospective employers apply for external funding (debt and/or equity), as an overwhelming majority that apply for funds get offers of external funding. So, it is tempting to ask, is acquisition of external capital (debt and equity) actually a problem for new business founders? However, we do not know if they are offered enough financial capital and in terms that are acceptable for the new businesses. Another important element to take into account is related to the fact that growth aspiring businesses usually underestimate the amount of financial capital needed to develop their businesses (Shane and Cable, 2002). Moreover, compared with studies of small businesses in, for example, Sweden, the actual use of external equity in the initial stages is quite high, as almost 8 percent of non-prospective and 17 percent of the prospective employers have accepted offers of external equity.

At first sight, this study indicates that non-prospective employers follow a 'pecking order' reasoning put forward by Myers (1984). So, according to the pecking order framework this should be related to the degree of information asymmetry between new business founders and their financiers. However, we suggest that this rank of financial sources is primarily related to non-prospective employers' lack of growth aspirations. They have low ambitions and the vast majority of these firms will not at any point even consider bringing in external financiers. Moreover, a less munificent environment may explain why their ambitions are that low. However, we find the 'muddling through approach' put forward by Winborg (2000) a more fruitful approach when discussing why prospective and non-prospective employers differ in perceived and actual financial behavior. We have in this chapter been backing the claim that prospective employers have growth aspirations. Prospective employers seem to adjust their perceptions and actual financial behavior to the actual situation of their business. Consequently, prospective employers perceive external funding (debt and equity) as the right means in order to achieve their goals. A more positive perception towards external funding is also confirmed in their actual financial behavior.

We started this chapter by emphasizing the role of SMEs as a vehicle for economic growth and job creation. We show that the majority of new businesses will or cannot grow. Growth businesses are identified among the new business founders who initially perceive that they will become employers. Therefore, policy makers must reconsider the use of general means towards all new business founders and consider giving more active support (financially and non-financially) to prospective employers. By supporting prospective employers policy makers can stimulate economic growth and job creation.

Limitations

This is a Norwegian study and it is unclear to what extent the findings are applicable to other countries. Overall, the Norwegian context is not very different from other small, developed countries. However, if we compare legislations in the USA and Norway we will see large differences when it comes to hiring and firing employees. This means that a comparative study with data from the USA might be biased due to differences in legislation.

Even if this study indicates that external finance is not a large problem in the initial stages, there are probably subgroups that have severe problems with raising initial financial capital, for example, new technology based firms and born global firms (that is, young firms with international growth ambitions). Furthermore, there is a need for longitudinal studies in order to examine how perceptions and actual financial behavior develop over time. Finally, this study suffers from all the weaknesses associated with a self-report study; for instance, respondents could be influenced by perceptions of what seems to be a desirable response rather than the actual facts.

CONCLUSION

Using a unique sample of independent new business start-ups we found that prospective and non-prospective employers differ when it comes to financial preferences and actual financial behavior. Prospective employers compared with non-prospective employers reported a more munificent environment, a stronger perceived self-efficacy for investor relationships, less control aversion and higher perceived financial risk associated with the business founding. All these relationships were statistically significant at the 0.01 level of significance. Thus, Hypotheses 1–4 are supported. Furthermore, the group of prospective employers were significantly more active in searching for loans/credits and external equity compared with non-prospective employers. A significantly larger share of prospective employers had received offers concerning loans/credits as well as external equity. With regard to accepted offers concerning loans/credits and external equity, prospective employers are significantly more likely to have accepted offers than non-prospective employers. Finally, a significantly larger share of prospective employers has received external financing. These results support Hypotheses 5a–d.

REFERENCES

Bandura, A. (1997), *Self-efficacy: The Exercise of Control*, New York: W.H. Freeman and Company.
Bandura, A. (2001), 'Guide for constructing self-efficacy scales (revised)', available from Frank Pajares, Emory University.
Berggren, B., C. Olofsson and L. Silver (2000), 'Control aversion and the search for external financing in Swedish SMEs', *Small Business Economics*, **15**(3), 233–42.
Binks, M. (1996), 'The relationships between UK banks and their small business customers', in R. Cressy, B. Gandemo and C. Olofsson (eds), *SMEs – A Comparative Perspective*, Stockholm: Nutek, pp. 127–44.
Birch, D. (1979), *The Job Generation Process*, Cambridge, MA: MIT Program on Neighborhood and Regional Change.
Birch, D. (1987), *Job Creation in America*, New York: The Free Press.
Brønnøysundregisterene (2004), available at http://www.brreg.no/ (accessed 27 April 2004).
Brown, T.E. and B.A. Kirchhoff (1997), 'The effects of resource availability and entrepreneurial orientation on firm growth', in P.D. Reynolds, W.D. Bygrave, N.M. Carter, P. Davidsson, W.B. Gartner, C.M. Mason, and P.P. McDougan (eds), *Frontiers of Entrepreneurship Research*, Wellesley, MA: Babson College, pp. 32–46.
Cassar, G. (2004), 'The financing of business start-ups', *Journal of Business Venturing*, **19**, 261–83.
Cressy, R. (1995), 'Business borrowing and control: a theory of entrepreneurial types', *Small Business Economics*, **7**, 291–300.
Cressy, R. and C. Olofsson (1996), 'Financial conditions for SMEs in Sweden', in R.

Cressy, B. Gandemo and C. Olofsson (eds), *SMEs – A Comparative Perspective*, Stockholm: Nutek, pp. 113–26.

Davidsson, P., L. Lindmark and C. Olofsson (1994), 'New firm formation and regional development in Sweden', *Regional Studies*, **28**, 195–210.

De Noble, A.F., D. Jung and S.B. Ehrlich (1999), 'Entrepreneurial self-efficacy: the development of a measure and its relation to entrepreneurial action', in P.D. Reynolds, W.D. Bygrave, S. Manigart, C.M. Mason, G.D. Meyer, H.J. Sapienza and K.G. Shaver (eds), *Frontiers of Entrepreneurship Research*, Wellesley, MA: Babson College, pp. 73–87.

Greene, P. and T. Brown (1997), 'Resource needs and the dynamic capitalism typology', *Journal of Business Venturing*, **12**, 161–73.

Hall, G. (1989), 'Lack of finance as constraint on the expansion of innovatory small firms', in J. Barber, J. Metcalf and M. Porteus (eds), *Barriers to Growth in Small Firms*, London: Routledge, pp. 111–29.

Holmes, S. and P. Kent (1991), 'An empirical analysis of the financial structure of small and large Australian manufacturing firms', *Journal of Small Business Finance*, **1**, 141–54.

Lumme, A., C. Mason and M. Suomi (1998), *Informal Venture Capital: Investors, Investments and Policy in Finland*, Dordrecht: Kluwer Academic Publishers.

Myers, S. (1984), 'The capital structure puzzle', *Journal of Finance*, **39**, 575–92.

Myers, S. and N. Majluf (1984), 'Corporate financing and investment decisions when firms have information that investors do not have', *Journal of Financial Economics*, **13**, 187–221.

Paul, S., G. Whittham and J. Wyper (2007), 'The pecking order hypothesis: does it apply to start-up firms?', *Journal of Small Business and Enterprise Development*, **14**(1), 8–21.

Reed, G. (1996), 'Mature micro-firms and their experience of funding shortages', *Small Business Economics*, **8**, 27–37.

Shane, S. and D. Cable (2002), 'Network ties, reputation, and the financing of new ventures', *Management Science*, **48**(3), 364–81.

Sørheim, R. (2003), 'The pre-investment behaviour of business angels: a social capital approach', V*enture Capital: An International Journal of Entrepreneurial Finance*, **5**(4), 337–64.

Storey, D. (1994), *Understanding the Small Business Sector*, London: Routledge.

Van Osnabrugge, M. and M. Robinson (1999), 'Do serial and non-serial investors behave differently? An empirical and theoretical analysis', *Entrepreneurship Theory and Practice*, **22**, 23–42.

Wiklund, J. (1998), 'Small firm growth and performance: entrepreneurship and other explanations', PhD dissertation, Jönköping International Business School, Jönköping, Sweden.

Winborg, J. (2000), 'Financing small businesses – developing our understanding of financial bootstrapping behaviour', unpublished PhD dissertation, SIRE/University of Lund, Sweden.

13. Advice to new business founders and subsequent venture performance

Lars Kolvereid, Espen J. Isaksen and Hannes Ottósson

INTRODUCTION

This chapter investigates the association between the number of advisers providing valuable advice to founders during the new business start-up process and subsequent new business performance in terms of invested capital, sales turnover and employment. The chapter also examines if there are diminishing returns to scale between the advice obtained and subsequent business performance. A number of studies have investigated the influence of advice on entrepreneurial or business performance, but research on diminishing returns to scale with regard to advice remains scarce. The idea of diminishing return implies that an excessive number of sources of advice may be counterproductive (Watson, 2007). The aim is to specifically address this issue. Further, one of the goals of our investigation is to expand this field of research, attempting to identify an optimal number of sources of advice.

In this chapter hypotheses are derived from the emerging theory of outsider assistance (Chrisman, 1999). The application of a sample of representative new businesses in a different context than previous studies implies a rigid test of theory and an examination of the extent to which previous findings can be generalized to other settings.

This chapter contributes to the entrepreneurship literature by using longitudinal research design and a robust measure for valuable advice. Within the entrepreneurship field general recommendations for research design have been common. Recommendations include applying approaches that acknowledge the complexity of the business start-up process by using multi-level studies (Low and Macmillan, 1988; Bouchikhi, 1993). The use of longitudinal research design has been encouraged to catch the dynamics of the start-up process, thus increasing the integration of outcome and process oriented research (Hoang and Antoncic, 2003).

A second contribution of this chapter relates to the sample of businesses utilized in this research. The use of an appropriately representative sample of entrepreneurs has been urged (Gartner, 1989). Most studies of business performance exploring factors associated with superior levels of business performance have used a sample of existing firms rather than start-up businesses. In this investigation the sample consists of new, small independent businesses entering a Norwegian business register. Registering a business can be viewed as an indication of business birth (Isaksen and Kolvereid, 2005). This research design issue reduces the chance for hindsight biases (Bazerman, 1994) since the entrepreneurs report information regarding valuable advice prior to the time when the outcomes of the start-up process are known.

LITERATURE REVIEW

Attempts have been made to map all perspectives of new business founding (Gartner, 1985). Most studies on the subject roughly fall into one or more of the following four areas: (1) research focusing on the process of new venture start-up; (2) research focusing on the individual entrepreneur; (3) research focusing on the organization or (4) research focusing on the environment of the new start-up. This study focuses on the process dimension, but central issues included in the other perspectives will be taken into consideration.

The process dimension covers factors related to the start-up activity performed by entrepreneurs during business formation (Carter et al., 1996; Reynolds et al., 2004). Therefore, the process dimension covers factors such as discovering and utilizing entrepreneurial opportunities (Ardichvili et al., 2003; De Carolis and Saparito, 2006), accumulation of resources (Davidsson and Honig, 2003) and gestation activities (Alsos and Kolvereid, 1998; Delmar and Davidsson, 2000). Obtaining outsider advice is an important part of the start-up process dimension.

The business start-up process is often studied in Panel Study of Entrepreneurial Dynamics (PSED) type datasets. In these datasets a probability sample of ongoing early stage business start-ups is obtained through screening telephone interviews with a very large number of adult members in households. Answers to the screening questionnaire determine whether respondents are nascent entrepreneurs or not. Those who are classified as nascent entrepreneurs are reinterviewed at regular intervals, typically every 6–12 months over two to five years to follow the business gestation process and asset outcomes (Reynolds, 2009). Davidsson and Gordon (2009) identified and reviewed 69 peer-reviewed published or accepted/in press journal articles, which were based on PSED type datasets. Among these articles, 31 concerned business creation process outcomes. In these studies only previous start-up experience is consistently found to predict progress in the business creation process.

Other studies on very new businesses and nascent entrepreneurs are scarce because of the difficulty involved with identifying representative samples of new businesses at the time of start-up. Previous analyses of the data used under the present circumstances have indicated that business ownership experience, business similarity, search for external funding, starting in teams and aiming at a local market are positively associated with early business performance, in terms of obtaining finance, sales turnover and employment (Isaksen, 2006). The only factor in these analyses which was found to be negatively associated with early business performance was perceived novelty of the venture.

Outsider Assistance

The emerging theory of outsider assistance as a knowledge resource suggests that outsider assistance leads to the creation of knowledge that positively influences business survival and performance (Robinson, 1982; Chrisman, 1999). Entrepreneurs starting a business will lack knowledge to get through the process. This knowledge gap represents the difference between the knowledge possessed by entrepreneurs and knowledge required for successful venturing. If entrepreneurs acknowledge that gap, an opportunity will be created to generate and transfer knowledge. Some of that knowledge will be provided by external advisers. Advice utilized will create a resource that allows the entrepreneur to perform better (Chrisman and McMullan, 2004).

The theory of outsider assistance suggests that outsider assistance leads to the creation of knowledge that provides a basis for sustainable competitive advantage, which will, in turn, influence business survival and performance (Robinson, 1982; Chrisman, 1999). Advice received and utilized will then create a resource that allows the entrepreneur to perform better.

Whatever capabilities new ventures possess reside with the entrepreneur. Entrepreneur knowledge is considered by many to be the single most important resource the venture can draw upon for potential success (Minniti and Bygrave, 2001). Narrowly, entrepreneurial knowledge has been defined as the ability to recognize opportunities and to organize and combine resources (Alvarez and Busenitz, 2001). However, entrepreneurial knowledge is based on a wide foundation. It can include the knowledge that the entrepreneur possessed before the start-up, such as formal education (Cooper et al., 1994; Gimeno et al., 1997) and prior start-up experience (Westhead and Wright, 1998; Delmar and Davidsson, 2000). It also includes the knowledge the entrepreneur acquires during the process of business formation.

Empirical support for outside assistance having positive influence on performance has been reported in several previous studies, using a variety of performance measures. In a study of 2025 nascent ventures Chrisman (1999) found strong support for outsider assistance having positive influence on the likelihood that individuals with entrepreneurial intentions will start a business a year after receiving the assistance. In a comparison study outsider assistance was found to positively influence survival after ten years of operation. The results suggest that the group that benefited from outsider assistance had an approximately 65 percent survival rate, which was significantly higher than the comparison group which had a survival rate of approximately 47 percent (Chrisman and McMullan, 2004). Using a sample of 159 clients of the Pennsylvania Small Business Development Center (SBDC) Chrisman et al. (2005) found a significant positive relationship between the amount of time entrepreneurs received counseling from the center and performance in terms of sales and employment.

Based on this it seems reasonable to expect a positive relationship between advice received by entrepreneurs and subsequent performance. Therefore, the following hypothesis was formulated:

Hypothesis 1: The number of advisers that provide the founder with valuable advice during the business gestation process is positively related to subsequent business performance.

Diminishing Returns

At some point in the learning process an entrepreneur will have obtained most of the relevant information, and the theory of outsider assistance postulates that obtaining advice beyond this point will have a detrimental effect on performance (Chrisman et al., 2005). Entrepreneurs who seek too much advice may reach a point of information overload, which could make them indecisive and unable to formulate a clear strategy for obtaining competitive advantage (Chrisman et al., 2005). Watson (2007) reported evidence of an inverted U-shaped relationship between network size and performance in terms of survival and growth among small and medium-sized enterprises (SMEs). He concluded that there may be an optimum level of resources that a small business owner should devote to networking (Watson, 2007).

While utilizing networking to some extent may be beneficial, it has been suggested, consistent with the law of diminishing returns, that excessive networking is likely to be counterproductive (Watson, 2007). Economists have argued that time is a scarce economic resource and how individuals allocate their time can influence economic outcomes. Relationships require time, energy and attention to establish and maintain, and because these resources are limited, relationships involve costs (McFadyen and Cannella, 2004). Entrepreneurs cannot spend excessive amounts of time networking without limiting their efforts concerning other crucial start-up activities. Beyond some point marginal benefit from further networking may be negative (Watson, 2007).

The concept of diminishing returns, diminishing marginal returns or the law of diminishing return, can be traced back to the classics in economics. More recently (Solow, 1956) presented a model in relation to his theory of economic growth. The key assumption of the model is that inputs are subject to diminishing returns. Given a fixed stock of input – such as labor or capital – the impact on output of the last unit will at a certain point become less than the one before. Beyond some limit each additional unit of input yields less and less output. It has been suggested that diminishing returns apply to a wide range of phenomena, including experience (Berman et al., 2002) and education (Menzies and Paradi, 2003).

Limited work has been done on the concept of diminishing returns of advice received by entrepreneurs. Chrisman and McMullen (2004) found a significant, negative association between advice received measured as squared number of hours received and the probability of survival. With sales and employment as performance measures, they further found that when both the amount of time receiving advice and advice squared were entered into a regression, they found a positive effect of counseling on performance, but a negative effect of advice squared, supporting the idea that counseling beyond a certain point has a detrimental effect on performance. They estimated that the optimal amount of counseling from the SBDC was between 136 and 143 hours (Chrisman et al., 2005). Measuring respondents' activated social networks, Watson (2007) also found support for an inverted U-shaped relationship between network size and performance in terms of survival and growth among SMEs in Australia. He concluded that there may be some optimum level of resources that a small business owner should devote to networking, and stated that 'accessing more than six networks during a year is likely to be counter-productive' (Watson, 2007, p. 870).

Based on the theory of outsider assistance, as well as the empirical studies reviewed above, the following hypothesis was formulated:

Hypothesis 2: There are diminishing returns to scale between the number of advisers that provide the founder with valuable advice during the business gestation process and subsequent business performance.

METHODOLOGY

The initial data collection took place during four successive weeks in May/June 2002. The sampling frame consisted of all sole traders, partnerships and unlisted limited liability companies registered in Norway during the four weeks. One week after the register supplied information questionnaires were mailed out (in four rounds) to the businesses. Three weeks after the initial mailings a reminder with a new copy of the questionnaire was mailed in four rounds to the non-responding businesses. In total 3121 businesses were approached and 1048 completed questionnaires were received. The follow-up interviews took place during weeks 5–8 in 2004, that is, approximately 19 months after the initial mailings. A professional vendor was engaged to tele-phone the respondents who participated in the postal survey. The vendor attempted to reach 980 of the 1048 respondents to the postal questionnaire. As a result of being de-registered from the business register, 29 businesses were removed from the initial sample. Six businesses were removed because they had more than 50 percent missing data, and the vendor failed to reach 33 of the respondents since they were not listed in any of the available telephone directories. Among the 980 candidates, 275 were inaccessible and 54 refused to participate. In total, the vendor collected data from 651 businesses, among which 557 reported to be in operation. Several requirements were used in order to ensure an appropriate sample for testing the hypotheses. Respondents were removed if they stated that: (1) they were not responsible for the new business start-up (15 businesses); (2) the new business was a daughter of another business (25 businesses); (3) the business was neither started from scratch nor an acquisitive entry (32 businesses) and (4) at the time of the follow-up interview the interviewees reported not to be owners of the busi-nesses (8 businesses). Finally, removing 168 respondents who failed to supply complete data reduced the final sample to 309 respondents.

In order to check for possible response bias, t-tests and Chi-square tests were performed comparing the final sample with non-respondents. The inde-pendent and control variables as well as legal form and county were compared across the two groups and no differences were detected at the 0.05 level of statistical significance. Therefore, the sample seems representative of new businesses in Norway.

Measures

Advice was measured asking respondents along a 7-point scale (1 = not at all, 4 = to some extent, 7 = to a very large extent) to indicate the extent to which 12 different actors gave valuable advice during the business gestation process. The actors included banks, family, private investors, venture capital compa-nies, industrial partners, suppliers, educators in business start-up and various government support agencies. In order to calculate a measure of advice the responses to these 12 questions were recoded into 12 dummy variables, where 1 to 3 were given a value of 0, and 4 to 7 were denoted a value of 1. The responses on the 12 dummy variables were then added together. Hence, the measure of advice can vary from 0 (no valuable advice) to 12 (valuable advice from 12 different sources). This measure reflects the number of advisers that have provided the businesses with valuable advice. In addition, in order to test the hypothesized inverted U-shaped relationship between number of advice and subsequent performance, number of advice squared was calculated. In order to minimize the effect of collinearity between advice and advice squared in the regression models, the latter variable was centered (mean = 0) prior to calculating its squared value.

The control variables included gender (0 = female, 1 = male), whether the firm was started from scratch (*de novo* = 1) or was an acquisitive entry (*de novo* = 0), and industry (manufacturing or trade, with service as the reference group).

The human capital variables included the number of years with management experience, at least some education at the university level (education = 1), whether or not the respondent is a novice entrepreneur (novice = 1), and whether or not the respondent reported to have a parental role model for entrepreneurship and self-employment (role model = 1).

The measures of business characteristics included a measure of whether the business was started by a single person or a team (team = 1). Perceived novelty was measured asking the following questions adopted from Reynolds et al. (2002) along a 7-point scale (where 1 = completely disagree to 7 = completely agree): (1) customers are familiar with the product or service to be provided; (2) there are few or no competitors that offer the same product or service and (3) the technology is not readily available. The reliability of this scale was satisfactory, with a Cronbach's alpha of 0.76. The final measure of characteristics with the business was urban location, defined as businesses located in municipalities with 10 000 or more people (urban location = 1). This statistical definition has previously been used by several authors, including Westhead and Wright (1998).

Three indicators of business performance were obtained by the vendor in the telephone interviews 19 months after the questionnaire survey: (1) the amount of capital invested in the business; (2) the annual sales turnover of the business in 2003 and (3) the current number of employees. To approximate a normal distribution the amount of capital invested and sales turnover in 2003, reported in Norwegian kroner (NOK), was recoded into an 11-point scale: 0 = 0; 1 through 24 999 = 1; 25 000 through 49 999 = 2; 50 000 through 99 999 = 3; 100 000 through 199 999 = 4; 200 000 through 399 999 = 5; 400 000 through 799 999 = 6; 800 000 through 1 499,999 = 7; 1 500,000 through 2 499 999 = 8; 2 500 000 through 4 999 999 = 9; 5 000 000 through highest = 10. Assuming that an average full-time employee works in the business 37.5 hours per week and that a part-time employee on average works half of that, the following formula was used to calculate the total employment, measured in hours per week in the business: The number of hours the respondent works in the business per week + (the number of full-time employees)*37.5 + (the number of part-time employees)*18.75. In order to approximate a normal distribution, employment was also recoded into an 11-point scale: $0 = 0$; 0.1 through $9.9 = 1$; 10 through $19.99 = 2$; 20 through $29.99 = 3$; 30 through $39.99 = 4$; 40 through $49.99 = 5$; 50 through $69.99 = 6$; 70 through $99.99 = 7$; 100 through $139.99 = 8$; 140 through $179.99 = 9$; 180 through highest $= 10$.

RESULTS

Descriptive statistics and correlations among the analysis variables are shown in Table 13.1. The correlation matrix offers preliminary support for Hypothesis 1. The correlations between advice and the three performance indicators are in the expected direction and all are statistically significant at $p < 0.05$.

The hypothesis was tested using OLS regression. The highest variance inflation factor (VIF) value found was 2.36, so multicollinearity was not a problem in the analyses. In order to formally test Hypothesis 1, control variables, human capital variables, business characteristics variables and the advice variable were entered into the three regression models where financial capital, sales turnover and employment were the dependent variables. The results are shown in Models 1A, 1B and 1C in Table 13.2. The models are all statistically significant at the 0.001 level and have an adjusted R square of 0.246, 0.17 and 0.103, respectively. Further, the advice variable is statistically significantly associated with financial capital ($p < 0.01$), sales turnover ($p < 0.05$) and employment ($p < 0.05$) in the expected direction. Hence, Hypothesis 1 is supported.

In order to check the sensitivity of the findings, alternative measures of advice were attempted. Alternative measures of advice were created by using different recoding of the original items, so that advice#1 was recoded as $1 = 0$ and $2,3,4,5,6,7 = 1$, advice#2 as $1,2 = 0$ and $3,4,5,6,7 = 1$ and advice#3 as $1,2,3 = 0$ and $4,5,6,7 = 1$. Except for the measure advice#3, which was not a statistically significant predictor of sales turnover, all the alternative measures of advice were significant predictors of all three measures of business performance. Therefore, the results obtained are not very sensitive to the measure of advice applied.

An examination of the relationship between each of the 12 items comprising the advice measure used and the dependent variables revealed that only advice from banks was significantly positively associated with all the three dependent variables. Moreover, the correlations between advice from banks and the dependent variables were higher than the correlations between any of the other sources of advice and the performance indications. This suggests that advice from banks is particularly valuable for new business founders.

Table 13.1 Descriptive statistics and correlation coefficients (n = 309)

	Mean	SD	1	2	3	4	5	6	7	8	9	10	11	12	13	14
Control variables																
Gender (1 = male)	0.77		1.00													
De novo	0.91		-0.02	1.00												
Manufacturing	0.20		0.20**	-0.14*	1.00											
Trade	0.13		0.03	-0.10	-0.20**	1.00										
Human capital																
Management experience	5.92	7.80	0.17**	0.05	-0.11	-0.03	1.00									
High education	0.55		-0.09	0.20**	-0.27**	-0.20**	0.12*	1.00								
Novice founder	0.73		-0.11*	0.00	0.06	-0.06	-0.32**	0.08	1.00							
Role model	0.37		-0.03	-0.12*	0.13*	0.02	-0.10	-0.08	-0.09	1.00						
Business characteristics																
Team	0.22		0.07	-0.10	0.02	0.12*	0.12*	-0.02	-0.29**	-0.01	1.00					
Perceived novelty	2.89	1.71	-0.13*	0.11*	-0.26**	0.08	0.12*	0.12*	-0.07	-0.03	0.01	1.00				
Urban location	0.73		-0.11	0.10	-0.13*	-0.02	-0.04	0.20**	0.02	-0.13*	0.01	0.08	1.00			
Sources of advice	1.74		-0.01	-0.10	0.17**	0.05	0.01	-0.16**	-0.05	0.02	0.07	0.06	-0.03	1.00		
Performance																
Financial capital	3.61	2.55	0.20**	-0.27**	0.14*	0.14*	0.18**	-0.12*	-0.20**	0.01	0.25**	-0.20**	-0.20**	0.20**	1.00	
Sales turnover	4.76	2.70	0.13*	-0.18**	0.03	0.19**	0.05	-0.07	-0.10	-0.01	0.21**	-0.28**	-0.03	0.13*	0.56**	1.00
Employment	3.91	2.65	0.07	-0.16**	0.03	0.17**	-0.05	-0.14*	-0.01	-0.02	0.17**	-0.20**	-0.03	0.15**	0.46**	0.72**	1.00

Note: Level of statistical significance: * $p < 0.05$; ** $p < 0.01$ (two-tailed).

Table 13.2 Regression results. Financial capital, sales turnover and employment as dependent variables (n = 309)

	Financial Capital		Sales Turnover		Employment	
	Model 1A	Model 2A	Model 1B	Model 2B	Model 1C	Model 2C
Control variables						
Gender (1 = male)	0.105*	0.100	0.079	0.091	0.040	0.055
De novo	−0.198***	−0.181***	−0.122*	−0.108*	−0.091	−0.074
Industry-manufacturing‡	0.048	0.046	−0.055	−0.057	−0.066	−0.067
Industry-trade‡	0.116*	0.116*	0.171**	0.158**	0.127*	0.111
Human capital						
Management experience	0.141*	0.145**	0.038	0.041	−0.030	−0.026
High education	0.032	0.047	0.043	0.056	−0.068	−0.053
Novice founder	−0.107	−0.107	−0.049	−0.048	0.034	0.034
Role model	−0.038	−0.033	−0.027	−0.023	−0.036	−0.032
Business characteristics						
Team	0.151**	0.139**	0.154**	0.144**	0.154**	0.142*
Perceived novelty	−0.191***	−0.169**	−0.304***	−0.285***	−0.207***	−0.185***
Urban location	−0.145**	−0.139**	0.001	0.006	0.009	0.014
Advice						
Sources of advice	0.158**	0.332***	0.132*	0.278**	0.143*	0.317***
Sources of advice squared		−0.232**		−0.195*		−0.233**
R^2	0.276	0.299	0.202	0.219	0.138	0.162
Adjusted R^2	0.246	0.268	0.170	0.184	0.103	0.125
ΔR^2		0.023**		0.017*		0.024**
F value	9.345***	9.681***	6.245***	6.346***	3.949***	4.374***

Notes: Standardized regression coefficients (betas) are displayed in the table. ‡ The reference category is service. Level of statistical significance:
* $p < 0.05$; ** $p < 0.01$; *** $p < 0.001$ (two-tailed).

In order to test the second hypothesis, advice squared was added to the regression equations. The results are reported in Models 2A, 2B and 2C in Table 13.2. All the three models are statistically significant at the 0.001 level. A significant improvement in R squared is reported in Model 1A (financial capital $\Delta R^2 = 0.023$, $p < 0.01$), 1B (sales turnover $\Delta R^2 = 0.017$, $p < 0.05$) and 1C (employment $\Delta R^2 = 0.024$, $p < 0.01$). Moreover, regarding all the three dependent variables, advice remains to have a positive significant effect, while advice squared has a statistically significant negative effect. Therefore, Hypothesis 2 receives strong support. To calculate the peak of number of sources of advice, advice and advice squared (not centered) were included as independent variables predicting invested capital, sales turnover and employment. The graphs are shown in Figure 13.1. The peaks are at between five and six sources of advice for the three dependent variables. That is, on average, there seems to be a positive effect of advice on performance up to approximately five different sources of advice. The results indicate that utilizing more than six sources has a negative effect on performance.

To investigate the possibility that a certain source of advice has stronger diminishing return to scale than other sources, additional regressions were run where the independent variables were the individual advice items and the items squared. The results showed that none of the single items had diminishing return to scale. Therefore, the findings indicate that there is no single source of advice that causes advice overload, but that seeking advice from too many different advisers can have a negative effect on subsequent business performance.

CONCLUSION

The purpose of this chapter was to explore the influence of advice received and utilized by entrepreneurs on subsequent venture performance. Of particular interest were the diminishing returns of advice on performance. The hypotheses were tested using a representative sample of new businesses in Norway.

The advice variable is significantly positively associated with financial capital, sales turnover and employment. Moreover, regarding all the three dependent variables, advice remains to have a positive significant effect up to an average of approximately five different sources of advice, while an average of approximately six or more different sources has a significant negative effect. This suggests that there are diminishing returns to scale between the amount of the advice received and subsequent business performance.

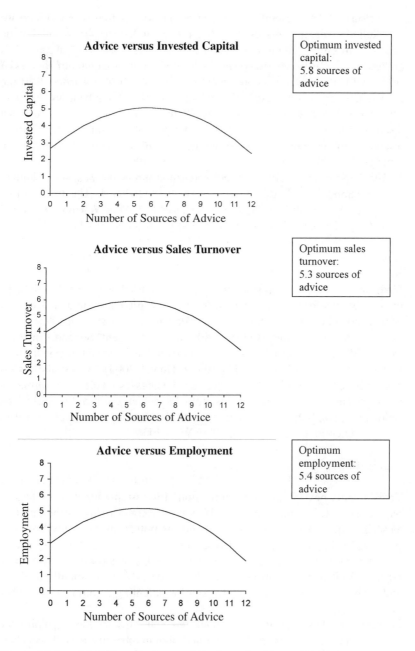

Figure 13.1   Modeling the inverted U-shaped relationships among sources of advice and the dependent variables

Not surprisingly, resources provided by outside advisers seem to increase the likelihood that the business founding process will be a success and that the venture will grow. Having too few outside advisers limits the entrepreneur's opportunities to gain necessary knowledge and a higher amount of sources of advice will increase these opportunities. However, at a certain point in the process the costs of increased advice seem to outweigh the benefits. To identify, develop and maintain relationships the entrepreneur has to exhaust resources that could be used elsewhere. Because of the interaction effect of resources, the entrepreneur could possibly use different means to reach the same goal.

The importance of advice to entrepreneurs during the business founding process supports findings reported in previous research (Chrisman, 1999; Chrisman and McMullan, 2004; Chrisman et al., 2005; Watson, 2007) and strengthens the claim that the findings hold for different contexts.

Limitations

First, due to the position-generator approach, the advice variable might be imprecise since each respondent was offered a predetermined selection of contacts to choose from. This list is of course not exhaustive and some entrepreneurs may have more contacts with one single agent. Second, since the sample of new businesses refers to survived businesses the results may suffer from survival bias (Davidsson and Honig, 2003). Hence, the results can only be generalized to surviving businesses. Third, performance measures such as those used in this study have been criticized for being too rigid, and a combination of more subjective and process oriented measures has been encouraged (Robinson, 1999; Witt, 2004).

Implications

These results have important implications for entrepreneurs. They should pay attention to the number of advisers they use and focus on the quantity as well as quality of advice. Further information from more advisers may prove redundant and the cost of resources used to access this information may outweigh the benefits. Entrepreneurs who seek too much advice may reach a point of information overload, which could make them indecisive and unable to formulate a clear strategy for obtaining a competitive advantage.

Based on these results it is suggested that further research could be focused on using a comparable research design in other contexts. Taking into consideration the limitations of this study and the use of slightly different measures might furthermore prove fruitful. Similar results in other countries will substantiate these findings and further contribute to the literature on advice received by entrepreneurs. Opportunities for future studies may include subjects such as: (1) interaction effects between entrepreneurs' resources and advice; (2) relation between entrepreneurs' experience and utilization of advice and (3) relation between entrepreneurs' competence and what kind of sources of advice to utilize.

There is a universal acceptance of the importance of entrepreneurship for the economy. However, resources are scarce during business gestation. This study underlines the importance of advice received and utilized by entrepreneurs during business formation. Furthermore, it is important to maximize the effect of advice, by focusing on optimal amount and intensity. The findings can help policymakers to identify efficient policies and measures regarding support initiatives. Authorities might consider changing the focus of advice services and network programs to better reflect the needs of entrepreneurs.

REFERENCES

Alsos, G.A. and L. Kolvereid (1998), 'The business gestation process of novice, serial and parallel business founders', *Entrepreneurship Theory and Practice*, **22**(4), 101–14.

Alvarez, S. and L. Busenitz (2001), 'The entrepreneurship resource-based theory', *Journal of Management*, **27**, 755–75.

Ardichvili, A., R. Cardozo and S. Ray (2003), 'A theory of entrepreneurial opportunity identification and development', *Journal of Business Venturing*, **18**(1), 105–23.

Bazerman, M.H. (1994), *Judgement in Managerial Decision Making*, 3rd edn, New York: John Wiley & Son.

Berman, S.L., J. Down and C.W.L. Hill (2002), 'Tacit knowledge as a source of competitive advantage in the national basketball association', *Academy of Management Journal*, **45**, 13–31.

Bouchikhi, H. (1993), 'A constructivist framework for understanding entrepreneurship performance', *Organization Studies*, **14**(4), 549–70.

Carter, N.M., W.B. Gartner and P.D. Reynolds (1996), 'Exploring start-up event sequences', *Journal of Business Venturing*, **11**(3), 151–66.

Chrisman, J.J. (1999), 'The influence of outsider-generated knowledge resources on venture creation', *Journal of Small Business Management*, **37**(4), 42–58.

Chrisman, J.J. and W.E. McMullan (2004), 'Outsider assistance as a knowledge resource for new venture survival', *Journal of Small Business Management*, **42**(3), 229–44.

Chrisman, J.J., W.E. McMullan and J. Hall (2005), 'The influence of guided preparation on the long-term performance of new ventures', *Journal of Business Venturing*, **20**, 769–91.

Cooper, A.C., F.J. Gimeno-Gascon and C.Y. Woo (1994), 'Initial human and financial capital as predictors of new venture performance', *Journal of Business Venturing*, **9**(5), 371–95.

Davidsson, P. and S.R. Gordon (2009), 'Nascent entrepreneur(ship) research: a review', available at www.http://eprints.qut.edu.au/view/person/Davidsson,Per. html (accessed 2 November 2009).

Davidsson, P. and B. Honig (2003), 'The role of social and human capital among nascent entrepreneurs', *Journal of Business Venturing*, **18**(3), 301–31.

De Carolis, D.M. and P. Saparito (2006), 'Social capital, cognition, and entrepreneurial opportunities: a theoretical framework', *Entrepreneurship Theory and Practice*, **30**(1), 41–56.

Delmar, F. and P. Davidsson (2000), 'Where do they come from? Prevalence and characteristics of nascent entrepreneurs', *Entrepreneurship and Regional Development*, **12**, 1–23.

Gartner, W.B. (1985), 'A conceptual framework for describing the phenomenon of new venture creation', *Academy of Management Review*, **10**(4), 696–706.

Gartner, W.B. (1989), 'Some suggestions for research on entrepreneurial traits and characteristics', *Entrepreneurship Theory and Practice*, **14**(1), 27–37.

Gimeno, J., T.B. Folta, A.C. Cooper and C.Y. Woo (1997), 'Survival of the fittest? Entrepreneurial human capital and the persistence of underperforming firms', *Administrative Science Quarterly*, **42**(4), 750–83.

Hoang, H. and B. Antoncic (2003), 'Network-based research in entrepreneurship – a critical review', *Journal of Business Venturing*, **18**(2), 165–87.

Isaksen, E. (2006), 'Early business performance. Initial factors affecting new business outcomes', PhD dissertation, Bodø Graduate School of Business, Norway.

Isaksen, E. and L. Kolvereid (2005), 'Growth objectives in Norwegian start-up businesses', *International Journal of Entrepreneurship and Small Business*, **2**(1), 17–26.

Low, M.B. and I.C. Macmillan (1988), 'Entrepreneurship – past research and future challenges', *Journal of Management*, **14**(2), 139–61.

McFadyen, M.A. and A.A. Cannella (2004), 'Social capital and knowledge creation: diminishing returns of the number and strength of exchange relationships', *Academy of Management Journal*, **47**(5), 735–46.

Menzies, T.V. and J.C. Paradi (2003), 'Entrepreneurship education and engineering students', *International Journal of Entrepreneurship Education*, **4**, 121–32.

Minniti, M. and W. Bygrave (2001), 'A dynamic model of entrepreneurial learning', *Entrepreneurship Theory and Practice*, **25**(3), 5–16.

Reynolds, P.D. (2009), 'Screening items effects in estimating the prevalence of nascent entrepreneurs', *Small Business Economics*, **33**(2), 151–63.

Reynolds, P.D., W.D. Bygrave, E. Antio, L.W. Cox and M. Hay (2002), *Global Entrepreneurship Monitor 2002 Executive Report*, Babson College, MA and London Business School: Ewing Marion Kaufman Foundation.

Reynolds, P.D., N.M. Carter, W.B. Gartner and P.G. Greene (2004), 'The prevalence of nascent entrepreneurs in the United States: evidence from the panel study of entrepreneurial dynamics', *Small Business Economics*, **23**(4), 263–84.

Robinson, K.C. (1999), 'An examination of the influence of industry structure on eight alternative measures of new venture performance for high potential independent new ventures', *Journal of Business Venturing*, **14**(2), 165–87.

Robinson, R.B. (1982), 'The importance of "outsiders" in small firm strategic planning', *Academy of Management Journal*, **25**, 80–93.

Solow, R.M. (1956), 'A contribution to the theory of economic growth', *Quarterly Journal of Economics*, **70**(1), 65–94.

Watson, J. (2007), 'Modelling the relationship between networking and firm performance', *Journal of Business Venturing*, **22**(6), 852–74.

Westhead, P. and M. Wright (1998), 'Novice, portfolio, and serial founders: are they different?', *Journal of Business Venturing*, **13**(3), 173–204.

Witt, P. (2004), 'Entrepreneurs' networks and the success of start-ups', *Entrepreneurship and Regional Development*, **16**(5), 391–412.

Index